Questions of Business Life

Exploring Workplace Issues from a Christian Perspective

Richard Higginson

First Published in 2002 by Spring Harvest Publishing Division and
Authentic Media

08 07 06 05 04 03 02   7 6 5 4 3 2 1
Authentic Lifestyle is an imprint of Authentic Media,
PO Box 300, Carlisle, Cumbria, CA3 0QS, UK
PO Box 1047, Waynesboro, GA 30830-2047, USA
www.paternoster-publishing.com

British Library Cataloguing in Publication Data

A catalogue record for this book is available from
the British Library

ISBN 1-85078-477-9

All Bible references are taken from NIV, NRSV and RSV.

The diagram on page 124 is taken from *All the Hours God Sends?*
by Peter Curran and reproduced by the permission of the
Publishers, Inter-Varsity Press, UK

Cover design by Diane Bainbridge
Printed in Great Britain by
Cox and Wyman, Reading

Contents

Contents

ACKNOWLEDGEMENTS

An enormous number of people have contributed to the writing of this book. More than most books, it is the fruit of a collaborative process, an ongoing engagement with people in the business community, mainly through the seminars and conferences we have held at Ridley Hall over the last six years. It is no exaggeration to say that every participant has played their part, to a greater or lesser extent. So thank you to each and every one.

There are some individuals who have made a substantial contribution, as partners in regular debate about particular questions of business life. They have spoken on our seminars and commented on chapters in which their views are reported. I would like to express special appreciation to Bob Cumber, Peter Curran, Mark Greene, Nick Isbister, Sir Michael Latham, David Murray, Simon Peyton Jones, David Runton, Peter Warburton, David Welbourn and Clive Wright. Others who have made helpful comments on parts of the manuscript include James Allcock, Sue Halliday, Peter Heslam, Calvert Markham and Mark Winter.

The first half of the book was written while on sabbatical in Melbourne, Australia. I would like to thank Graham Cray (then Principal), my other colleagues and the Council of Ridley Hall for releasing me to do this, as well as their counterparts at the other Ridley College in the University of

Melbourne, who provided support and congenial company –
notably Gordon Preece (with whom I did an exchange),
Graham Cole and Lindsay Wilson.

Thank you to Authentic Lifestyle and to Spring Harvest, for
publishing the outcome of these labours. Here I must single
out Steven May-Millar and Simon Warner for their support
and advice during the final stages of writing.

Finally, I owe a huge debt of gratitude to my wife, Felicity,
and our five children, Hannah, Daniel, Peter, Simeon and
Lydia, for their love and companionship over the years, and
for bearing with me on a project that has run and run!

                                                   Richard Higginson

INTRODUCTION:
QUESTIONS OF BUSINESS LIFE

The 1990s were billed as the decade of Christian evangelism. On the whole, this description promised rather more than it delivered. They were years in which the Christian churches seemed to lose ground rather than gain it, in which church membership fell rather than grew. But there were some notable exceptions to this trend. The Alpha courses pioneered by Holy Trinity Brompton have proved a very effective way of attracting people to the Christian faith. Alpha revolves round a simple, straightforward explanation of Christianity, explored within a context of friendship. It is based on Nicky Gumbel's book *Questions of Life* – one of the Christian bestsellers of our time.

I do not intend it as a criticism, but I believe it's an accurate observation that Alpha has been a particularly effective means of evangelism among professional people, many of whom work in, or on the periphery of, business. Holy Trinity Brompton itself throbs with such people. This raises a question about the impact of their Christian faith – whether newly discovered or well established – on working life. It's wonderful when people come to faith, and the lively charismatic worship typical of churches that use Alpha is often exhilarating, but how does this operate in terms of weekday discipleship? What happens to this faith in the hard grind of Monday to Friday, or under pressure from work that often encroaches far into the evening and maybe weekends as well? How are Christians being equipped for this highly testing arena?

This book unashamedly takes the Alpha strapline, *Questions of Life*, and inserts within it the word *business*. I take my hat off to Alpha and to other excellent evangelistic initiatives for what they are doing, but I wish to go a stage further. I want to explore the implications of Christian faith and discipleship for many of the tough and complex issues that confront businesspeople in their everyday circumstances. I don't promise easy answers, just an honest and thoughtful grappling with the issues. Throughout I have tried to be faithful to the principle that John Stott commends, that of *double listening*: careful listening to what is going on in business, and the testimony of practising businesspeople, on the one hand; and equally attentive listening to what God is saying, especially through the words of Scripture, on the other hand.

The Ridley Hall Foundation – Phase One

It's not the first time I have ventured into this area. To explain the background to this book and my credentials for writing it, I need to say something about the Ridley Hall Foundation, whose work I direct. Ridley Hall is an Anglican theological college in Cambridge. Its primary task is training people for the ordained ministry, and part of my job is teaching them courses in Ethics and Leadership. But Ridley has also spawned a number of projects that reflect a passionate concern to relate Christian faith to key aspects of contemporary culture. Two that have borne fruit are the Centre for Youth Ministry and the Theology Through the Arts project. Business is the third area.

Hugo de Waal, the then-principal of Ridley Hall, contacted me in 1988 to ask if I might be interested in heading up a new project. The idea for his 'God on Monday' project, which had been developing in Hugo's mind for many years, was fuelled by two major concerns. Both of these I fully share: which helps explain why, with some hesitation and trepidation, but also a great sense of anticipation and excitement, I took on the job.

The first concern was that the idea of lay ministry, or ministry of the laity, had largely been hijacked. In the 20 years during which it came to prominence, it had come to mean lay people helping clergy in their traditional tasks of preaching, leading services, leading home groups, leading youth groups, and so on. Do not misunderstand. It is good if lay people get involved in these areas. The danger is that the focus on church activities becomes a distraction. The main area where lay people should be exercising their ministry is actually the wider world, not the church; in particular, their place of work. Do they see their job as an arena for Christian service, and what is the quality of the work and witness they offer? Or to make it more personal, *do you and I* see our jobs as an arena for Christian service, and what is the quality of work and witness *we* offer?

The second concern is that among the types of work people do, the church has a peculiar difficulty knowing how to relate specifically to the business sector, the world of commerce and industry. The church feels a sense of unease about business, a hunch that business is contaminated by its pursuit of profit or by full immersion in an unjust global system. But the church also knows that it cannot do without business. To some extent it depends on business. We shall investigate the ironies, complexities and historical roots of this ambivalent relationship in this book. Sufficient to say that there is an issue here: an issue Ridley Hall believes should be confronted and not ignored.

Out of this twofold concern emerged the idea of a project that seeks to do the following:

- develop a carefully worked out Christian perspective on business and business issues
- bring practising businesspeople, ordinands, theological educators and other interested academics together in a process of dialogue and mutual learning
- offer businesspeople both support and challenge: fundamental encouragement in the work that they do, and a

willingness to question what business does and how it
operates wherever the Christian faith demands it
● equip future clergy for a more effective ministry to and with
businesspeople.

Hence the vision of a project concerned with the interconnec-
tion of faith, values and business practice in what might at first
sight seem an unlikely setting for continuing management
education, a theological college.

The project's main focus is running residential seminars.
The frequency, length, size and focus of these have varied in
the 13 years we have been operating, but there are consistent
features. The seminars, which have something of the character
of a think-tank, bring together people of expertise, experience
and insight to share best practice and take thinking forward.
Delegate numbers range from 10 to 50, depending on the
theme, but the seminars are always highly participative. We
arrange a programme of distinguished speakers, who provide
crucial input, but allow plenty of time for discussion in which
speakers interact freely with delegates. Because the seminars
are usually spread over two days (during 1989-93 they
actually took the best part of a week), delegates have an
opportunity to discuss issues in depth and get to know each
other well. Bonds of fellowship and friendship develop during
these events – often continuing to mutual benefit afterwards.

The subjects tackled in the early years were fairly broad.
During the early 1990s we ran a number of themes several
times: *Values in Business Today, Issues of Leadership, Managing
the Dynamics of Change,* and *Success and Failure in Business.* Out
of these seminars, I wrote three books:

● *Transforming Leadership,* a write-up of the 1994 London
Lectures in Contemporary Christianity, in which I reflected
on those four themes in an attempt to set out a Christian
approach to management in the secular world
● *Called to Account,* a down-to-earth application of Christian
theology to the realities of the business world, drawing on
every major doctrine of the creed

● *Mind the Gap*, a popular booklet making connections between faith and work, designed for use by home groups and Christian fellowships in the workplace, and focused on four key doctrines: creation, fall, reconciliation and our future hope.

These three books effectively sum up Phase One of the project.

The Ridley Hall Foundation – Phase Two

In the mid-1990s the work of the project moved on. First, we changed our name. 'God on Monday' was effective in getting attention, but less helpful in being treated seriously in corporate circles. We therefore became the more sober-sounding Ridley Hall Foundation, with 'Faith in Business' as a subtitle cum logo. This was not intended as a statement of idolatry, as though faith in business should replace faith in God, but is a deliberate *double entendre*. It sounds the dual notes of support and challenge. It seeks to convey a positive attitude to business, based on the conviction that business *does* have a legitimate role in God's purposes, and a concern to explore the application of faith and values *in* business. *Faith in Business* is also the name of a quarterly journal launched in 1996 in partnership with the Industrial Christian Fellowship, the longest-standing organisation in the area of relating faith to work. The journal has an excellent reputation and is the only publication of its type in the field.

Second, we changed the focus of the seminars. Through listening carefully to our 'market', we found a declining demand for events on broad themes and increasing interest in sharply focused seminars on a business sector, corporate function, ethical problem or topical issue. A positive response has provided the opportunity to test some of the more general assertions made about the relevance of Christian faith and discover how these stand up in detailed situations. Whereas *Called to Account* was more deductive in style, starting with the grand themes of Christian doctrine and then applying them to

what is happening in business, *Questions of Business Life* begins
with the topical issues and then works back to see what wisdom, if any, Christianity has to offer on the subject.

This book, then, is an update on the work of the last six
years. Each year we run two or three seminars. After each I
write a report in which I chronicle the progress of the seminar
and seek to sum up the key insights to emerge from it. This is
circulated to the delegates, and sometimes further afield as
well (often, for instance, in *Faith in Business*). In compiling
these reports I have been very aware that there was more work
to be done.

A term's study leave in Melbourne, Australia, from
September to December 2000, gave me the opportunity to do
further reading, research and reflection on each topic. I read
widely in the areas of history, theology, sociology, cultural
studies, management studies, and business ethics. Making
sense of the contemporary business world is a multi-discipli-
nary endeavour. I have sought to incorporate the most
important writing to appear since the seminars. Throughout I
have tried to make the material as accessible as possible,
notably through the use of personal, real life *stories*. The writing I started in Australia has now been brought to completion.

Since 1996, the Ridley Hall Foundation has run these seminars:

- The Ethics of Marketing   13-15 March 1996
- Transforming Leadership   26-28 June 1996
- Christians in Consultancy   12-14 March 1997
- The Stakeholder Economy   21-23 May 1997
- Establishing Trust in the
  Construction Industry   11-13 March 1998
- Vocation: Christian Calling in the
  Secular World   19-20 June 1998
- Tackling Corruption in Business   17-19 March 1999
- The Portfolio Lifestyle   18-19 June 1999
- Managing the Supply Chain   15-17 March 2000
- Business in Cyberspace   23-25 June 2000
- The Changing Faces of Loyalty   14-16 March 2001

- Business and Sustainable
  Development   23-25 May 2001
- Spirituality and the Workplace   22-24 June 2001

Looking back over these topics, it became clear that they divided – none too artificially – into three groups.

The first group consists of certain crucial issues about *doing business corporately*:

- The nature and purpose of a company: the stakeholder debate
- Changing stakeholder relations: the development of supply chain management
- Can partnership really work? Establishing trust in the construction industry
- The changing faces of loyalty: reshaping the employee relationship.

The second comprises equally fundamental issues in *doing business globally*:

- Fuelling the consumer society: the ethics of marketing
- Tackling international corruption: doing business without bribes
- Saving the future of the planet: business and sustainable development
- Business without frontiers: the growth of e-commerce.

The third group is more about *doing business individually*:

- Influencing organisations for good? The role of the consultant
- Changing patterns of work: the portfolio lifestyle
- Spirituality and the workplace: a new paradigm at work?
- The revived idea of vocation: calling in the business world.

While these three areas overlap, each has a coherent focus. I believe they embrace most of the crucial issues that have preoccupied people in business for the last few years, and devote a chapter to each.

In writing this book, I became aware of two significant omissions. I realised the need for a preliminary chapter to put our present circumstances in historical perspective. I must explain why we are in a situation where we need to assert that Christianity is relevant to business and cannot simply assume it. Its marginalisation is the result of a long-term process. Another chapter is required to bring the global dimension to the fore. Globalisation has become a buzz-word, and was the topic of the most recent Ridley Hall seminar in June 2002. There's no question that globalisation is the context for all the other scenarios, and so is the subject of Chapter 2

1

PUSHED TO THE EDGE:
THE MARGINALISATION OF CHRISTIANITY BY BUSINESS

This book is a protest – against the marginalisation of Christianity by business, and the marginalisation of business by Christianity.

The business world finds little of significance for its activities in the Christian faith or the Christian church. The church feels the same. This sometimes takes the form of indifference, causing business and Christianity to scarcely consider each other at all. It also emerges as suspicion and hostility, so there is a conscious relationship but it is one of alienation. Either way, marginalisation prevails. This chapter considers the factors that led to the sidelining of Christianity by business. By marginalise I mean 'push to the edges'.

This gulf is the result of momentous developments during the last 250 years. Before that came several centuries of positive interaction between business and Christianity. While the medieval church exalted the contemplative life above the active life, it could not avoid questions relating to the practice of trade, not least because the church, like other institutions, was dependent on the creation of wealth for its survival. While monastic orders were committed to vows of poverty, they engaged in business. The Cistercians, by grazing sheep, helped pioneer the English wool industry. Dominican and

Franciscan professors of theology in Paris developed a tradition of commentary on issues of economic morality. These scholastic theologians of the Middle Ages had plenty to say about property rights, justice in the levelling of prices and wages, and the charging of interest (usury).

Thus medieval theologians such as Thomas Aquinas:

- affirmed the right of people to own private property, though this was qualified by concern for the common good. Aquinas recognised a general duty to provide for those in need, and said a person in dire need might be justified in taking what was not his (i.e. stealing) if the public failed to meet that obligation. Not everyone agreed with this latter point, and some writers emphasised the rights of property-holders
- developed the concept of a *just price*, which both rewards the seller and satisfies the customer. A seller may guard against loss, but should not take advantage of a buyer's need. The price should be based on the cost of raw materials and labour. The underlying belief was that it was possible to determine objectively what a worker ought to earn, depending on their social status. If goods were sold at a price higher than warranted by these two costs, it represented unnatural profit
- used the same concept of acting contrary to nature in condemning lending at interest. Aquinas followed Aristotle in his belief that money was essentially barren, so it was 'unnatural' to make money out of money. But not all the scholastic theologians were convinced by this argument. Some said there should be exceptions. These were justified as compensation for the lender's risk (a category known as *damnum emergens*) and his loss of the gain if the loan had not been made (*lucrum cessans*). In general, though, it was believed that the practice of usury ran contrary to Christian duties of love and mercy.

Though the church might have been critical of some of what went on in the world of finance and trade, this thinking shows that it was engaged in a constructive way.

The Protestant Ethic

There is solid ground for believing that Christianity – or a particular version of it – contributed to the rise of capitalism during the 300 years before 1800. This was certainly the conviction of the German sociologist Max Weber, author in 1905 of *The Protestant Ethic and the Spirit of Capitalism*, one of the most influential and provocative books ever written. Weber started by observing that in modern Europe the owners of capital and higher grades of skilled labour were overwhelmingly Protestant, rather than Catholic. Many have since disputed this observation, but it can be defended in general terms. Weber's explanation was that Protestantism created the psychological conditions that facilitated the development of capitalist civilisation. By capitalism Weber did not mean primarily the impulse to acquisition or the desire to get rich, which he recognised to be habits as old as history. Rather, he meant the pursuit of profit, and persistently renewed profit, by means of thought out, forward-looking enterprise: in particular the organisation of notionally free labour by the owners of capital.

According to Weber, Protestantism encouraged this because of the sort of character it produced: rational, sober, industrious and thrifty. Calvin's Geneva, along with cities modelled on it, was a breeding-ground for merchants who used their time, money and talents to maximum effect. Hard work yielded prosperity, but the prosperity did not spawn a life of idle leisure. Instead, money was invested in businesses that lasted several generations. In Weber's view, two theological ideas provided impetus for such a lifestyle: the Lutheran concept of 'calling' and the Calvinist doctrine of 'predestination'.

Luther on vocation

Martin Luther was an Augustinian monk who discovered that scrupulous religious observance didn't lead to any assured sense of salvation. His life was transformed through reading the New Testament. He discovered the good news of justification by grace through faith, spelt out in the letters of Paul. His subsequent break with the Roman Catholic Church included a rejection of the monasticism that he believed had led him astray, with a revolutionary reappraisal of the well-established demarcation between 'sacred' and 'secular' work. Luther came to emphasise the great variety of occupations in which it is possible to work hard and serve God. The mother suckling her baby, the maid wielding her brush and the magistrate passing sentence were doing something of real value if they performed these tasks in response to God's command and to his glory.

The German word that Luther used to describe everyday work was *Beruf*, or 'calling'. Until then, this had been a concept restricted to monks, nuns and priests. Luther set his understanding within the context of a 'spiritual' calling, which is God's call to receive personal salvation through believing the gospel. This call is essentially the same for all believers. What distinguishes Christians from each other is the calling that comes through their particular 'station' in life, the various family, social and occupational positions in which people find themselves. The duties of the station become God's commandments to one person or another.

Such thinking may strike us as conservative, as a way of sanctifying a hierarchical society. In Luther's case, it did not produce a particularly positive attitude to business, not least because he saw the leading German merchants (families such as the Fuggers) as greedy rascals. But we need to grasp that in a sixteenth century context his teaching on vocation was heady stuff. It invested everyday work with a significance and dignity it had previously lacked. It opened the way for regarding every task or job as important in the sight of God.

Calvin on predestination

The other great Protestant reformer, John Calvin, agreed with Luther in all essentials of his teaching on worldly vocation. Calvin saw work – potentially at least – as a means of bringing glory to God, in and through his creation, and in the process adding to the wellbeing of that creation. Like Luther, he emphasised the initiative and sovereignty of God in bringing about the experience of human salvation. But Calvin developed this into a doctrine of predestination whereby all of humanity was split into the saved and the damned by the eternal decree of God. Personal salvation was received by faith, but ultimately depended not on one's own decision but on God's. Some people might have a counterfeit faith that fails the test of time. In Weber's view, the psychological effect of this doctrine was 'a feeling of unprecedented inner loneliness of the single individual' (*Protestant Ethic*, p.104). Unable to be entirely sure whether he was saved, what could the individual do?

The only answer seemed to be a sober life full of good works. They might be useless as a means of attaining salvation, but were significant as a sign of election. Weber called good works the means 'not of purchasing salvation, but of getting rid of the fear of damnation' (p.115), adding that a series of isolated good works was no use but only a unified system of them. The process of sanctifying life took on the character of a business enterprise. And for many a Reformed Christian it took place within a business setting. What Weber called 'worldly asceticism' was well suited to making money. Working hard produced results. Moreover, God's call for people to develop their talents pointed towards specialisation of occupations. That in turn helped justify the division of labour characteristic of modern capitalism. Wealth was seen as a source of temptation, never to be sought as an end in itself, but wealth as the by-product of labour devoted to a calling could be seen as a sign of God's blessing. Since Protestants in business did not, on the whole, fritter away their wealth in consumption, they accumulated capital through saving. This capital could then be invested in equipment, plant and employees to further the life of a flourishing business.

The Quakers

A striking example of a Protestant group that had influence out of all proportion to their size is the Quakers. Historian James Walvin says: 'A mere century ago, the British people could easily have organised substantial parts of their material lives around the products and services of a number of Quaker commercial enterprises' (*Faith in Business* 3:4, p.8). They were prominent in banking, insurance, confectionery, drinks, engineering, railways, steel, soap, pharmaceuticals, shoes and textiles. Many of the great Quaker names of eighteenth and nineteenth century commerce – Lloyds, Barclays, Cadbury, Rowntree and Clarks – survive and flourish to this day. Yet British Quakers were always a very small proportion of the total population; during the second half of the nineteenth century, when they were at the height of their commercial influence, they numbered less than 20,000 people. In addition, they were one of the more eccentric groups thrown up by the English Reformation. They wore distinctive clothing, used an old-fashioned form of language and annoyed their supposed social betters by refusing to bow, remove their hats or acknowledge titles. But within a generation they had developed a reputation for being prosperous. Why was this?

It is insufficient, though accurate, to point out that they were forced into business through being excluded by law and choice from a wide range of activities (e.g. universities, the law, and politics). Walvin concludes that Quakers did well in business for four main reasons:

- A fierce commitment to *honesty*. They took Jesus' instruction to 'let your "Yes" be "Yes", and your "No", "No"' (Mt. 5:37) with a literal seriousness, and were accepted as honest even by those who disliked them. During the eighteenth century, when there was a growing demand for financial services and the number of banks mushroomed, this reputation made the public ready to trust Quakers with their money. Honesty also stood them in good stead in other areas of commerce. Their word could be trusted, their goods were what they purported to be, and their prices were both fixed and reasonable

- A system of *mutual accountability*. They kept checks on each other, and had to answer for their commercial conduct to the local Quaker meeting. Anyone who brought shame and discredit on the Quaker community was rapidly disciplined. Prominent Quakers met regularly, passed on business advice, and warned against dubious prospects or traders. This Quaker network stretched across the Atlantic

- An emphasis on *education*. From the first, Quakers formed a highly literate society. This is partly an offshoot of the Protestant emphasis on reading the Bible for yourself. The Quakers set up their own schools (for girls as well as boys) and developed apprenticeships for their offspring. Sons were often sent to a Quaker associate to learn a trade before returning to run the expanding family business. This pattern contributed to another Quaker trend, dynamic marriages between the children of different business families

- Ambivalence over *luxury goods*. The Quakers believed in plain dress and a simple lifestyle, and generally stayed true to these principles. But this did not stop them supplying the needs and wants of those who sported a more affluent lifestyle. Chocolate is a luxury item associated with Quaker names above all others. Quaker shopkeepers also sold a range of luxurious clothes, frills and elaborate dress. It can be called a paradox, hypocrisy or just plain bowing to economic pressures, but the Quakers actually contributed significantly to the growth of luxurious consumption in British life.

Wesley's Dilemma

The link between business activity and this particular strand of Christian faith had its difficulties. John Wesley, the great eighteenth century Methodist, identified a crucial tension. In his famous sermon on 'The Use of Money', he exhorted Christians to *gain* all they can and to *save* all they can. Only if they did so would they fully employ their God-given talents. But Wesley saw some undesirable consequences in this. In a passage that Max Weber said 'might well serve as a motto' for the whole of his thesis, Wesley observed:

'I fear, wherever riches have increased, the essence of religion has decreased in the same proportion. Therefore I do not see how it is possible, in the nature of things, for any revival of true religion to continue long. For religion must necessarily produce both industry and frugality, and these cannot but produce riches. But as riches increase, so will pride, anger, and love of the world in all its branches. How then is it possible that Methodism, that is, a religion of the heart, though it flourishes now as a green bay tree, should continue in this state? For the Methodists in every place grow diligent and frugal; consequently they increase in goods. ... We ought not to prevent people from being diligent and frugal; we must exhort all Christians to gain all they can, and to save all they can; that is, in effect, to grow rich.' (Southey, *Life of Wesley II*, p.308).

Wesley's answer to the problem was that Christians should *give* all they can. Money that had been gained and saved should be given away. Believers would thereby grow in grace and lay up a treasure in heaven. How satisfactory this is as a solution remains open to debate, but the link was there – Christianity was a formidable force at the centre of economic life – and can scarcely be disputed.

It would be wrong to allege that no such link exists today. There are parts of the world where Christianity exercises a similar function, providing the disciplined, energetic ethos so important to a newly industrialising country. For examples we must look to parts of South America and East Asia. Studies in Brazil and Chile by sociologist David Martin show that conversion to Protestantism brings about what can only be called a cultural revolution. Individuals who join these Protestant churches – mainly Pentecostal – change their behaviour abruptly, radically and in most cases permanently. Defying all the stereotypes about Latin American culture, they begin to act like eighteenth century Methodists. The character traits described by Max Weber emerge: an ethic of discipline and self-denial, of hard work, of favouring savings over consumption, and of systematic planning for the future. While in general the Pentecostal worship of South Americans is more overtly emotional than that of the Europeans Weber studied, the sober hard-headedness with which they conduct their weekday activities *is* comparable. The economic effects are beginning to be evident.

South Korea's economic growth between 1960 and 1990 was quite remarkable, recording an annual rate of 9%. Within one generation Korea had a level of development that it took most of today's advanced nations a century to achieve. Its economic 'miracle' was parallelled by the explosive growth of Christianity. Seoul, the capital, has the world's largest Methodist and Presbyterian churches (50,000) and Pentecostal congregations (500,000) – 25% of the population is Christian. Korean analyst Sang-Goog Cho argues that the two are linked. Christianity contributed to a growth-oriented strategy, an industry-oriented strategy, and an outward-looking strategy, all appropriate for the country's stage of economic development. He says Christian attitudes to work, thrift, vocation and positive thinking were critically important for the development of the Korean economy – notwithstanding its difficulties in recent years.

The Rise of Market Economics

So why was Christianity shoved to the margins of economic life in the West? Significant trends were active at the same time as the events Weber analysed so shrewdly. Religion contributed to the rise of capitalism, but capitalism was developing a life of its own. In particular, it was throwing off the restraints imposed by the medieval church – at least notionally – on the practice of trade.

The first shibboleth to fall was the prohibition on usury. Exceptions had been made even by scholastic theologians. Among the Reformers, Luther viewed lending at interest as unbiblical and morally suspect – he smelt the greed of merchants – but Calvin, who had a less jaundiced view of their activities, was more open to the practice. He saw the Israelite ban on interest as temporary rather than permanent, an aspect of their political constitution appropriate to their time and place. In sixteenth century Europe, Calvin said, it was permissible 'to make concessions to the common utility'. Loans at modest rates between parties who had good business reasons to lend and borrow were acceptable. His condition was that lending at interest should be subject to the Christian law of love; it should not infringe the principles of equity and charity. Thus the first *major* breach in the church's stand on usury came from one of its most influential theologians.

Effectively Calvin was exhorting people to conduct business by the spirit of the law rather than the letter, but it opened the way for abuse. A 'reasonable rate' of interest is a subjective matter. Rather than making a fresh decision in each case based on the interests and intentions of the parties, it seemed easier to set a standard figure. In 1571 the English Parliament accepted charges of interest up to 10%. Also underlying this gradual acceptance of interest was the view that money was a commodity. So money had its price and interest was the price for borrowing it. As commerce developed, so did the need for long-term investment: outlays might be considerable before profits began to flow in. Entrepreneurs needed money to get started, and the bankers who provided it could justifiably expect a return for their service.

Just price was the next favourite of moral theologians to come under fire. Seventeenth century philosophers gave the idea short shrift. Thomas Hobbes derided it as a meaningless abstraction: 'the value of all things contracted for, is measured by the Appetite of the Contractors, and therefore the just value, is that which they be contented to give' (*Leviathan*, ch.15). The same attack was levelled at the just wage: 'The value or worth of a man, is as of all other things, his price; that is to say, how much as would be given for the use of his power'. In other words, the price for goods or labour is whatever is agreed by a buyer and seller negotiating in the marketplace. Amounts will vary, depending on a host of circumstances. It makes little sense to measure these local variations by an abstract yardstick of justice.

Hobbes had a dark view of humanity. Life is 'nasty, brutish and short', he said, and it is the nature of human beings to prey upon each other. Private owners strive to increase their power over others. The resulting state of insecurity requires a strong state if life and property are to be secure, and contracts defined and enforced.

Adam Smith was the Scottish moral philosopher who wrote the seminal work *An Inquiry into the Nature and Causes of the Wealth of Nations* in 1776. Like Hobbes, he took human egoism as his starting-point. He contended that the pursuit of self-interest was 'the general principle which regulates the actions of every man'; 'the constant and uninterrupted effort to better his own condition' (*Wealth of Nations*, p.364). It was almost as strong a tendency as the readiness 'to truck, barter and exchange one thing for another', an area of life where self-interest dominates above all others.

In *A Theory of Moral Sentiments*, written 15 years earlier, Smith had acknowledged a different side to humanity. He said: 'To restrain our selfish, and to indulge our benevolent affections, constitutes the perfection of human nature.' In the economic realm, however, he saw no need for this perfection. Self-interest was sufficient, because it worked out for the general good. In Smith's famous words: 'It is not from the benevolence of the butcher, the brewer or the baker that we expect our dinner; but from their regard to their own interest. We address ourselves not to their humanity but to their self-love, and never talk to them of our own necessities but of their advantages' (*Wealth of Nations*, p.14). In addition, competition between those in the same trade serves the public, because it keeps prices down. Smith saw all this as providential: he talked about an 'invisible hand' that brought a harmony of personal gain and social benefit.

Because Smith believed the market was such a force for good, he thought it was best left largely to its own devices. His doctrine of the state is less interventionist than Hobbes'. He was concerned that governments defend the rights of property owners, but beyond that said business was best left free of regulation: 'The natural effort of every individual to better his own condition, when suffered to exert itself with freedom and security, is so powerful a principle, that it is alone, and without any assistance, not only capable of carrying on the society to wealth and prosperity, but of surmounting a hundred impertinent obstructions with which the folly of human laws to often encumbers its operations; though the effect of these obstructions is always more or less either to encroach upon its freedom, or to diminish its security' (*Wealth of Nations*, Book IV, ch.5).

Smith's thinking gave rise to a new discipline, economics. It was based solidly on the assumption that economic activity is governed by the behaviour of rational, acquisitive individuals seeking to maximise utility. Economics borrowed from Utilitarianism. According to Jeremy Bentham, a leading proponent of this prevalent philosophy: 'Nature has placed mankind under the governance of two sovereign masters, pain and pleasure. It is for them alone to point out what we ought to do, as well as to determine what we shall do' (*An Introduction to the Principles of Morals and Legislation*, opening words). Bentham believed that because maximising our own pleasure is our central preoccupation, it is misguided and futile to base a moral system on any other principle.

So-called classical economics has rarely deviated from this presupposition. Prices and wages emerge from a bargaining process between buyers and sellers, employers and employees, who all push their own interests as hard as possible. The scarcity or abundance of a commodity (whether human labour, land or a finished product) has a crucial effect on the outcome of the transaction: it determines who benefits most. By studying the pattern of these bargaining processes, economics is able to identify so-called laws of supply and demand. This in turn enables it to perform a predictive function. Economics claimed to be nothing more than an empirical or mathematical science, describing what was going on in the actual marketplace.

The revolution in thinking brought to a head by Adam Smith was summed up by a British parliamentarian, Edmund Burke, writing in 1800: 'The laws of commerce are the laws of nature, and therefore the laws of God' (*Thoughts and Details on Scarcity*, pp.31-2). The same words could have been spoken by a medieval theologian, but in the opposite order – starting from the laws of God. The laws of commerce would then look very different. Burke's ordering leaves the church with little to say about business. If Smith was right, market economics had usurped the place of moral theology.

The Rise of the Joint-Stock Company

A paradox – some would call it a contradiction – runs through Smith's thinking. Fundamental to his view of how to increase national prosperity is an approval of *division of labour*: the divide between the owners of production and the labourers who perform specialist functions. A logical outcome of this thinking is the assembly line, where value-adding actions are performed in a logical progression by groups of workers who do the same thing over and over again. Smith saw it as the means to increase efficiency. But despite his enthusiasm for the overall benefits of division of labour, Smith is under no illusions about the wretched lot of the poor factory workers. Repetitive work deadens the senses: 'The man whose whole life is spent in performing a few simple operations ... generally becomes as stupid and ignorant as is possible for a human to become' (*Wealth of Nations*, p.734). In addition, because employers are far more powerful than employees, workers are often paid bare subsistence wages and are especially vulnerable during times of recession or stagnation.

Somewhat unexpectedly, in language that could have come from the pen of Karl Marx, Smith describes at least the poorest sections of the working classes as thoroughly *alienated*: lacking in power, exploited, and estranged from themselves. But he offers no suggestion to overcome the alienation. Desperate conditions are for him simply the price workers must pay for society's economic progress. Not so for Marx. 'Faced with the alienating consequences of the division of labour, Marx chose differently than Smith had: he decided that division of labour had to go, and with it the whole structure of a market economy' (Miroslav Volf, *Work in the Spirit*, p.55). Marx saw the capitalist system as a necessary phase in economic development, but also as intrinsically exploitative and unjust because one social class is made to serve the purposes of another. He said the middle class (or bourgeoisie) creams off the 'surplus value' created by the working class (or proletariat). Employees are alienated from their work, so they find little satisfaction or meaning in it, and are deprived of a proper reward for it. Marx said this situation could not be sustained indefinitely. Eventually the proletariat would stage a revolution, seizing the means of production and owning it communally. Only then could their alienation be overcome.

Marx rejected the Christian faith wholesale. Regarding religious profession as subordinate to economic circumstances, he saw Christianity as a tool of social control, the 'opium of the people'. The employing class used it to distract the workforce from their plight, to inculcate obedience and channel emotions in a non-subversive way. But that is not an essential part of his theory, and it is possible – as Stephen Green says in his book *Serving God? Serving Mammon?* – to imagine a Christian version of Karl Marx, fulminating against the rich much like the eighth century Old Testament prophet Amos. But no major figure emerged. On the whole, Christian churches failed to develop a sustained, coherent, radical critique of the workings of nineteenth century capitalism.

The churches did not lose all influence overnight, and were never totally silenced by Adam Smith and the rise of free market economics. Christian individuals and groups did respond to the harsh working conditions described so accurately by Smith and condemned so passionately by Marx. In Britain, this response took three main forms.

Wilberforce and Shaftesbury
The first response was to press for legislation to curb the worst excesses of the free market. On the international front, the evangelical MP William Wilberforce led the campaign for the abolition of the slave trade against much resistance from landowners in the West Indies. Eventually he won. On the home front, an equally fervent evangelical, Lord Shaftesbury,

sought to mitigate many of the problems produced in the wake of the Industrial Revolution. He is best known for demanding statutory restrictions on the long hours worked in factories. In 1833 he carried a bill limiting children's employment to ten hours a day, and in 1842, one prohibiting underground work in mines for women and children. He helped enhance sanitary reforms in London and ensure acceptable conditions in lodging houses and mental asylums. A man of unflagging energy, who sacrificed his chances of political advancement to the cause of social reform, Shaftesbury thoroughly deserved the tribute of 'the working man's friend'. But he trusted his own judgment over that of the workers themselves. He campaigned on their behalf, not alongside them.

Christian socialism

The second response was a diluted form of Marxism, in the shape of the Christian Socialist movement. In fact, it is more accurate to say movements, because a variety of groups travelled under this name. Some, like the theologians F.D. Maurice and Maurice Reckitt, favoured workers' cooperatives and guild socialism. Others, like the Anglican high churchman Stewart Headlam, favoured public takeover of private enterprises and the land: what later became known as state socialism. Christian socialists – especially Nonconformists – were prominent in the early trade unions, organised in the late nineteenth century to balance the power of employers and to secure adequate wages and working conditions for their members. The claim is often made that the British trade union movement 'owed more to Methodism than to Marx', though other Christian churches – especially Roman Catholicism – could claim a significant influence. Out of this organisation of mass labour came the Labour Party in the final years of the nineteenth century. A whole raft of significant legislation followed: the redistribution of wealth through personal and corporate taxation, unemployment benefit, and monopoly and competition acts that limit the power of individual companies.

Paternalistic employers

Although employers often resisted both legislative reforms and workers' organisations, a few took a more enlightened approach. They felt a responsibility to ensure their workforce was decently paid, clothed, fed and housed. They were concerned too about the wider social environment. In Britain, the late Victorian and Edwardian eras saw the rise of several notable employers who created villages or suburbs to house their workforce, providing facilities for every aspects of their lives. Most of them were motivated by a lively Nonconformist faith They include Titus Salt (1803-76) in Saltaire, W.H. Lever (1851-1926) in Port Sunlight, George Cadbury (1839-1922) in Bournville and Joseph Rowntree (1834-1925) in York. Like Shaftesbury, these paternalist employers could be authoritarian in their sure assumptions about what was good for their employees. But they constructed an impressive alternative to inner-city slums, and showed that business was capable of taking the initiative in exercising social responsibility.

George Cadbury's Story

This letter from Quaker chocolate manufacturer George Cadbury to Charles Gore, the first bishop of Birmingham, gives us a rare glimpse into the mind of one of the great paternalist employers:

> Dear Lord Bishop,
> Those things which divide Christian men into various denominations appear infinitely small when we face problems such as the existence side by side of great wealth and extreme poverty, and why one portion of the community should have a superabundance of wealth which provides them with every comfort and luxury, while large numbers in so-called Christian lands should lack these things which are essential to health and morality. Problems like these are overwhelming, and one feels almost inclined to give them up in despair as "infants crying for the light, and with no language but a cry".

I have for many years given practically the whole of my income for charitable purposes, except what is spent upon my family, but this is not a satisfactory conclusion of the question. As a politician, I have strongly urged doubling the Death Duties, so that a portion of that wealth which men would not give during their lifetime shall be used at their death for the benefit of the nation to which they belong, and a graduated income tax. Nearly all my money is invested in businesses in which I can truly say the first thought is the welfare of the workpeople employed. Should Christian men sell all that they have, such businesses would probably come in the hands of unscrupulous men whose aim is to make dividends as large as possible, regardless of their workpeople. "Give me neither riches nor poverty' – either extreme does not conduce to happiness. "How hardly shall they that have riches enter into the Kingdom of God". The camel had to stoop to go through the Needles' Eye Gate into Jerusalem – the rich man can enter if he will humble himself before God.

I have never written such a letter before, and this must not be published, but I am delighted that godly men are facing problems such as these, and Christians might have a greater influence over the vast masses of our population who are living without God, if they faced these problems. Too often professing Christians, like the priest and the Levite in the parable "pass by on the other side". And do not know the wretched conditions of millions in our cities and towns which make it practically impossible for them to live clean, moral and healthy lives.

The heyday of the Christian paternalist employer was short-lived. Most of the companies they founded survive, but now look very different. Over three or four generations, their ethos has been severely diluted. This is not just because the sons or successors of a movement's founder rarely share his starry-eyed idealism in all its fullness, true though that is. It is also because these companies have changed their basic structure. They have made the transition from family controlled business to public limited company. The significance of this can hardly be overestimated.

In Britain, the 1862 Companies Act authorised the joint stock company. This enshrined the principle of limited liability for shareholders. Companies had discovered that once they reached a certain size, the only way they could secure the required infusion of capital for further expansion was through ensuring that the risk involved was substantially reduced. Limited liability provided this. The liability of shareholders was limited to their initial stake in the firm. This meant that members of the public could buy shares in companies, unfettered by fears about paying out sizeable sums if things went badly wrong. Initially a company was granted 'limited' status only by special charter from the crown or parliament. The same progression took place in France: until general limited liability was introduced in 1867, all such companies required a charter from the legislature. Corporate structures differ from country to country, but limited liability provides a basic framework that is now practised very widely around the world.

The concept of the public limited company (PLC) has been subject to serious moral question, on two main counts. The first is whether it is compatible with a proper sense of responsibility. Offering shares to the public is an effective means of raising capital, but is it right or fair that shareholders can walk away from debts to creditors if the firm goes bankrupt? In *Morality and the Marketplace*, Brian Griffiths notes the criticism of Sir Arthur Bryant, the English social historian, that the 1862 Companies Act completed the divorce between the Christian conscience and the economic practice of everyday life. In Griffiths' words, limited liability is 'an incentive for management to play for high stakes and allow the general public to pick up the bill' (*Morality and the Marketplace*, p.109).

The second objection is the gulf that the PLC creates between the roles of ownership and stewardship. Managers find themselves called to account by shareholders whose interest in the company may not extend beyond immediate financial returns. Diligent managing directors who have put much time and energy into running a company may rue their dependence on the fickleness of the stock market. Many shareholders (represented as they usually are by a financial institution) have no long-term concern for the welfare of the company. They measure its success simply by the current 'bottom line'.

In such conditions, the difficulty of preserving a distinctive corporate ethos based on Christian principles becomes clear. Once a company goes public, it has to answer the public. George Cadbury invested an unusual proportion of his profits in the welfare of his employees. If he were chairman of Cadbury Schweppes PLC today, he would be under intense pressure from the City to cut labour costs – and the pressure is increasing daily. A generation ago, an announcement of substantial redundancies would cast gloom over the stock market and send share prices diving. Today, it is seen as a mark of efficiency and a proper move for a company that needs to be lean and trim to flourish in the global marketplace. It usually sends share prices soaring.

The Rise of Pluralism

The third stage in the marginalisation of Christianity is more difficult to pinpoint. The first two are marked by key events: the publication of *Wealth of Nations* in 1776 and the passing of the Companies Acts in 1862. It took decades for the consequences of these events to emerge and only today can we see how momentous they were. The rise of pluralism lacks a defining moment, but the process is no less real, and no less significant.

I have identified pluralism and not secularisation as the third stage even though secularisation has been gathering pace for 200 years. In most of western Europe, decreasing numbers of people go to church or profess Christian belief. God's obituary has been written several times (with the year 2000 providing a convenient excuse) and most commercial life is practised as if he doesn't exist. Marginalisation is what one would expect for a declining faith. Os Guinness writes: 'Formerly the philosopher atheist would shout defiantly, "there is no God!" Now the practical atheist who is the modern manager, marketer, expert, or consultant says with quiet professional authority, "There is no need of God – and frankly, this is not the time or the place for such questions."' (*The Call*, p.207)

Secularisation is insufficient as an explanation for two reasons. First, a small group can exercise influence out of all proportion to its size if it thinks incisively and acts decisively. Consider the early Quakers; quality counts for more than quantity. Second, the level of Christian commitment has stayed much higher in the USA, where 75 million people, about 40% of the population, are estimated to be churchgoers. But there too Christianity is strangely marginalised, especially in the business arena. Some of the most objectionable – arguably unChristian – features of global capitalism are found in the USA. Sociologist Robert Wuthnow's well-researched study, entitled *God and Mammon in America*, concludes that Americans are a generally religious people who are also 'passionately committed to the almighty dollar' (*God and Mammon*, p.4). They appear to be serving two masters, something Jesus said we could not do (Mt. 6:24). Christianity still has an influence, but often not a constructive one as it leads more to ambivalence than to informed ethical decisions or distinct patterns of life. 'Feeling ambivalent, we therefore go about our lives pretty much the same as those who have no faith at all' (*God and Mammon*, p.5). For a variety of reasons, Christians in the USA are failing to make the impact on the way business operates that their numbers might warrant.

Pluralism is the more potent explanation for marginalisation, because pluralism describes a society marked by a considerable variety and diversity of views and outlooks. Different moral, religious and political philosophies and ways of life exist cheek by jowl; sometimes peacefully, sometimes jostling for dominance. As capitalism has become global, as societies have grown multicultural and companies multinational, pluralism has become a feature of the marketplace.

Christianity no longer occupies a privileged position. It has been upstaged by the media, which has probably replaced the family as the main transmitter of values to young people. In many families young children watch television for three or four hours a day, but only have five minutes of meaningful conversation with their father. A secular humanist basis for values, couched in a highly consumerist culture, is thought to attract most consent. Christianity is dumped in the same basket as Judaism, Islam, Hinduism and Buddhism – a religion with minority appeal. In the years following the Second World War churches set up industrial chaplaincies in many parts of the country, particularly large manufacturing firms. They are finding it much more difficult to gain access to companies today. When a workforce is multi-ethnic and includes adherents of several religions, why should Christianity be granted a special institutional presence?

There is a revival of interest in spirituality in the workplace, explored in greater detail in Chapter 13. Many companies are becoming sensitive to the spiritual dimension in their employees, and the desirability of their bringing the 'whole self' to work. Use of the word 'spirituality' varies and is notoriously difficult to pin down. It is often defined in terms of interconnectedness: a sense of being connected with the self, with others, with nature, and – quite possibly – with the divine. While such connections can be understood in a Christian way, most advocates of spirituality at work are much more sympathetic to ideas from Eastern religion, adopt 'New Age' thinking or even distinguish spirituality sharply from religion altogether. Where insights from the Christian faith are incorporated, it is usually in a syncretistic way, alongside concepts taken from other sources.

The extent to which Christianity is being marginalised in this process is also evident in bookstores. Shops in Australia and New Zealand reveal the same pattern as in Britain. If Christianity still has a section, it often consists of nothing more than some Bibles and a few other books. In contrast, large sections of shelf space are given over to 'Body, Mind and Spirit', 'New Age' and 'The Occult'. This prompts a serious question: 'Has the faith which was the basis of our Western civilisation been dismissed as old hat?' It is coming to look this way.

That is not the whole story. Some commentators see Christianity as a continuing influence in business, and regard that influence as distinctly unwelcome. Gordon Pearson is a director of Keele Management Centre at Keele University and a lecturer in strategic management. *In Integrity in Organisations: An Alternative Business Ethic*, he takes stock of what he calls the 'business ethics movement' and accurately describes the presence of three groups at business ethics conferences:

- senior managers from industry and commerce
- academics from the field of management studies and other disciplines, often adopting a philosophical approach to business ethics
- 'surprisingly large' numbers who 'come from various religious backgrounds, mainly from branches of the Christian churches'.

Pearson says: 'The religious community seeks both to learn and to proselytise. Their underlying motivation for attending such a conference is presumably to increase their understanding of the ways in which the world of business functions, or malfunctions, so that their efforts to improve humanity's moral worth, and in particular the ethics of business operations, might be better informed and more effective, so that they might increase their beneficial impact on the world.'

Business delegates are there to improve the ethical standing of their organisations, he says, and are 'sometimes puzzled, even dismayed, to find their concerns being hi-jacked by clerics and academics and turned into a subject which they do not understand and which seems to have little relation to practical business situations. Appealing to people to behave in a certain way because the creator of the universe wishes it so, is not helpful if most of the population do not believe in the existence of a superior being. Similarly, appeals to ethical behaviour on the often subtle and obscure grounds advanced by moral philosophers, may have only limited effect on managers who are largely unconcerned with philosophy' (*Integrity in Organisations*, p.25).

Pearson, claiming to represent the best interests of business practitioners, offers in contrast a hard-nosed approach that he claims, remarkably, to be 'value-free'. Within this, he has an important place for *integrity*, which was very much a buzz-word in company codes and mission statements throughout the 1990s. To be perceived as honest and trustworthy is of long-term commercial advantage in most stakeholder relationships. True, he recognises that for a company to be perceived as trustworthy it helps if it actually *is* trustworthy. But for Pearson, integrity is first and foremost a calculated image an organisation should cultivate.

His hostility to Christian influences resurfaces in his conclusion, where he warns: 'Beware the well-meaning "do-gooder" who puts your business at a competitive disadvantage for purely religious reasons. Beware the business ethicist who would prefer business did not exist – except that they earn their living from it – rather than see it act from self-interest to beat competitors or make a profit' (p.164). I think Pearson misrepresents these groups. The academics and religious people I have met at the conferences he describes are genuinely motivated to see business succeed and prosper, but have a deeper view of integrity than the one he recommends. But it is revealing to see how deep the suspicion goes. Pearson's clear, unambiguous message is that adopting Christian values could damage your organisational health, and its ability to survive in the rough, tough world of business.

A similar vein of antagonism runs through a book brazenly titled *Sin to Win*, by Marc Lewis, a young man who made his money starting and then selling Web Marketing, an internet company. Lewis pillories Christianity for inventing the seven deadly sins as a way of exerting social control and impeding progress. Avoiding these sins, he claims, will stop you realising your full potential. Pride, envy, gluttony, lust, anger, avarice and sloth are powerful motivating factors enabling you to realise your personal goals, whatever they are. All successful companies commit at least one of the seven deadly sins.

Lewis explains: 'What does Rolls Royce stand for, if not pride? When Avis decided to beat Hertz and pledged to try harder to become the world's biggest car rental company, they displayed nothing less than naked envy. When Richard Branson enters into court actions against British Airways or Camelot, he fights for even greater personal and corporate success with anger. When Shell, BP and Esso preserve their margins by ignoring fuel protestors and hiding under governmental skirts they employ sloth with unrivalled skill. It was covetousness that spurred Ford to try to buy Ferrari and it was Fiat's corporate lust that beat them, forcing Ford to vent their envious desires on Aston Martin and Jaguar instead. And if Microsoft doesn't prove there's nothing wrong with a good strong dose of old-fashioned gluttony, nothing ever will' *(Sin to Win*, p.xiv).

'Forget what you learnt at Sunday school,' he adds (p.xv), and later crows 'At the turn of the twentieth century, 56% of British children attended Sunday school. At the turn of the twenty-first, that figure stands at less than 4%' (p.203). Lewis says this is because Christianity relied on fear to sell its message, but now we have no need to fear. Consumerism is the new religion, 'our pursuit of happiness, peace and contentment through the shared experience of the superstore or the television show or the website or the text message' (p.209). The seven deadly sins are the necessary baggage that go with this new consumerist evangelism.

This isn't just the marginalisation of Christianity in business by today's pluralist society, it amounts to a contemptuous dismissal. While it is tempting to dismiss Lewis' book as sensationalist and silly, he touches a raw nerve. Many people today, including many business practitioners, have overtly abandoned any restraint on selfish impulses. Virtues and vices are being inverted. Greed is good and sin to win: the gauntlet has well and truly been thrown down. How can Christianity meet this challenge?

2

THE GLOBAL ECONOMY TODAY:
CAPITALISM UNDER THE MICROSCOPE

Defining Capitalism

Feudalism: You have two cows. Your lord takes some of the milk.

Fascism: You have two cows. The government takes both, hires you to take care of them and sells you the milk.

Communism: You have two cows. You must take care of them, but the government takes all the milk.

Capitalism: You have two cows. You sell one and buy a bull. Your herd multiplies, and the economy grows. You sell them and retire on the income.

Enron Capitalism: You have two cows. You sell three of them to your publicly listed company, using letters of credit opened by your brother-in-law at the bank, then create a debt equity swap with an associated general offer so that you get all four cows back, with a tax exemption for five cows. The milk rights of the six cows are transferred

through an intermediary to a Cayman
Island company secretly owned by the
majority shareholder, who sells the rights
to all seven cows back to your listed company. The Enron annual report says the
company owns eight cows, with an
option on one more!

For most of the 1990s it was thought that capitalism had tri-
umphed over its rivals. Karl Marx said capitalism was a
necessary stage in economic development that would be
replaced by communism, but it has actually outlasted its ideological foe. Many of the countries that pursued a system of
democratic socialism, practising a mixed economy of private
and publicly owned companies, have shifted in a capitalist
direction over the last two decades. Labour governments
today practise what a generation ago would have been
described as Conservative-style economics – Tony Blair's
British government being a notable example.

Capitalism is an elusive concept. It is a word much bandied
around, both orally and on the written page, but people very
seldom stop to define what they mean by it. Capitalism can be
variously described as:

- A system concerned to increase the amount of capital
  (money and resources that can be converted into money) a
  trading organisation has. There is therefore a fundamental
  concern with economic growth. This distinguishes it from a
  system that is content simply to stay at current levels of
  production or consumption, or operates on a bartering principle
- A system in which the capital is in the possession of private
  owners, who employ others as means of production. This
  distinguishes it from a system where capital is in the hands
  of the state (state socialism) or capital is shared among the
  whole workforce (a co-operative system)
- A system that emphasises the freedom of individuals and
  companies to produce, sell and buy goods and services in

the marketplace with a minimum of government interference. This distinguishes it from a system where the government frequently intervenes to restrict individual freedom or influence the workings of the economy

• A system that allows considerable autonomy to the market, and in particular patterns of supply and demand, in terms of deciding where resources are allocated and of determining levels of prices and wages. This distinguishes it from a system that assumes to know what a 'just' price or wage is, or which seeks to distribute wealth equally to people.

The four key features of capitalism turn out to be economic growth, private possession of capital, individual freedom and the autonomy of the market. On reflection, most people would probably recognise the importance of each of these features – but the one they emphasise or which is dominant in their understanding of capitalism will vary. If one of them *is* to be picked out, the logic of the word 'capitalism' suggests that it should be the first: the central concern of the system is with an increase in capital.

The word has been with us a long time, but only during the last few years have we begun to speak of global capitalism. *Globalisation* has entered our language and become a major area for debate. Why? Partly because the media has made us aware of the extent and nature of global trade, and technological advance has accelerated this, making it easier to buy and sell goods across geographical barriers. Partly because financial markets are increasingly deregulated and interconnected, facilitating the buying and selling of shares and currencies on a global scale. Partly because some of the world's most powerful organisations are multinational corporations, doing business and setting up units and subsidiary companies in a host of different countries. And partly because cross-cultural spread has created near-universal habits of consumption, so the three best-known icons in the world today are probably the Coca-Cola logo, the golden arches of McDonalds, and the swoosh of Nike.

Loose Talking

In much of the talk about capitalism in recent years, I have observed three interconnected trends that together amount to a loose use of language.

First, there is a tendency to talk about capitalism or its closely related concept 'the free market' (often shortened to the market) as if it were a personal agent. Capitalism is described as liberating or enslaving, as providing or stifling, as winning or losing. It is made to sound like a system with a life or mind of its own, independent of the lives and decisions of those who operate within it. This is understandable, both because it is a useful form of shorthand and because capitalism is characterised by forces or patterns of behaviour so powerful and prevalent that they seem difficult to withstand. But there is a danger of taking this language too literally.

Second, there is a tendency to underestimate the impact of specific cultures on capitalism.

An illustration of the first tendency is how huge salaries for chief executives are justified by saying 'the market' determines how much they should be paid. I heard the chief executive of the Institute of Directors doing this. The implication is that if companies won't pay these salaries, they won't get the person they want. But the market varies a great deal from country to country, even between countries of comparable economic stature. The market rate for a chief executive is about one-third more in America than in any other country. It is 27 times more than the average American worker. A chief executive gets 17 times more than an average worker in the UK, 13 times in Japan, 9 times in New Zealand and 7 times in Sweden. It is individuals, not the market, who demand certain levels of pay, with some being able to get what they want and others not. While what individuals demand is undoubtedly influenced by the behaviour of their peers, this in turn is influenced by the culture of the country in which they live. In some countries a huge salary is regarded as fair game if you can get it. In others, it is denounced as greedy and socially divisive. That is just one example.

In their fascinating book *The Seven Cultures of Capitalism*, Charles Hampden-Turner and Fons Trompenaars argue convincingly that capitalism is not one seamless robe but has countless variations, rooted in different national histories and cultures. This is reflected in the relationship between governments, financial institutions and companies typical of different countries. For instance, banks are major holders of equity in Germany in a way that is unusual in Britain; companies are typically small and family-based in China, but large and outweighing family loyalties in Japan.

Third, there is a tendency to underestimate personal responsibility for what happens in a capitalist system. Of course, once we have demythologised the language of the market, we may criticise the 'fat cats' for creaming off a company's profits. But the critics of capitalism too easily distance themselves from the system, or delude themselves about the extent to which they are active participants and probably beneficiaries from the system. Anglican clergy in Britain include many more critics than supporters of capitalism. I do not hear many protesting that their pension comes from the Church Commissioners' investment of church money in a wide variety of companies on the Stock Exchange. We are active players as investors, even if other people made the investment on our behalf; and even more fundamentally, we are active players as consumers. Every time we visit a supermarket our purchases play their part in the ebb and flow of global capitalism – for better or worse, for richer or poorer, sometimes even contributing to people's sickness and health. To what extent if at all do concepts of 'fair trade' influence our purchases?

Where do the outspoken, militant critics of global capitalism who have surfaced in recent years – the protestors at the World Trade Organisation meeting in Seattle, the World Economic Forum meeting in Melbourne, and the G8 meeting in Genoa, or the anarchists who make a date to smash up the City of London once a year – shop and eat? Their protests are often as muddled and ignorant as they are strident. 'I don't know what the World Bank does but I hate the rich', a banner at Seattle proclaimed. Even Naomi Klein, an outspoken critic of the business world in her best-selling book *No Logo*, says of the Seattle protestors: 'Trapped in the headlights of irony and carrying too much pop-culture baggage, not one of its anti-heroes could commit to a single, solid political position' (*No Logo*, p.83).

We cannot simply dismiss the anti-capitalism movement, however. Several substantial criticisms of the current state of global capitalism have been made, and deserve to be taken seriously.

The Dark Side of Capitalism

The overall thrust of these criticisms is that under global capitalism the gulf between rich and poor is widening. Adam Smith's central thesis is untrue: pursuit of self-interest has not worked for the general good. His subsidiary thesis – which is in tension with the first – has proved accurate: the lot of the poor has grown more wretched. Internationally, the historical statistics are startling. Per capita income 250 years ago varied between the richest and poorest nations by about five to one. Today it is 400 to one. According to UN statistics, inequality between rich and poor has doubled in the last 15 years. More than one billion people lack access to basic health and education, safe drinking water and adequate nutrition. The poorest countries, with 20% of the world's population, saw their share of world trade fall from 4% in 1960 to less than 1% four decades later. Even within the richer countries a comparable widening of the gulf has taken place.

Over 200 years after Adam Smith, Harvard historian David Landes has written a wide-ranging investigation into *The Wealth and Poverty of Nations*. He asks: How did the rich countries get so rich and the poor countries so poor? In particular, why did Europe (the West) take the lead in changing the world? Most answers fall into one of two schools, he says: 'Some see European wealth as the triumph of good over bad. The Europeans, they say, were smarter, better organised, harder working. The others were ignorant, arrogant, lazy, backward, superstitious. Others see it as a triumph of bad over good. The Europeans, they say, were aggressive, ruthless, greedy, unscrupulous, hypocritical; their victims were happy, innocent, weak – waiting victims and hence thoroughly victimised' (*The Wealth and Poverty of Nations*, p.xxi).

Those who condemn the capitalist system take the latter view, saying the process continues to this day. Global capitalism is a system in which the North – probably a better word to use now than the West – exploits the South – probably better to use than the Third World. (Both couplets have their problems: Australia for instance belongs with the North.) The charge is that the North abuses its position of power, and leaves the underdeveloped countries of the world poorer, not richer. In particular, this accusation is levelled at a variety of powerful agents within the system.

Currency dealers
Currency dealers on the world's money markets have grown steadily in power and influence over the last 30 years. Before 1970, financial markets were geared towards domestic economies. Most money stayed at home. The world's major currencies were also controlled by a system of fixed exchange rates. When these failed to reflect a country's underlying financial position, currencies were adjusted by devaluations, but these were occasional, one-off events. With the abandonment of rigid exchange rates in the early 1970s, power shifted from national governments to currency dealers. Currencies were allowed to 'float'. Some attempts have been made to revert to a more fixed system, as with the European Exchange Rate Mechanism (ERM) in the late 1980s and early 1990s. But what happened there was very instructive. The British government discovered that it was impossible to maintain the pound's exchange rate at a level linked to the German mark in the face of the overwhelming view of the dealers that it was over-valued. On 16 September 1992, following futile attempts to maintain the pound at an artificially high level by jacking up interest rates, it was forced to concede defeat to the market and leave the ERM.

In theory, flexible exchange rates should have led to much smaller, if more frequent, changes in exchange rates that were less disruptive than the large, occasional changes made by governments. Over thirty years it is difficult to maintain this has been the case. Lester C. Thurow, not an enemy of capitalism but an astute observer of it, says: 'The speculators who were supposed to be looking at long-run real values and off-setting the effects of the short-run, herd-mentality speculators simply didn't exist. Once a rush to the door started, everyone jumped on the trends regardless of fundamentals. Currencies roared up and down' (*The Future of Capitalism*, p.224).

In late 1994 and early 1995 Mexico experienced a major financial crisis caused by a mass sale of Mexican pesos. Objective analysis suggests this was actually quite arbitrary: Mexico's economy had its problems, but it was in no worse state than several countries of comparable status. Similarly, the Asian crisis of 1998 was caused as much by the volatility of financial speculation as the underlying strength or weakness of the region's economy.

Whatever one may think of the currency dealers' judgment, there is no doubting the huge scale of their operations. On an average day worldwide, the world's capital markets trade around $1.5 trillion. In a little over two days, according to Thurow, 'the world's capital markets move as much money as all of the world's economies move in a year' (p.223). To the critics, this is casino capitalism. It is betting on which way the wind of trading will blow; and has nothing to do with the creation of wealth in any meaningful sense of the phrase. The most powerful centres of currency dealing are in the North.

Multinational companies

The largest multinational companies are said to be dangerously powerful, handling financial assets greater than those of many countries of the South. Their power has eclipsed that of the nation-state. They are said to be footloose and fancy-free, able to manipulate money round the globe to pay as little tax as possible. The fact that they are international means they often lack a sense of accountability to (or in) any one country. They feel no responsibility to preserve jobs in a 'home' country, relocating plants and services wherever it makes business sense. They are investing capital in the countries of the South, but – it is alleged – to exploit rather than help those countries. This exploitation takes the form of profiting from those countries' natural resources; making use of the cheap labour found in the South; and taking advantage of weaker legislation or sometimes a complete lack of legislation relating to health, safety, environmental and advertising standards.

There is a lot of truth in these accusations. We all know horror stories about multinational companies, including:

- The tragic explosion at the Union Carbide factory at Bhopal, India, in 1984, where culpable corporate negligence led to the deaths of hundreds of people and damaged the health of thousands
- Nestlé's pressing of its infant formula foods on mothers in countries where poor sanitation made them dangerous to use
- The meagre wages paid by sports shoe manufacturers to children in Asia for their part in making trainers that sell for inflated prices in the North. The $20 million that Nike allegedly paid basketball star Michael Jordan for promoting their sports shoes in 1992 exceeded the entire annual payroll of the Indonesian factories that made them
- The insidious advertising tactics used by tobacco manufacturers such as Philip Morris to persuade people in the South to take up the deadly habit of smoking. More about this in Chapter 6
- The Southern farmers being exploited by Northern agribusiness, which lures them to buy hybrid cotton seeds or patents life forms and indigenous knowledge. In the fifth Reith Lecture, Vandana Shiva claimed: 'The knowledge of the poor is being converted into the property of global corporations, creating a situation where the poor will have to pay for the seeds and medicines they have evolved and have used to meet their own needs for nutrition and healthcare.'

- As an example of the sin of omission rather than commission, the way pharmaceutical companies target their research and development efforts overwhelmingly at medical ailments of the North, and neglect tropical diseases such as malaria that cause about 50% of the world's illnesses. Such diseases attract 3% of the world's medical research money.

Environmental damage caused by business activity has long-term implications for the whole world. The extent is disputed, but there is no doubt that land degradation, deforestation, species extinction, water degradation, global toxification, and the alteration of the earth's atmosphere are all happening on a serious scale. Global warming, linked very likely to a release of greenhouse gases through the burning of fossil fuels and a reduction in the world's forests, is producing a hole in the ozone layer that particularly threatens low-lying countries in the southern hemisphere. Over the last 200 years human activities have increased the amount of carbon dioxide in the atmosphere by over 30%. Although measures are being taken to slow down this trend, they look like being too little too late. Multinationals are made to bear much of the blame for this.

There is strong resistance, not just from business but from people in general, to significant reductions in energy consumption. The USA appears to be in denial about the environmental crisis, as shown by the price of petrol at the pump, where it is below one dollar a gallon at the time of writing. In the UK petrol costs two and a half times as much, mainly as a result of government-added tax, and in the autumn of 2000 this led to serious protests. It is interesting, however, that the government refused to defend this on environmental grounds. Instead of saying the tax is necessary to deter people from driving, it said it is to provide more public money for schools and hospitals.

Another charge made against global capitalism is that of disrupting indigenous cultures and producing a dreary uniformity of consumerist culture. Perhaps no company illustrates this more aptly than McDonalds, whose zeal in producing an unlimited supply of burgers has been linked to the clearing of forests in South America for grazing cattle, and who open new restaurants every day somewhere in the world. The North foists its products on the South, and while many in the South appear eager for them these products often cause more harm than good or become prized ahead of more basic needs. This is evident in shanty towns where everyone has a television set, but there is no clean water and the roads are dangerous to drive on. White people introduced Australian Aboriginals to the delights of alcohol, and this has caused particular devastation in that community because the Aboriginals have a genetic predisposition which makes them especially vulnerable to alcohol addiction. And in general terms, the Northern habit of associating personal identity and status with the possession of certain material goods is becoming all too pervasive.

International institutions

Along with the financial markets and multinational companies, a formidable measure of power lies with certain international financial institutions. Set up at the Breton Woods conference in New Jersey just before the end of the Second World War, these are the third major target for capitalism's critics. One institution is the World Bank: originally the International Bank for Reconstruction and Development. After the war it provided substantial sums in loans and gift aid to enable the countries of Western Europe to rebuild their damaged economies. Its loans were chiefly to finance public infrastructure. A second is the International Monetary Fund (IMF). It also lent money, but was more concerned about short-term liquidity problems in government expenditure and national income. The core functions of both the World Bank and IMF are unchanged, but most borrowers are now the poor countries of the South rather than the rich countries of the North. It is in this capacity that they are much criticised, as the major creditors in the phenomenon of global debt.

The basic facts are familiar. Over the last 20 years, debt in the South has grown ruthlessly until those countries now pay

the North three times as much in debt services as they receive
in aid payments. The net flow of money is therefore from the
poor to the rich, not the rich to the poor. National governments
and commercial banks are among those getting the money, but
the World Bank and IMF are the major players. Since the mid-
1980s their response to the plight of impoverished countries
has generally taken the form of 'structural adjustment programmes' that require these countries to reduce their public
spending and increase their crop exports to improve their
balance of payments. This has often meant cuts in basic education, health and water supply programmes, with allegedly
catastrophic results: it is estimated that 8 million children may
have died last year as an indirect result of their country transferring resources. The scale of problem is such that for around
fifty Heavily Indebted Countries (HIDCs) with limited capacity to earn foreign currency it is difficult to see how the debt
can ever be repaid.

In response to the Jubilee 2000 campaign, these creditors
reduced or renegotiated some of the debt to a limited extent.
But there has been a signal unwillingness to cancel, or as some
would say 'forgive', debts outright. Unlike individuals or
companies, there is no way a country can be declared bankrupt. If it stops financing its debts, the debts stay on the books
and the country risks exclusion from the world economic community. It will then be unable to borrow any more money in
the foreseeable future.

The Breton Woods conference also set up a General
Agreement on Tariffs and Trade (GATT), which was intended
to reduce barriers to international trade. During several
rounds of discussions sustained over nearly fifty years it did
indeed preach a gospel of free trade, and gradually succeeded
in getting countries to dismantle tariffs and quotas. But exceptions were frequently made to special interest groups, notably
farmers in the North to protect them against imports from the
South. This evoked the obvious criticism that there was a disparity of power among the negotiating parties. GATT was also
criticised for overruling national legislation designed to safeguard ethical concerns. For instance, environmentalists were

incensed when an American law requiring tuna sold in the USA to be caught using sophisticated nets that avoided ensnaring dolphins was overthrown by GATT following an appeal by Mexico, whose fishermen used more economical nets that tended to catch dolphins along with the tuna. (The problem occurs because tuna and dolphins have the habit of swimming together.)

GATT's successor, the World Trade Organisation (WTO), has also been charged with the crime of indifference to the processes by which products available in world trade are made – though usually with reference to the exploitation of human labour rather than the destruction of animals. The WTO is a significant step forward from the Breton Woods institutions in one sense as it formally alters the balance of power, because every member country from the richest to the poorest has one vote. But as the virulent protests in Seattle and elsewhere have shown, it is still regarded as being weighted in favour of the interests of the North. Whether justified or not, it has become a symbolic scapegoat for those determined to vent their fury on the capitalist system.

The Radical Christian Critique

It is not surprising that criticism of global capitalism is building up a considerable head of steam, even among countries doing well out of it. Christian voices can be heard among the outcry. A system characterised by exploitation of the weak, devastation of the world's ecosystem, expansion of materialism and worsening of poverty is one that doesn't sit comfortably with the Christian faith, which has the core values or virtues of love and justice at its heart. The specific evils of global capitalism stand under the judgment of various strands of biblical teaching:

● God's bias to the poor – God's special concern for the poor, shown both in the message of the prophets and the ministry of Jesus, and his demand that they be treated with mercy, dignity and respect

- Human beings' responsibility for creation – the responsibility God has given to humanity, found both in the creation stories and some of the psalms, to be faithful stewards or managers of the earth
- The doctrine of the divine image – the belief that our value is found in the fact that humans are made in God's image and is demonstrated by his becoming man, in the person of Jesus, in order to redeem us. Our identity is therefore not to be found in the material things of this world, which offer temptations to idolatry
- The paradigm offered by the institution of Jubilee – the example found in the Old Testament law of a periodic release from debts which provides restoration from the inequalities created by the practice of trade, and enshrines the principles of justice, mercy and hope in dealing with those who have fallen on hard times.

Some Christian theologians are so struck by the contrast between these biblical motifs and present-day realities that they have nothing good at all to say about global capitalism. It provokes their fierce condemnation.

A Confessional Issue?

Prominent among the critics is German Lutheran theologian Ulrich Duchrow. As far back as 1986, he argued in his book *Global Economy* that the global economic system is so serious an embodiment of evil that it ought to be a confessional issue for the churches. This is theological speak for an issue so serious that support for it is deemed incompatible with being an authentic Christian church. Duchrow says: 'Sometimes ... a system can become so totally perverted as to fall, so to speak, into the hands of demons. Christians and churches must then dissociate themselves clearly by their words and deeds from such a system, either at specific points or even completely' (*Global Economy*, p.92).

Recent examples of political systems where Christians have largely agreed about their utter abhorrence are Nazism and apartheid. On the global economy, Duchrow finds instead a worrying acquiescence, people even defending a 'cut-throat' system in Christ's name. He calls on us to wake up to the fact that: 'We inhabitants of industrialised nations, together with a few tiny elites in the countries of Asia, Africa and Latin America, are exploiting the majority of the world's population just as systematically as the white South Africans exploit the majority of the people in South Africa. The demon of profit for the few at the expense (i.e. the impoverishment) of the many has the whole world economic system firmly in its grip, with all the sideeffects in the shape of discrimination and the suppression of human rights' (p.93). Duchrow even talks about a new form of global fascism, consisting of a coalition of big business and big government.

Choosing life is the theme of *Capital and the Kingdom*, by Anglican theologian Timothy Gorringe. His biblical basis for this is Deuteronomy 30:19: 'I call heaven and earth to witness against you this day, that I have set before you life and death, blessing and curse; therefore choose life, that you and your descendants may live.' Like the Israelites addressed in Deuteronomy, Gorringe thinks that we stand clearly before two ways, a way of life and a way of death. 'At the present time thirty million human beings die each year from preventable hunger, resources are transferred systematically from the poor to the rich, and the earth's respiratory system is being destroyed. This is no tragic accident but stems from the way in which the world economy is structured, and the distribution of resources between rich and poor countries' (*Capital and the Kingdom*, p.viii).

He sees the underlying assumptions and imperatives of conventional economics as leading the world to catastrophe. Like Duchrow, he bemoans the triumph of the ideology of self-interest, the autonomous market, and the concealed exercise of powerful forces within it. He consistently presents the North as an exploiter and pillager, and the South as the unfortunate victim. In his final chapter, Gorringe calls for replacing the present economic order. He wants to eradicate the distinction between managers and managed, replace the multinational economy as the central focus of interest with the local economy, and abolish usury. He claims that none of these proposals is Utopian. Anticipation of such schemes already exists in some places, as in the long-standing association of co-operatives in northern Spain. 'At the moment they are forced to exist under the hegemony of the market, but the need to generalise their practice must be understood not as impractical idealism but rather a sober programme for survival' (p.168).

Are these assessments justified? My own view is that global capitalism does indeed exhibit abundant evidence of the dark shadow cast by what Christian theologians call the fall: the fact that human beings fall far short of their high calling and deviate from God's purposes for them and his world in a great variety of ways. The workings of the international economy reveal much that is selfish, much that is cruel, much that is cynical or manipulative, much that displays the flagrant exploitation by vested interests of their position of power – often deceiving both themselves and others that this is what they're doing. However, I do not believe that a Christian response to global capitalism should consist simply in joining in a widespread denunciation. For me, that fails on at least two counts.

First, if this position were widely adopted it is guaranteed to cement the increasing marginalisation of Christianity from business. Wholesale rejection would prevent the churches and their members from voicing a constructive protest within it. Some of the small-scale alternatives Duchrow recommends are worth trying, but are likely to remain small-scale and so unlikely to have much impact on the mainstream global economy. Gorringe's final chapter is indeed Utopian. The reality is that capitalism is not going to lie down and allow itself to be replaced, especially in light of the collapse and perceived failure of communism. To talk of a new economic order begs two critical questions – how do we move from the current order to the new one, and how do we prevent the new order reverting to the old one. Some crucial aspects of human nature would resist the creation of the egalitarian, non-competitive ideal for which Gorringe longs.

Wholesale rejection of the current system might be justified if its evils were as undiluted as Duchrow and Gorringe allege. We rightly regard collaboration with Nazism or apartheid as morally unacceptable. But the analogy, thoughtful and provocative though it is, breaks down. My conviction is that global capitalism is a much more complicated phenomenon about which to make an overall judgment. A measure of ambivalence in one's judgment is therefore appropriate. This should not be misread as a sign of moral or intellectual cowardice.

This leads to my second point, which is that radical critics fail because they are selective with the facts. It is tempting to carve the world up into rich baddies and poor goodies, but life is not that simple. There is a serious moral issue at stake here. How concerned are we to speak the truth, even when we encounter evidence that refuses to fit our predetermined categories of good and evil? In discussing global capitalism, it befits Christians to be as fair and judicious in their assessment as possible, to recognise and praise what is good as well as exposing and criticising what is bad. We have a responsibility to give as balanced an account of what is going on as we can muster. If that sometimes means saying things that are unfashionable or may be misunderstood, so be it. We should not be found wanting in the virtue of courage.

Signs of hope

I offer the following signs of hope, not retracting my critique of the 'dark side of capitalism' but balancing it and illustrating some scope for self-correction observable within global capitalism:

First, it is clearly wrong to tar all practitioners with the same dark brush. I have met many people in business who are remarkably idealistic, exhibit a high degree of integrity, and care deeply about the people affected by their activities. I have met many corporate people with a strong sense of responsibility to all the different groups they do business with: not just a responsibility to themselves or their shareholders, but also to customers, employees, suppliers and the local or wider community.

It is also unfair to tar all the financial institutions with the same brush. I shall confine myself to a balancing comment regarding multinational companies (though a defence could also be made of currency dealers and international institutions). Alongside those that warrant censure, there are companies whose activities are having positive effects in the countries of the South where they have a presence. Where they hold high standards of health, safety and environment they practise across the world, they usually outperform local standards and can have the effect of raising standards in those countries. Comparative surveys by the International Labor Organisation (ILO) and the UN Centre for Transnational Corporations have shown this to be the case. The attempt by radical critics to pin all the blame for environmental pollution on the North also flies in the face of the facts. The cities of economically backward eastern Europe have much dirtier air than those of western Europe. During the early stages of industrialisation, countries tend to see the alleviation of pollution problems as a lower priority. Responsible multinationals can help move it higher up the agenda.

While positioning specific functions in the countries of the South often has an element of taking advantage of cheaper labour – paying employees less than in the North – it also has the fundamental effect of creating jobs. It offers those countries the prospect of a crucial competitive advantage. In relation to this *The Judas Economy: The Triumph of Capital and the Betrayal of Work*, written by American business journalists William Wolman and Anne Colamosca, makes a salutary read. Its major theme is what the authors see as the betrayal of Western (principally American) workers, as multinational companies turn to increasingly well-educated and qualified workers in emerging economies. They take software engineers and research scientists in Bangalore, India, as a case in point. The overall widening of the gulf between rich and poor should not obscure the fact that there are some major shifts of wealth going on within that spectrum. Not all the countries that would have been described as poor in 1960 are poor any longer. There has been the emergence of the four 'Asian tigers' (Taiwan, Hong Kong, Singapore and South Korea), as well as significant advances made in most Asian countries, including those slumbering giants of China and India. Some South American countries also now come into the 'middle income' category. Africa remains a continent beset by poverty and serious development problems, and that is a major cause for concern, but the rest of the globe is not standing still. Although Wolman and Colamosca, from a narrow national perspective, lament the fact that the gap between America and the rest of the world is narrowing, the fact is that multinationals – by their very nature – lack this preoccupation with protecting national interest. They are ready to use and encourage talent wherever they identify it.

Child Labour

An important issue, and one which readily arouses the indignation of critics of multinational companies, is child labour in underdeveloped countries. Children in their early teens or even younger are used in many countries (particularly on the Asian continent) to perform hard, laborious work. In India, for instance, low-caste children as young as nine are effectively bonded into slavery to manufacture *beedis*, a local cigarette. Abusive employers often force these children to crouch on the floor for hours in poor light and bad ventilation, breathing in tobacco fumes. Some child labour is used to make consumer goods for the export market, which is where the multinationals come in. The answer to this evil seems obvious: hound the companies into changing their practice by organising consumer boycotts, and ban goods known to entail child labour. Reality is more complex. The solution may leave the children in a worse situation, not a better one. When the USA took a decision in 1995 not to import garments made by workers under fifteen, the Bangladeshi clothing industry was badly hit.

At least 50,000 child workers were sent home, affecting 1.5 million families. Many of the children went from earning between $30 and $40 a month to a meagre income as garbage collectors or a morally degrading one as prostitutes.

The point is that eradicating bad practice – though desirable – is insufficient alone. Positive alternatives need to be found. If there are no schools for children or the underlying cause is family poverty, banning child labour wholesale is a misguided gesture.

There is now a trend for companies to work with NGOs and national governments on a more responsible, long-term strategy towards ending child labour. Rugmark is a labelling initiative established in 1994 to eliminate the illegal use of child labour in the carpet industry in South Asia. The Rugmark Foundation has established a system of labelling that guarantees carpets are free of child labour. Manufacturers and exporters in India and Nepal make commitments not to use child labour, and importers in Europe and the USA commit themselves to purchasing only carpets with the Rugmark label. Both exporters and importers make a financial contribution to Rugmark, which uses the money to pay for the inspection of looms to ensure that no child labour is used and to set up schools and rehabilitation centres for former child labourers. Another constructive approach has been adopted by the charity Save the Children in relation to the manufacture of hand-stitched footballs in Sialkot, Pakistan. In partnership with the ILO, UNICEF and the Sialkot Chamber of Commerce and Industry, Save the Children is working to phase out the use of children under fourteen in the football stitching centres. At the same time this partnership is phasing in education and alternative sources of income (see Save the Children's *Big Business, Small Hands* for more information).

In response to criticism, some multinational companies now go to considerable lengths to improve their practice. Nike, pilloried in the early and mid-1990s for paying Asian children a pittance, has a team of nearly 100 people working on the social dimension of its operations. Many of these deal with labour issues in the company's supply chains. Nike carries out regular social audits of its suppliers. Not surprisingly, it is now calling for an international inspectorate to ensure that its competitors meet the same exacting standards. At the UN Global Compact meeting in July 2000, Nike CEO and Chair Phil Knight said: 'We believe in a global system that measures every multinational against a one set of universal standards using an independent process of social performance monitoring akin to financial auditing. This would bring greater clarity to the impact of globalisation and the performance of any one company' (Quoted by Simon Zadek in *The Civil Corporation*, p.97).

Engaging with the Critics

Much remains to be done in the area of international child labour, but events in recent years offer some cause for hope in the shape of a patient, detailed, nitty-gritty improvement of a harmful practice.

Examples of multinationals about which something good deserves to be said are Shell and BP, two of the world's biggest corporations. To some critics they stand indefensible, condemned automatically because they make most of their money out of non-renewable resources – oil and gas. Exploitation of fossil fuels beyond doubt contributes significantly to world pollution levels, as detailed in Chapter 9, but it also gives us heat and light at affordable cost, keeping us warm, helping us see, keeping equipment going – until alternative sources of energy became a reality. I do not believe the core business of extracting natural gas and oil is to be condemned *per se*, though the strategy applied from now on is very much an area for legitimate debate.

Clearly there are specific failings for which Shell and BP can be taken to task. Shell attracted a lot of adverse publicity in 1995 for its plan to sink the Brent Spar oil platform in the North Sea (a plan it had to abandon following an effective, if not entirely honest, campaign by Greenpeace) and for its alleged complicity in the circumstances that led to the execution of Ken Saro-Wira and eight other protestors in the Ogoniland area of Nigeria. The public criticism surrounding these events prompted a great deal of soul-searching in the company. Protests from some shareholders added to this. Widespread consultation took place both within and outside the company about what should be included in a revised Statement of General Business Principles. I was involved in this process myself.

Since then, Shell has radically changed character. It used to be highly inscrutable, but has become much more open and responsive to the public. It produces an annual ethical audit, *People, planet and profits*, that assesses its performance in living up to the nine professed principles in the company statement. Shell is remarkably candid and precise about things that have gone wrong and the action the company is taking to put things right. For instance, the audit tells you how many

- Shell employees have been sacked worldwide for soliciting or accepting bribes
- contracts were cancelled because contractors failed to adhere to Shell's policies on health and safety or human rights
- employees and contractors have died doing Shell business, mainly in road accidents.

Shell is clearly giving sustainable development a higher profile and increasing its investment in the exploration of renewable resources – though inevitably it is still making nearly all its money out of non-renewable ones. Shell also invites the public to use its website (www.shell.com) to express their views on Shell's policy and performance, and some do so in extremely critical terms, without any attempt at censure.

Many of the developments at Shell have parallels in BP. BP is producing a comparable report integrating its financial, social and environmental performance; taking a lead in trying to eradicate the payment of bribes from its worldwide operations; and endeavouring to tackle the problem of environmental pollution. BP too now has a website which is interactive with the general public. During the year 2000, this offered an opportunity to question Sir John (now Lord) Browne, BP's chief executive. He guaranteed to answer one question a day for 100 days. Examples of some of the questions include:

- Why is the stock price going the reverse direction of crude oil price?
- Why do you insist on investing in PetroChina and developing oil in China? Do you care at all about human beings?
- Does gasoline cause a problem for the environment? If so, what are you doing to help solve it?

Sir John's answers on the BP website (www.bpamoco.com) could well be described as a mixture of the sensitive and robust.

These websites are hopefully a sign of what is to come. They comprise one of the positive effects of the internet: an opportunity for companies to become more accountable, not just to their shareholders but the general public, for what they are doing. They offer scope for constructive conversations, much more than has taken place in the past either through shareholder annual general meetings or confrontations where critics and companies sound off and simply talk past each other.

A company doing something unusually altruistic is Merck, the American pharmaceuticals giant. During the 1980s Merck developed a drug that is effective against river blindness, which used to afflict many people in the countries of West Africa. It then discovered that the governments of these countries were unable to afford the drug so Merck made it free, deciding that the money spent on research and development did not need to be recompensed. The UN has devoted significant money ($340 million since 1975) to fighting river blindness, which has now largely been eradicated from Africa. About 1.5 million people affected by the illness have recovered, and many others were saved from going blind. The river valleys are also opening up again for agricultural use. It is an all too rare good news story from Africa. There are isolated examples of other drugs companies collaborating with the World Health Organisation to give medicines away.

Among signs of hope is the Jubilee 2000 campaign, limited though it has been so far in its practical effects. The campaign does show that when a groundswell of public opinion is marshalled by a combination of different pressure groups coming together in a well-organised coalition, governments are forced to sit up and take notice. International debt also illustrates the complexity of many global issues, and the fact that fault does not all lie on one side. The debt problem is the result not just of the hard-heartedness of the governments and banking institutions of the North, but also the moral failings of governments in the South, and the failure of these countries to use resources effectively. Many Southern countries fell into serious debt because their leaders syphoned money off for their own personal vainglory or to finance capital projects that were not necessarily in the country's best interest. The problems of debt and corruption are connected, because the lure of bribes often influenced an unwise choice of projects. Resolution of the debt problem is much needed, but it requires a recognition of mutual human failure and the insertion of safeguards to ensure that, once remitted, the whole cycle of borrowing, lending and indebtedness does not simply happen again.

Radical theologians who are selective in their choice of facts are equally selective in their choice of texts. The Bible often depicts the poor as the victims of rich and powerful people who oppress them. To sample that strand of the Bible, read through the book of Amos. But it does not assume that poverty is necessarily the result of exploitation; it may sometimes be the consequence of indolence, failing to make the most of God-given resources. To sample that biblical strand, read through the book of Proverbs. Consider too the ministry of Jesus. Jesus made a special point of emphasising that the message he brought was good news to the poor, and he showered his love upon the socially marginalised. He overthrew the tables of the money-changers partly because he saw their practice as exploitative, making the temple into a den of thieves.

But he also told the parable of the talents, which is a powerful spur to responsibility in God's service, and is a warning against sloth, whether induced by laziness, fear of change, or unwillingness to take risks. It may be a cause of embarrassment that the parable includes the words 'For to him who has will more be given; and to him even what he has will be taken away' (Mt. 25:29), but that is what happens when the equivalent of the servant with the one talent buries that talent in the ground. Or take Paul's words, probably directed at clients sponging off their rich patrons: 'He who is not willing to work shall not eat' (2 Thes. 3:10). American theologian Daniel Finn makes the unfashionable but accurate observation that 'sinfulness not only tempts the wealthy and powerful to exploitation; it also tempts all of us to shirk our rightful responsibilities if we were given a guarantee that we could share equally in the prosperity which the hard work and effort of others has brought about' (*Just Trading*, p.56).

The Devil Lies in the Detail

All of which leads to this. While the state of global capitalism gives me grave cause for concern, I do not see it as so unrequitedly wicked that Christians should have nothing to do with it. More constructive than any of the alternatives commended by Duchrow and Gorringe is a consideration of how we can influence that system for good, and in the process bring about a state of affairs where Christianity is no longer considered so marginal to business. We need to think seriously about ways in which aspects of the current system might be humanised, improved, renewed and reformed. The programme run by the Ridley Hall Foundation has constructively probed many aspects of contemporary business, avoiding broad-brush aspersions and engaging in a detailed, in-depth examination of what actually goes on.

The chapters that follow explore in much more depth many of the themes I have introduced briefly. 'The devil lies in the detail', it is often said, with some justification. To evaluate the business world aright we need detailed investigation, not dismissive generalisation. But we need to be open to finding the footprints of God – not just those of the devil – in the detail as well.

3

THE NATURE AND PURPOSE OF A COMPANY:
THE STAKEHOLDER DEBATE

What is a Company?

So those who welcomed his message were baptised, and that day about three thousand persons were added. They devoted themselves to the apostles' teaching and fellowship, to the breaking of bread and the prayers.

(Acts 2:41-42, NRSV)

The original company was established by Peter and the apostles at Pentecost. The word derives from the Latin *cum panis*, which means 'breaking bread together'. The fellowship entailed in breaking bread together is fundamental to the purpose of a company. We find resonances of this in the phrase 'the glorious company of the Apostles' in the Anglican canticle the *Te Deum*. Some 1,600 years after Pentecost the phenomenon of the ship's company preserved something of the original idea. Members of the company did not just work together aboard ship. They ate and lived together.

Of course, words change their meaning over time. We may well object that the essence of a company has altered enormously since those heady far-off days described in the early chapters of Acts. Christians might try to score a point by calling the church the biggest multinational of them all, but we all know that multinational companies are dedicated to very different goals than are churches. That does not stifle debate, but gives it fuel.

At the centre of much recent debate and an area of major controversy in Britain in the mid and late 1990s is the word *stakeholder*. In the lead-up to the 1997 General Election the leader of the opposition Labour Party, Tony Blair, used the word in a famous speech and made it for a time a political football. But it had been circulating for a long time beforehand, both in the academic and business communities. The word 'stakeholder' raises crucial questions about the nature and purpose of a company that aren't as straightforward as they may seem. There is a surprising lack of unanimity about the purpose of business both among practising businesspeople and commentators on business.

Friedman and Freeman

A good way into the stakeholder debate is through a 1970 article by Milton Friedman in *The New York Times Magazine* headlined 'The Social Responsibility of a Business is to Increase its Profits'. Although Friedman never used the word 'stakeholder', his target being more the concept of corporate social responsibility, many writers have responded to his views by talking in stakeholder terms. Friedman's line of argument is essentially simple:

- Shareholders own the company, and any profits belong to them
- A manager's responsibility is to increase the profits for the owners: 'In his capacity as a corporate executive, the manager is the agent of the individuals who own the company, and his primary responsibility is to them'
- Social responsibility is a matter for government, not business. It is for governments to decide on the redistribution of wealth through taxation. It is no business of business to take on the roles of legislator, executor and jurist – it would

probably make a mess of these functions if it did. The expertise of business lies elsewhere. The doctrine of corporate social responsibility, taken seriously, would extend the scope of politics to every human activity, which would be quite undesirable

- 'There is one and only one social responsibility of business – to use its resources and engage in activities designed to increase its profits so long as it stays within the rules of the game, i.e. engages in open and free competition without deception or fraud'. With the proviso that they observe relevant laws and established moral customs, companies should have a single-minded focus on the objective of maximising profits.

Providing a clear contrast to Friedman's views is the American academic R. Edward Freeman. He has put forward his ideas on stakeholder theory in various places but in an article he wrote with William M. Evan, entitled 'A Stakeholder Theory of the Modern Corporation: Kantian Capitalism', the argument runs as follows:

- The property rights of a company are legitimate but not absolute
- Legal developments recognise corporate responsibility to a variety of groups. The fact that there is legislation protecting the interests of customers, employees and local communities (e.g. the USA's clean air and clean water acts) indicates that these groups have rights in relation to companies. These rights constrain the pursuit of shareholders' interests by management
- All these groups have a legitimate 'stake' in a company's activities – hence the appropriateness of the word *stakeholder*. Freeman has both a wide definition of stakeholders (those groups or individuals who benefit from, or are harmed by, corporate actions, and whose rights are violated or respected by them) and a narrow definition (those groups who are vital to the survival and success of the company)

- All stakeholders should be treated as ends in themselves, not merely as means to an end. Here Freeman and Evan draw on a famous moral 'truth' stated by the Enlightenment philosopher Immanuel Kant: that all human beings should be treated as ends and never merely as means. It is an axiom that has been widely recognised as consistent with a fundamental human dignity – that dignity which Christian thinkers ground in the belief that men and women are made in the image of God. The conclusion Freeman draws is that the interests of other stakeholders should never be subordinated to those of shareholders. To do so would be treating them as mere means
- The company is a vehicle for coordinating stakeholder interests. In general, management must keep the relationship among stakeholders in balance. Freeman and Evan acknowledge that this is a difficult matter and calls for the wisdom of a King Solomon. As structural mechanisms to assist this, they suggest a stakeholder board of directors and a redefinition of corporate law to include recognition of the rights of stakeholders.

Other academics occupy positions across the spectrum between the two extremes of Friedman and Freeman. Without attempting to be comprehensive, this table sums up some of the main distinctions made. It incorporates positions taken up by Kenneth Goodpaster, Jack Mahoney, and Tim Ambler with Andrea Wilson (see diagram at the end of the chapter).

Charles Handy and the RSA

The world of business, certainly in Britain, largely ignored this ongoing academic debate until Professor Charles Handy, perhaps Britain's foremost business guru and a man whose views command wide respect, gave a high-profile speech on 5 December 1990. Delivering the Michael Shanks memorial lecture at the RSA (Royal Society for the Encouragement of Arts, Manufactures and Commerce), he spoke on 'What is a

Company For?' Handy questioned the wisdom received from his American business school in the 1960s that the purpose of business is 'to maximise the medium-term earnings per share'. He said he was now convinced this is wrong: 'The principal purpose of a company is not to make a profit – full stop. It is to make a profit in order to continue to do things or make things, and to do it even better and more abundantly' ('What is a Company For?', p.233).

Handy argued against two 'pervasive myths'. First that profit is the company's purpose, which he saw as a case of mistaking means for ends. Second, that those who pay the money own the company. Shareholding, he said, should not be construed in terms of owning property. Most UK shareholders are more like punters, diverting money from proper investment with their expectation of high dividends.

Handy professed a lack of enthusiasm for stakeholder theory, saying: 'I don't really know who all the stakeholders are or who would properly represent them. Stakeholders language is a nice way of talking about the balancing act that companies have to perform, but I don't think, myself, that it answers the question "what is a company for?" except in a very blurred way' (p.235). He saw a company as operating in a hexagonal ring, surrounded by competing pressures from so-called stakeholders. 'Within that ring I want to see the development of "the existential corporation", the corporation whose principal purpose is to fulfil itself, to grow and develop to the best that it can be, given always that every other corporation is free to do the same. It owes something to each of the ring-holders, but is owned by no one. It is in charge of its own destiny, and it is immortal or would like to be. It is not a piece of property, inhabited by humans, it is a community, which itself has property' (p.236).

He argued that managers should be accountable to a board of trustees, whose task is oversight with the ultimate power to replace any management that fails in the task of 'growing the community'. Examples of communities that were truly self-determining (e.g. the John Lewis Partnership and the Baxi Partnership) were not public limited companies, he noted. Handy called for a wholesale review of corporate governance and change of company law to make business less like an 'auction ring'. Ultimately, each corporate community must answer for itself the question 'what is a company for?' – once it had been set free legally to do so. That purpose ought to be the major concern of the company's board of trustees.

Charles Handy further develops his views about the purpose of business in his best-selling book *The Empty Raincoat*. Chapters 8 and 9 are on 'The Meaning of Business'. There he argues that the different systems of capitalism need to move closer together, borrowing the best of each other's traditions, in order to forge a new image of capitalism that is more obviously in the service of society but still flexible and efficient. Handy pursues his theme that companies should aim for immortality. To achieve this, they have to deserve it. 'A company will only be allowed to survive as long as it is doing something useful, at a cost which people can afford, and it must generate enough funds for their continued growth and development' (p.143). A company therefore needs to seek 'stakeholder symmetry', a phrase Handy says doesn't get the blood beating any faster than 'shareholder value,' which is why he prefers to speak of immortality.

Handy drew attention to the fact with which we began this chapter – that the word company originally meant a fellowship, a group of companions or members one of another. Membership gives meaning and responsibility to those who work in the business. Handy thinks this concept is found much more among charitable and non-profit organisations and says that just as these organisations are becoming more 'businesslike', so companies may usefully look to the non-profit arena to find new models for themselves.

Tomorrow's Company

Such was the interest created by Handy's Michael Shanks memorial lecture that RSA decided to launch an inquiry. It asked the question: Would a change in our view of the purpose and responsibilities of the company contribute to long-term wealth creation – in other words, to a more sustainable basis for the creation of wealth in the UK and beyond?

The inquiry began with a meeting of senior executives from 25 leading UK companies under the leadership of Sir Anthony Cleaver, then chairman of IBM UK, in January 1993. A wide-ranging consultation exercise over two years involved more than 8,000 business leaders and opinion shapers. The findings were published in the report *Tomorrow's Company* (originally *Rethinking the Company*) in June 1995. It was written mainly by RSA Programme Director Mark Goyder.

The report begins: 'There are too few world-class companies in the UK. We are not creating enough new ones.' The obstacles preventing UK companies from being globally competitive include complacency and ignorance of world standards, over-reliance on financial measures of performance, and a national adversarial culture. The report identifies 'the increasing need for companies to maintain public confidence in the legitimacy of their operations and business conduct – in other words, to maintain their *licence to operate*' as a major force for change. It argues that the companies which will sustain competitive success in the future are those that focus less exclusively on shareholders and on financial measures of success. Instead they will include all their stakeholder relationships, and a broader range of measurements, in the way they think about their purpose and performance. The report calls this the *inclusive approach*.

To maintain the impetus created by the report, RSA set up the Centre for Tomorrow's Company in 1996. This aims to inspire and enable companies to be globally competitive through applying the inclusive approach. It does this through a variety of services including questionnaires, workshops and help offered by 'professionals'.

Shareholder Focus

In the mid-1990s the stakeholder approach was enthusiastically endorsed by a variety of influential thinkers, including

Will Hutton, John Kay and John Plender. Despite becoming widespread, it cannot be said to have carried the day.

Elaine Sternberg is a notable thinker who is totally opposed to it. In *Just Business*, a rigorous if repetitive book, Sternberg claims that 'by introducing conceptual clarity to business ethics' she 'provides solid arguments for rebutting trendy, but unethical demands, for "social responsibility in business"' (p.3). Sternberg takes a teleological approach, arguing that what constitutes ethical conduct in business depends critically on business's definitive purpose. On the nature of business, she claims that business is a very specific, limited activity whose defining purpose is to maximise owner value over the long term by selling goods or services. Business is not an association to promote social welfare, spiritual fulfilment or full employment; it is not a family, a club or a hobby, nor is it to be confused with government. Sternberg deliberately sets herself against a stakeholder theory of business which typically – in her presentation – holds that business is accountable to all its stakeholders, and that the role of management is to balance their competing interests. Rather, business is being true to its defining purpose in seeking to maximise long-term value for owners (a wider category than shareholders), and should be unapologetic about this. Nevertheless, it is necessary to take into account behaviour towards so-called stakeholders, because behaviour that alienates stakeholders or discourages repeat business is unlikely to be in the owners' long-term interests. Sternberg sees the fundamental principles of business ethics that should undergird such behaviour as distributive justice and ordinary decency.

In a later booklet, *The Stakeholder Concept*, Sternberg refines and reinforces these arguments, claiming that stakeholder theory is incompatible with a company holding substantive objectives and exercising proper corporate governance, and that it ultimately undermines private property, moral agency and the creation of wealth. In the process, she attacks the Tomorrow's Company approach as an 'extreme form of stakeholder theory' (p.15).

In the context of this increasingly polarised debate, the Ridley Hall Foundation held a two-day consultation on the stakeholder economy in May 1997. It reviewed the state of the debate, addressed the fundamental question 'is stakeholder a useful concept?' and considered the claims of the various groups often described as stakeholders.

Argenti vs. Goyder

The main protagonists at the consultation were John Argenti, a management consultant, and Mark Goyder, the RSA report author representing the Centre for Tomorrow's Company.

Argenti's views are similar to Sternberg's, and promoted with similar passion. He said the view that companies should benefit all stakeholders, not just shareholders, was disastrous on several counts. It makes it impossible to measure corporate performance: there are too many conflicting factors, there is even disagreement on how many different stakeholders there are, and in any case, only shareholder performance can be measured with any accuracy. Argenti illustrated this by comparing the performance of two hypothetical firms against five different stakeholder criteria, and then asking which was the better company.

Company Performance Indicators	Return on shareholders' capital	Customer approval rating	Employee enjoyment index	Supplier satisfaction survey	Community contentment	Total
	%	%	Units	Category	Deciles	
Company A	21	44	12	B	8th	??
Company B	7	88	24	E	4th	??

All stakeholder performances are measured in different units, he said, and who knows what weighting is to be given between them? There are no objective rules for trading off the different scores. Even after 50 years of social accounting, he said, we are no further forwards. The reason for this failure is not that people haven't tried hard enough. It is because whereas all shareholders are treated equitably (their rewards are calculated *per share*), all the other stakeholders – employees, customers, suppliers and especially the community – are heterogeneous. They do not form a homogeneous 'set' or category and never will. In Argenti's precise words: 'Not now, not ever.'

Every organisation, he claimed, needs a clear expression of purpose and must distinguish between two different groups, the *intended* and the *collateral* beneficiaries. Intended beneficiaries are those for whom the organisation exists, its *raison d'etre*. In the case of a company, these are the shareholders. In the case of schools, it is children. Collateral beneficiaries are those who *may* benefit from an organisation's activities – with a company, the so-called stakeholders – but it is not essential that they do so.

Argenti closed by acknowledging that the idea that organisations, especially companies, should not be run for the benefit of a small clique, but for everyone concerned, is immensely attractive. He said the stakeholder approach was extremely seductive but irredeemably flawed.

Goyder began his contribution by saying that the RSA inquiry into Tomorrow's Company and the Centre for Tomorrow's Company are often associated with the stakeholder approach. In fact, though the word 'stakeholder' appears in some of their literature, he prefers the phrase 'inclusive approach'. He explained why.

The word 'stakeholding' has its origins in the frontier days of American history. As settlers moved into new territory, they staked their claim to land and marked it out with posts or stakes. The term was then taken up by management thinkers to describe claims on the company by different groups and grew from there. The problem as Goyder sees it is that we then get into stakeholder rights. It seems inappropriate to define all the relationships a company has in terms of having a stake. Sir Michael Angus, the chairman of Whitbread, has commented: 'Just because I go into a newsagent and buy a Mars Bar doesn't mean I have a stake in the Mars Corporation.' The fact is that many customers have an exceedingly fleeting, superficial and uncommitted relationship with the companies whose products they purchase.

What the Centre for Tomorrow's Company is strongly committed to is this. A company that neglects key relationships with so-called stakeholders misses opportunities and incurs risks, putting it at a competitive disadvantage. The companies that will succeed in the future are those that include all their key relationships in the way that they think and talk about their purpose and performance – as the *Tomorrow's Company* report is at pains to emphasise.

The RSA inquiry found a significant barrier to change is that many chief executives and boards of directors believe their duty in law compels them to concentrate on pleasing the body of shareholders. This is a misconception. A director's duty is owed to the company, not any specific third-party group. They must, as fiduciaries, have regard to the interest of shareholders, but that obligation is not related to the holders of shares at one particular time. There is nothing in company law to prevent directors having regard to other interests if they judge reasonably and in good faith that to do so is conducive to the health of the company. Their duty is to arrive at a balanced judgment about maximising the company's value on a sustainable basis, and not necessarily to take a short-term view of maximising returns for current shareholders. Once these obligations are properly understood, it becomes clear that the adoption of an *inclusive* approach is more than simply beneficial for the company: it is essential for the proper discharge of their duties.

Goyder argued that no two companies are the same. The marketplace is big enough to embrace both an Anita Roddick and a Rupert Murdoch. Companies are started by entrepreneurs, and the motives that drive them vary. Some are genuinely excited by the product they have to offer, especially if it is a new product or service they have been instrumental in developing. The size of profits or dividends for shareholders are not usually the dominant factor. A company – as Handy encouraged – can choose its own purpose. Nevertheless, for most companies of any significant size, creating long-term shareholder value is likely to be crucial in sustaining success.

Goyder says: 'To achieve this, a company needs leadership that pays close attention to the quality of its relationships with investors, customers, employees, suppliers and the community. 'In other words, the inclusive approach pays dividends in the long run. If your customers abandon you, you don't have a business. If your employees don't work effectively, you'll never get anything done. If you abuse your relationship with your local community it can make life very difficult for you, and the inconvenience if a supplier goes bust because you didn't pay it on time is obvious. We believe that all these things are not attended to at the expense of long-term shareholder value but are essential to it.' ('The Inclusive Approach', p.13)

Dart Boards and Bull's-Eyes

The nature and scale of the differences between Argenti and Goyder were identified by other contributors to the symposium. This was crucial to avoid a deadlock.

Chris Marsden, then director of the BP Corporate Citizenship Unit, made a very helpful contribution using a model of a dart board. His argument runs like this. If the traditional model of the Anglo-American joint-stock company sees its purpose as the maximisation of shareholder value – a combination of dividends and share price growth – then this can be depicted as a dart board. Shareholder interests are represented by the 'bull's-eye' (p.63 opposite) and the object is to hit the bull's-eye (satisfy the shareholders) as often as possible.

An alternative model (opposite) redefines the bull's-eye as a better society, with better variously described as fairer, kinder, more humane or more sustainable. Whatever the description, shareholders become one of several organisations the company is seeking to serve with no order of preference.

Analysis of Goyder's position shows that he subscribes more to the first model, and Goyder and Argenti's differences are less marked than perhaps they anticipated. Marsden's bull's-eyes helped to reveal this. Argenti saw the other targets on the board, the primary stakeholders, as needing to be hit just often enough to stop them being dissatisfied, but the bull's-eye remains the target most frequently in one's sights.

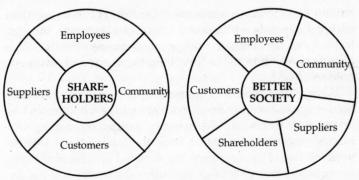

Goyder in contrast saw the indirect approach as being the route to satisfying the shareholders. The various stakeholders need to be hit first, before attempting to go for the bull's-eye. It is almost as if the rules of the game insist that one do so. Too direct an approach is a recipe for self-destruction: one will end up missing the mark. The Centre for Tomorrow's Company says their claim is backed by empirical evidence. Kleinwort Benson, the investment bank, analysed companies in terms of whether they exhibited an inclusive approach to business (a so-called Tomorrow's Company characteristic) between 1992 and 1996, and found that shares of the 32 firms with the characteristic rose 90% while the FT share index gained 38% overall.

A significant ideological gulf separates Argenti and Goyder, but it's not a big as that between the two dart boards. The number of companies that subscribe to the second model may be small, but includes such big names as The Body Shop, Ben and Jerry's, and The Co-operative Bank. Marsden pointed out that powerful forces are shifting companies in this direction. Green consumers, ethical investors, special interest NGOs and local communities are all demanding that companies contribute towards the creation of a better society. So are the radical critics of capitalism. The strongest pressures are certainly from the other direction, the financial markets and those insisting on short-term shareholder value, but that is not the whole story. Marsden showed how the juxtaposition of opposing forces means that companies are having to perform a sensitive balancing act. Because their survival depends – ultimately – on social approval, they are learning to do dialogue with a whole range of stakeholder groups in addition to the investment analysts and the share-holders' AGM.

What I find especially interesting is that since the stake-holder consultation there is evidence of the two groups, the financial investors and the pressure groups, converging. The human resources director at Exel, the international logistics group, tells me the company has received an 'absolute storm' of requests since 1999 from institutional shareholders for cor-porate evidence that a cluster of ethical policies are in place. These policies relate to environmental issues, community involvement, ethical standards, treatment of staff, and health and safety requirements. Exel finds itself under constant pressure to set targets, monitor progress, and improve per-formance.

The City's growth of interest is reflected in the FTSE4Good index. This is a listing for social responsible investment designed by FTSE, one of the world's leading global index providers. It comprises a series of benchmark and trading per-formance indicators, facilitating investment in companies with good records of corporate social responsibility. The FTSE4Good selection criteria cover three areas:

- Working towards environmental sustainability
- Developing positive relationships with stakeholders
- Upholding and supporting universal human rights.

Profit and Service

It is not easy to identify a distinctively Christian position in the stakeholder debate. This was illustrated at the consultation when the Christian participants found themselves occupying different points on the spectrum. A few years after the event, I think I see the issues more clearly than I did when I wrote my original report.

Argenti certainly threw down the gauntlet with his distinction between shareholders as intended beneficiaries and stakeholders as collateral beneficiaries. But when he compared a company and a school, I felt the analogy broke down. Aren't customers more comparable to children in their position as principal and direct beneficiaries? It is they, after all, who receive and make use of the company's products and services. John Davis would doubtless agree. A former senior executive with Shell, he came to the conclusion early in his career that the essential purpose of a company 'has to be the complete satisfaction of all the needs of customers and potential customers relating to our product and service. Making money can no more be a purpose than breathing is the purpose of life. Both are conditions of survival; means and not ends' (*Greening Business*, p.41).

In support of this position, remember that Jesus was a distinctly topsy-turvy sort of teacher who loved to stand conventional wisdom on its head. (Love your enemies. Give, and it will be given to you. The last will be first, and the first will be last. Whoever would be great among you must be your servant, and whoever would be first among you must be slave of all.) When it comes to the relationship between profit and service, Christians might say that we too should have the courage to turn conventional wisdom on its head. Instead of seeing service as the means to profit, we could say that service (i.e. aiming to give the client or customer the best possible quality service) is the goal and profit is the means. A very necessary means, certainly: no company that fails to return a consistent healthy profit will have the wherewithal to make the necessary investment in people, technology and products to maintain a high level of service. Profit is a constraint that ensures a company continues to attract sufficient reserves of fresh capital. But properly understood, profit has a subordinate status. Serving other people is the goal, and serving other people, according to the New Testament, is the pathway to glory. As Paul says in Philippians 2, Jesus Christ humbled himself and took the form of a servant, and though it led him to death on the cross, it led ultimately to a state of glorious exaltation.

This radical view of business is an attractive if challenging one. I have advocated it myself in the past. But I have come to the conclusion that a simple inversion of the profit-service relationship is precisely that: too simple. First, it flies in the face of common sense. When one's customers are actually other companies (selling within industry rather than to the public) it seems distinctly odd to put their interests *before* one's own. Second, too strong an emphasis on service makes it difficult to distinguish business from the many not-for-profit organisations that make serving different groups in the community their hallmark. Although I believe that Sternberg is too prescriptive about what a business is, she is right to insist that a commercial concern to increase owner value marks it out from a club, society or other voluntary organisation. Third, there *is* a proper self-interest in business, and it needs to be distinguished from selfishness. We recognise this on the individual level, where a concern for my own welfare (e.g. keeping myself healthy) both displays a proper self-respect and enables me to be of use to others (e.g. family and friends). It is also true on the corporate level, where managing directors seek corporate success both for their own benefit (in terms of financial reward and personal reputation) and for the good of those most closely associated with the company (shareholders and employees). Self-interest can very easily degenerate into selfishness, but if kept in proportion, it is a legitimate and powerful motivating force.

It may be possible to refine the idealistic view that subordinates profit to service so that profit and service are on exactly comparable levels. In other words, both are corporate goods, both are equally important. The chairman of Start-Rite, the children's shoe manufacturer, was asked what came first in his business: profit or concern for children's feet? He replied: 'Neither. They work simultaneously. We're unashamedly out to make a profit *and* we're very concerned about the health of children's feet and posture. We run the business on both concerns.' (Quoted by Laura Nash in *Good Intentions Aside*, p.152) This approach might be described as profit-seeking streaked with altruism, or enlightened self-interest. I believe, on reflection, that this is the view most compatible with a Christian approach. It strikes a chord with Jesus' identification of the second commandment: 'You shall love your neighbour as yourself' (Mt. 22:39). He did not say love your neighbour *instead* of yourself. Consultant David Murray drew the consultation's attention to where Paul says, 'Each of you should look not only to your own interests [the implication being that they will], but also to the interests of others' (Phil. 2:4). Paul was addressing the church in Philippi, but the words have a broader social relevance. As David said, 'What better text could there be to put at the head of a paper on responsibilities to stakeholders?'

Accountability and Responsibility

Most of us were struck during the consultation that the term 'stakeholder' covers a diverse collection of groups. A company has significantly different relationships with shareholders, employees, suppliers, customers, the community, and the environment. Some relationships are contractual; others are not. Most are with human beings; but not all: the environment is the exception. As various contributors to the consultation made clear, each relationship has its particular nuance. The word 'stakeholder' may still be useful as a form of shorthand. Now that it has passed into the common vocabulary of business, it saves us spelling out all the different groups every time. But the diversity means we can make only the most generalised statements about relationships with stakeholders and obligations. In particular, when the word is defined in its stricter, more literal sense – i.e. those who have a legitimate stake in a company's activities, as distinct from those who are simply affected by those activities – then the nature of the stake needs identifying very carefully.

Among the different groups, shareholders or – to use a more general term – investors clearly occupy a special position. They have put up the risk capital that the company uses as a platform for trading activity. They have the right to know whether that has been put to good use and how it has been handled. In normal trading conditions, they have the right to expect a reasonable return on their investment. The company is therefore *accountable* to investors in a way that is not true of any of the other stakeholder relationships. Those who invest money have a right to call to account, to question, or to investigate. The biblical parable of the talents (Mt. 25:14-30) comes to mind. Those who manage a company are in the position of faithful or unfaithful stewards, giving account to their master, who has entrusted his property to them, and being judged by the profitable use to which they put that property. A faithful steward adds value: an image that in Christian understanding also describes the position of humanity managing the world on God's behalf. (More on this in Chapter 9.)

But in relation to other stakeholder groups, it is more appropriate to talk of corporate responsibility than accountability. The responsibilities are real, and in some cases protected by law. As virtually everyone in the stakeholder debate acknowledges, companies simply cannot afford to ignore the interests – even the legitimate claims – of employees, customers, suppliers or the local community. So, for instance, they ought to:

- ensure employees work in a safe environment
- provide customers with quality products
- pay suppliers within agreed times
- avoid polluting the environment where they are based.

It is a matter of basic personal integrity – and something that ought to be axiomatic to Christians – that we treat people honestly, fairly and with dignity simply because they are people. Duties to stakeholders are justified not so much on the grounds of corporate social responsibility as from our fundamental human responsibility. However, acknowledging all those duties does not amount to stating that the company is strictly accountable to those interested parties in a formal sense.

Balancing the Interests of Others

In distinguishing between responsibility and accountability, I agree with Elaine Sternberg. The version of stakeholder theory she attacks is the one that asserts that a company is equally accountable to all the stakeholders. But I part company with her, and find myself on the other side of the debate, when she goes on to attack the view that 'the proper objective of management is to balance stakeholders' competing interests'. It may not be the only objective of management, but it is a very important one.

A company's responsibility to stakeholders other than investors often necessitates a delicate balancing act. Sometimes there is no serious conflict between the interests and expectations of different groups in relation to the company. At other times, especially when trading conditions are difficult, there will be a clash. Faced with the need to cut costs, a company may have to choose between lower shareholder dividends, staff redundancies, and higher prices for certain goods. A strategic choice may sometimes suggest a sharp prioritisation of interests; more often a spreading of the burden of cost. Companies are rightly reluctant to abandon any one group in favour of another, because maintaining confidence among all parties is crucial to future health.

Sternberg and Argenti claim the notion of balancing interests is unworkable. Managers, they say, cannot be expected to juggle so many balls without taking their eyes off the one ball that really matters, maximising shareholder value. But as David Murray observed, management cannot have it both ways. Senior managers justifiably claim their handsome salaries are warranted because of the complexities of their job. They have to manage the demands of cost, conflict and change in a fast-moving and highly competitive marketplace. 'There can, however, be no logic in arguing the complexity case when setting levels of financial reward, but claiming the impossibility of handling complexity when faced with the challenge of multiple stakeholders' ('Looking to the Interests of Others', p.10). Outstanding businessmen and women realise the strategic importance of all the key stakeholder relationships, and respond accordingly. Sternberg makes the task of balancing the different interests sound impossible, but the best managers consistently belie her in practice – probably with a minimum knowledge of stakeholder theory, or even of the generic word 'stakeholder'.

This is not to say that coordinating stakeholder interests is straightforward. Freeman and Evan wrote something more profound than perhaps they realised when they said it calls for 'the wisdom of a King Solomon'. It does indeed require a practical wisdom that cannot be summed up in any easily applicable model. Here again the Christian faith has something important to say. It counsels us to admit the limitations of our own understanding and to seek the wisdom that comes from God. That was the source of Solomon's wisdom. He consciously asked God for a 'wise and discerning mind' (1 Kgs. 3:12) to equip him to govern the Jewish people. In the New Testament we are told: 'If any of you is lacking in wisdom, ask God, who gives to all generously and ungrudgingly, and it will be given to you' (Jas. 1:5). Wisdom applies knowledge and experience to life, with a view to living wholesomely and harmoniously. It is a quality that senior management needs every bit as much as national rulers or church leaders.

Such wisdom cannot be reduced to a formula. There is no foolproof decision-making process that can be learnt and then applied as and when required. Nor is wisdom acquired overnight. It is the fruit of a whole series of small decisions that together make for a settled character, good habits that come to be practised almost unthinkingly and therefore take much of the heat out of many potential moral dilemmas. If I have a settled disposition to be faithful to my wife this reduces the likelihood that I'll need to seriously agonise over every temptation to be unfaithful that comes my way. (This does not amount to making the foolish claim that such habits make me immune from temptation – anyone is capable of a moral lapse or being ensnared.) The point remains that the integration of Christian virtues into an individual's lifestyle is part of the formation of the Christian conscience, which acts as a prompt and a guide when hard decisions are called for. Where such a process has taken place, we do not start from a blank sheet. The same can be true in corporate life.

Clive's Story

'The integration of key values and principles into the bloodstream of a company's decision-making processes should be similar to the process that establishes the Christian's conscience. It is too late to start thinking about what are the principles to be followed only when a crisis has arisen,' writes Clive Wright, a former director of public affairs at two leading chemicals companies.

'I used to be director of a successful chemical company which was largely engaged in the production of intermediate chemicals, that is to say chemicals which were then used in other processes to manufacture the final product for the consumer. One of our products was extensively used as a carrying agent in medicines, as a food ingredient and in cosmetics. For such a sensitive product the highest standards of purity and quality were clearly necessary, and it was manufactured to an extremely demanding specification prescribed by the US regulatory authorities. The product was sold on behalf of our company through distributors who supplied it to food manufacturers, pharmaceutical companies and so on.

'A serious problem arose when a batch of product was returned by one of our agents who had detected an unusual smell. The product still met the very demanding specification to which we were required to work. But analysis showed trace quantities of an unknown impurity to be present, the properties of which had not been tested for the kinds of use to which our product was put. We clearly had a serious problem on our hands.

'The ethical dilemma was complex. From a purely legal perspective the product was within the required specification. But the impurity was an unknown one. What were its properties? It had possible links to chemicals that were considered to be harmful to human beings. The imperative to protect human health was clear. We had to find out the properties of the impurity. But what was the extent of the problem? How had the impurity got into the product? Had product containing the impurity been used in a sensitive application? The implications were enormous and could affect the future existence of our company. Indeed the future of other companies that had used the product could also be at risk. Given the uncertainties regarding the nature of the impurity, how widely should the situation be notified? Against the need to warn, we had to consider the dangers of unnecessarily alarming people.

'The company had a very well-established code of ethics and some very clear statements of principle that underpinned that code. The president of the company was absolutely steeped in those principles and in the application of the code. Thus, at the first meeting of the crisis team called to manage the situation, he affirmed the company principle that financial considerations were secondary to those of health, safety and the environment. The expense involved in setting up the necessary testing procedures, in recalling all product and in carrying out any actions we deemed necessary, was a secondary consideration to that of health and safety. He also worked to the imperative of the Golden Rule – do to others as you would have them do unto you. He was a man who respected the worth of every human being as an integral part of his way of doing business. In this instance, any risk to people should be established as soon as possible and every possible step taken to minimise that risk.

'There is no need to describe in detail the evolution of the dilemma and how we handled it. One aspect of our decision-making may serve to illustrate how we worked. A key question lay in deciding how many people should be told about the situation. It could be argued that we should have told the whole world. That would have involved alarming many people before we were able to explain all the relevant facts about the impurity. But there were many people who had to know the situation: distributors, end-use-customers, competitors, regulatory bodies and so on. We therefore worked on the basis of telling those who needed to know about the situation because they might have action to take. There was no obvious 'right answer' so we were obliged to work out the practical application of the principles that we had developed for our guidance in the corporate code of ethics. Transparency was at the heart of those principles.

'The outcome of the crisis was a happy one. The impurity turned out to be harmless. It had arisen as the result of improper storage procedures by one distributor, which had caused the build up of abnormal concentrations; there was no general problem. The necessary corrective steps were taken to avoid any recurrence and all other companies who dealt with the product were advised of the outcome to enable industry practice to be modified.

'My point in recounting this incident is to illustrate that in a crisis of that nature, immediate decisions were called for. Those decision were, as far as we were concerned, matters of life and death. We did not have time to work out a value system uniquely for that situation. We worked to values that had been honed and integrated into the way we worked. Those values were akin to the functioning of a Christian conscience in an individual. It also happened that both the values that the company had articulated and the character of the president of the company were easily recognisable as values fully consistent with the traditions of Christian understandings on ethical behaviour. This case illustrates that there is a critical place in the world of business for Christian virtues and Christian formation.'

Clive's shrewd analysis leads me to a final observation. It looks as if the shareholder versus stakeholder debate has run its course. If the balance between shareholder accountability and stakeholder responsibility I have advocated is sound, then the way forward may be to focus on the virtues required of the 'good' manager and the 'good' organisation. We need to work out and spell out the virtues particularly relevant to corporate existence. For instance, David Murray, with a lifetime's immersion in business on the one hand and an in-depth knowledge of the Bible on the other, suggests seven core principles of business integrity: consideration, creativity, interdependence, justice, service, stewardship and truth ('Looking to the Interests of Others', p.10). It is in discerning the meaning and teasing out the practical implications of such values that Christians can draw on a rich moral tradition, and potentially have much to offer the wider community.

The Stakeholder Spectrum

FRIEDMAN	GOODPASTER	AMBLER/ WILSON	MAHONEY	FREEMAN
Shareholders are owners of the company	*Strategic stakeholder synethesis:* stakeholder interests considered, but are subordinate to shareholder interests	No clear evidence whether Friedman's or Freeman's approach produces better results for shareholders or stakeholders	Shareholders better understood not as owners but as trustees	Property rights of a company legitimate but not absolute
Corporate profits belong to the shareholders	*Multi-fiduciary stakeholder synthesis:* all stakeholders have equally important interests	Stakeholders cannot have rights without responsibilities	Many stakeholders feel part in ownership of company	Legal developments recognise corporate responsibilities to a variety of groups
Responsibility of managers is to increase profits for owners	*Stakeholder paradox:* managers have special (fiduciary) responsibility to shareholders and real (non-fiduciary) responsibility to stakeholders	Rights have to be earned through contribution to the company's welfare and by participation in its activities	Shareholders, customers and employees all have responsibilities	All these groups have a legitimate stake in the company's activities – hence stakeholders
Social responsibility is a matter for government, not business	Fiduciary duties are those which agents have to principals	Participants need identifying and registering	Distinction between *Active stakeholders* (entitled to benevolent treatment) and *Passive stakeholders* (entitled to non-malevolent treatment)	All stakeholders should be treated as ends in themselves, not means to an end (cf. Kant)
Only onstraints are 'staying within the rules of the game' – law and moral custom	Responsibilities to stakeholders defined in non-malevolent terms	Distribution of power and benefits can then be addressed		Company a vehicle for co-ordinating stakeholder interests

4

CHANGING STAKEHOLDER RELATIONSHIPS:
THE DEVELOPMENT OF SUPPLY CHAIN MANAGEMENT

'It's problems in the supply chain that keep you awake worrying at night,' a senior executive told me.

Small suppliers bemoan the big companies that fail to pay bills on time, often putting them out of business due to a cash-flow crisis.

The most hidden stakeholder relationship is that between a company and its suppliers. It is the relationship the public probably thinks about least. But for those in business it is of critical importance.

The supplier relationship is fascinating, not only as an illustration of stakeholding in action but also because of the sea change taking place in the nature of that relationship. Not everyone welcomes that change or regards it as positive. The supply chain, like other areas of business, is the scene of a major ideological battle. In March 2000, the Ridley Hall Foundation and the Warwick Manufacturing Group jointly ran a seminar to examine supply chain management – probably the first time a university manufacturing department has linked up with a theological college to run a course designed to help people in business.

Recent management theory and practice has concentrated on obtaining or adding value. Increasingly, theorists and practitioners are moving away from analysis of internal company performance to concentrate on all the activities a company is involved in, from raw materials at one end to the supply of products and services to eventual customers at the other. In short, they are wrestling with the question of how to make the supply chain smoother and more efficient.

Lean Supply in Theory and Practice

Our first speaker from Warwick, Robin McKenzie, drew attention to the way that supply chains have changed, looking particularly at the automotive industry since it continues to be a lead industry in this respect. Nissan in Sunderland has reduced the number of direct suppliers from 1,200 to 200, but other suppliers feed into those to create as many as four tiers of suppliers. This means the supply chain has become longer, with all parties along the chain seeking to subcontract some of the work as individual companies focus on core competencies. Distribution has become another specialist area and few producers still have their own transport fleet.

Organisations are becoming more open, or 'leaky'. There is more sharing of personnel between organisations and more sharing of information with suppliers, because these changes only bring a benefit with greater exchange of information. New technology allows information to be sent easily and quickly. Relationships are structured for flow and continuity, rather than checking for failure. With the removal of waste and reduced inventories, materials and products are expected to arrive *just-in-time*. There is of course often a thin line between this and *just-too-late*!

New thinking is being applied to the retail industry through a process called Efficient Customer Response (ECR). Until recently, US supermarkets were characterised by excessive inventories (average three months stock), massive use of promotional coupons (98% of which went unused), and a proliferation of new me-too brands (90% of which lasted less than two years). This has now changed. The ECR programme took

$30 billion of wasteful expenditure out of the grocery supply chain by:

- Continuous but flexible replenishment of the product from manufacturers, with no stock holding at retail or wholesale level
- Collaborative planning by retailers and manufacturers aimed at making available groups of products actually wanted by customers, rather than brands which were the darling of manufacturers
- A drastic reduction in the number of coupons and special offers, with the substitution of lower pricing.

An example of taking customer pricing seriously was the discovery that the public doesn't need five different sizes of jar containing the same brand of coffee, nor do they want 129 different sizes of cereal box!

Toyota led the way in pioneering 'lean production' in the car industry. The story of how this happened is well told by James Womack, Daniel Jones and Daniel Roos in *The Machine that Changed the World*, a book based on a $5 million study undertaken by the Massachusetts Institute of Technology (MIT) into the global car industry. They pay particular attention to the processes followed by the Japanese car manufacturer and its underlying philosophy. Womack and Jones followed this up with *Lean Thinking: Banish Waste and Create Wealth in Your Corporation*.

Toyota's War on Waste

The MIT research found that in the 1950s Eiji Toyoda and Taiichni Ohno developed a way of operating at Toyota that was markedly different from the mass production so characteristic of Ford and General Motors. Toyota encouraged assembly workers to assume responsibility and take initiative so that defects were dealt with immediately, rather than caught at the end of the line as in mass production. It organised suppliers into functional tiers, and encouraged them to share relevant information and discuss ways to improve design rather than simply issuing instructions (as in mass production). Toyota structured career paths to promote strong team players who were good at coordinating processes rather than people who displayed brilliance in a single area of engineering without regard to their function in a team (as in mass production). The company worked closely with its dealers, who adjusted their sales pitch to the firm's production capabilities and developed close relationships with repeat customers so their wishes influenced the design of future models. By the early 1960s, Toyota had fully worked out the principles of lean production. By the late 1980s, it was outperforming General Motors and many other global competitors by a staggering 2:1 in terms of productivity, 3:1 in terms of quality, and 40% more efficiency in space used with next to no inventory.

'Lean' refers to a way of thinking and operating that emphasises less of everything – fewer people, less time, less space, lower costs – with no loss of quality: rather the reverse. Lean *thinking* focuses on identifying value (best defined by the ultimate customer), lines up value-creating actions in the best possible sequence, and ensures that such activities are conduc-ted efficiently without interruption whenever they are requested. Pursuing this wholeheartedly has radical implications for the supply chain. Womack et al. say, 'Every participating firm has the right to examine every activity in every firm relevant to the value stream as part of the joint search for (the eradication of) waste.'

Womack and Jones identify eight key types of waste:

- defects – mistakes that require rectification
- over-production of goods that aren't needed
- inventories of goods awaiting further processing or consumption
- any processing steps not actually needed
- unnecessary movement of employees from one place to another
- transport of goods from one place to another without any purpose

- waiting by employees, either for a process to finish or because an upstream activity has not delivered on time
- the design of goods and services that do not meet the needs of the customer.

The first seven of these were identified by Ohno, who has been described as the most ferocious enemy of waste who ever lived.

Since the 1980s the competition has been emulating Toyota and has made considerable gains in closing the gap in performance. But it has become clear that improving performance is not just a matter of adopting new techniques. Interactions within and between organisations involve human beings, and attitudes of trust and openness do not develop overnight. They run counter to many traditional modes of operating. We need to grasp the underlying psychological and cultural conditions for making the theory of lean supply and production work in practice. Much of the seminar was devoted to this in an attempt to make good what is largely lacking in supply chain literature: sophisticated discussion of the relational elements involved.

An important contribution was made by Chris Sunderland, a theologian who is also a biological scientist. As such, he is interested in looking at parallels between the animal world and the human world. Sunderland showed a film about cooperation between a large turtle and a small finch pecking fleas off the turtle's skin. The immediate consequence is that the finch gets a good meal and the turtle experiences relief from itching. Sunderland asked what happens if payback is delayed. On the human level, it is immediately evident that most organisations are reluctant to take the risk of initiating trust.

Sunderland showed how structure is crucial in affecting whether or not it is sensible to trust. An example is whether key decisions are made in public. What broke the 1984 miners' strike was a change in union ballots from the traditional show of hands to a secret vote. People often act differently in secret from how they behave if they know people are watching. The prime minister of the time, Margaret Thatcher, knew this and based her change of legislation around it. Thinking about ways of encouraging trust needs to take the *systemic* element into account.

Trust as Social Capital

Two very different writers, Francis Fukuyama and Stephen Covey, use striking metaphors about the nature of trust that point in different directions but are highly complementary. They throw light on the mentality that pervades the approaches to car manufacture that Womack and Jones discovered in their global survey – mass production and lean production.

In his wide-ranging cultural survey *Trust: The Social Virtues and the Creation of Prosperity*, Fukuyama describes trust in terms of social capital as 'the expectation that arises within a community of consistent, honest and cooperative behaviour, based on shared norms' (p.26). He says it is transmitted through cultural mechanisms such as religion, tradition and historical habit. Some societies (and, by implication, some business sectors) display more trust than others. Fukuyama surveys many contrasting examples. Japan and Germany score highly in terms of their capacity to generate trust between companies and within companies, in contrast to Italy, France and China where trust does not come easily beyond the level of the family.

Fukuyama acknowledges that cooperation is possible on other bases, but says 'people who do not trust one another will end up cooperating only under a system of formal rules and regulations, which have to be negotiated, agreed to, litigated, and enforced, sometimes by coercive means' (p.27). This legal apparatus, serving as a substitute for trust, entails what economists call 'transaction costs'. Where widespread trust exists, doing business costs less.

Fukuyama clearly prefers the kind of moral community where social capital exists, but warns that it cannot be acquired, as can other forms of human capital, through a rational investment decision. Nor can trust be generated through individuals acting on their own because 'it is based on the prevalence of social, rather than individual virtues' (p.27). Fukuyama is quite pessimistic about the prospects of changing a culture marked by mistrust. It is not impossible, but moving from a low-trust culture to a high-trust culture is necessarily a slow process.

In a supply chain, low trust causes an adversarial approach to procurement. The relationship between buyer and supplier is marked by mutual suspicion, keeping each other at arm's length, maximising advantage at the expense of the other, and the emergence of openly hostile attitudes once a problem occurs. Typical features are:

- The buyer relies on a large number of suppliers, who can be played off against each other to gain price concessions and ensure continuity of supply
- The buyer allocates limited amounts of business to suppliers to keep them in line and avoid undue dependence on any of them
- The buyer uses only short-term contracts, and good performance is no guarantee of their renewal
- The focus tends to be on price to the neglect of other factors (product quality, value-added services, technological improvement, process innovations)
- The buyer often pays the supplier late, which may cause cash-flow problems
- The key business quality is seen as 'retaining trained staff with the ability to negotiate effectively in an adversarial manner' (John Ramsey, 'Partnership of Unequals', *Supply Management*, p.33).

Womack, Jones and Roos observe that in the West, most suppliers believe strongly that 'what goes on in my factory is my business'. Detailed questions from an assembler about a supplier's production problems or a request to observe their manufacturing process in action are distinctly unwelcome and would be regarded as meddling. It might uncover valuable data on the supplier's operation and costs – information that the assembler could use to bargain down prices for follow-up contracts.

The MIT authors' verdict, however, is that: 'The mature mass-production supply system is broadly unsatisfactory to everyone. The suppliers are brought in late in the design process and can do little to improve the design, which may be hard and expensive to manufacture. They are under intense cost pressure from a buyer who does not understand their special problems. As a result, implausible bids win contracts, followed by adjustments, which may make the cost per part higher than those of realistic but losing bidders. This process makes estimating costs accurately difficult for the assembler. Moreover, the effort to play bidders off against each other makes them very reluctant to share ideas on improved production techniques while a part is in production. In other words, they have no incentive to merge their learning curves' (*The Machine that Changed the World*, p.145). A system marred by an atmosphere of distrust doesn't have a lot going for it.

Trust as an Emotional Bank Account

A different view of trust is found in Covey's popular collection of home-spun wisdom, *The Seven Habits of Highly Effective People*. Covey uses the term 'emotional bank account' as a metaphor to describe 'the amount of trust that's been built up in a relationship. It's the feeling of safeness you have with another human being' (*Seven Habits*, p.188). By our behaviour we either make deposits into that account (i.e. we build trust up) or we make withdrawals (we break it down). Covey lists six key deposits: understanding the other person (or organisation), attending to the little things, keeping commitments, clarifying expectations, showing personal integrity, and apologising sincerely when a withdrawal (i.e. failing in the other respects) is made. Consistency in these areas contributes to a situation where a genuine relationship of trust exists.

You don't have to read Covey for very long to become aware of his untroubled confidence that adopting his 'powerful lessons in personal change' (the subtitle of the book) can make a genuine difference. He is far more optimistic than Fukuyama in his conviction that individuals can either make an impact on their culture or be successful in the face of it. He commends a win/win approach to life, including business, and 'a frame of mind and heart that constantly seeks mutual benefit in all human interactions' (p.207). This is based on 'abundance mentality' – a belief that there can be plenty for everyone – and maturity, which he defines as a mixture of courage (sticking up for one's own interests) and considera- tion (seeking others' interests).

In the context of the supply chain, a win/win attitude results in a *partnership approach* rather than an *adversarial* one. This approach may be summed up as an agreement between a buyer and supplier that involves a commitment over an extended time period, and includes the sharing of information along with a sharing of the risks and rewards of the relation- ship. Its typical features are:

Buyer and supplier

- commit themselves to continuous improvement and shared benefits
- exchange relevant information openly
- resolve problems by working together, rather than blaming and penalising the other or seeking a new supplier or buyer.

Suppliers are often

- reduced in number
- paid, as well as delivering, on time
- proactive – volunteering ideas for improvement.

There is an underlying assumption of loyalty built in, an expectation of repeat orders between the partners if things go well.

Womack, Jones and Roos show how the partnership approach works in the Japanese car industry. There, sup- pliers are selected at the outset of the process of product development – not on the basis of bids, but on the basis of past relationships and a proven record of performance. The car assembler and the main suppliers work together on the assumption that a rational framework exists for determining costs, price and profits. The lean assembler establishes a target price for the car and then – with the suppliers – works backwards, 'figuring how the car can be made for this price while allowing a reasonable profit for both assembler and suppliers. In other words, it is a "market price minus" system rather than a "supplier cost plus" system' (*Machine*, p.148).

It is important to note that for the system to work, the supplier must share a substantial part of its proprietary information about costs and production techniques. In return, the assembler respects the supplier's need to make a reasonable profit. By agreeing to share profits from joint cost-saving activities and letting suppliers keep profits from any additional activities they undertake, the assembler relinquishes the right to monopolise benefits of suppliers' ideas. On the other hand, the Japanese assembler gains from the increased willingness of its suppliers to come up with innovations and cost-saving suggestions and to work collaboratively.

A Win/Win Relationship

In preparation for *Managing the Supply Chain*, I wondered if there were any examples of customer-supplier relationships in the Bible that might prove instructive. The answer came to me one sleepless night at four in the morning. In 1 Kings 5, King Solomon commissions King Hiram to send wood to be used in the building of the temple at Jerusalem.

Solomon and Hiram

Now King Hiram of Tyre sent his servants to Solomon, when he heard that they had anointed him king in place of his father, for Hiram had always been a friend of David. Solomon sent word to Hiram, saying, 'You know that my father could not build a house for the name of the Lord his

God because of the warfare with which his enemies surrounded him, until the Lord put them under the soles of his feet. But now the Lord my God has given me rest on every side; there is neither adversary nor misfortune. So I intend to build a house for the name of the Lord my God, as the Lord said to my father David, 'Your son, whom I will set on your throne in your place, shall build the house for my name.' Therefore command that cedars from the Lebanon be cut for me. My servants will join your servants, and I will give you whatever wages you set for your servants; for you know that there is no one among us who knows how to cut timber like the Sidonians.

When Hiram heard the words of Solomon, he rejoiced greatly, and said, 'Blessed be the Lord today, who has given to David a wise son to be over this great people.' Hiram sent word to Solomon, 'I have heard the message that you have sent to me; I will fulfil all your needs in the matter of cedar and cypress timber. My servants shall bring it down to the sea from the Lebanon; I will make it into rafts to go by sea to the place you indicate. I will have them broken up there for you to take away. And you shall meet my needs by providing food for my household.' So Hiram supplied Solomon's every need for timber of cedar and cypress. Solomon in turn gave Hiram twenty thousand cors of wheat as food for his household, and twenty cors of fine oil. Solomon gave this to Hiram year by year. So the Lord gave Solomon wisdom, as he promised him. There was peace between Hiram and Solomon; and the two of them made a treaty. (1 Kings 5:1-12, NRSV)

Solomon is the customer and Hiram the supplier in a deal that clearly produces mutual satisfaction. The result of their doing business with each other was 'peace between Hiram and Solomon; and the two of them made a treaty.' I believe a plausible reading of the text suggests the following lessons for us:

A background of friendship

Solomon was able to build on something he had inherited from his father. The chapter begins with Hiram sending his servants to Solomon 'when he heard that they had anointed him king in place of his father; for Hiram had always been a friend to David' (v.1). An existing family friendship meant that

Solomon wasn't starting from scratch. In a positive customer-
supplier relationship, personal links can be very important in
forging the way.

A balance of power

Solomon sends word to Hiram explaining his intention to
build a temple – a project David had wanted but been unable
to carry out – and issuing the command 'that cedars from the
Lebanon be cut for me'. The tone sounds peremptory: here is
a king at the height of Israel's power who expects others to
do as he says. But he immediately acknowledges that the
power is not all on one side. Hiram occupies a niche position
in the market, because as Solomon says, 'There is no one
among us who knows how to cut timber like the Sidonians.'
Israel is willing to pay for this specialist skill: 'My servants
will join your servants, and I will give you whatever wages
you set for your servants' (v.6). Solomon has the money, and
Hiram has the skilled workers: this makes for an equilibrium
where neither is at a bargaining disadvantage. It is when
there is a severe imbalance between companies (either in
terms of size or distinctive competence) that the relationship
often ends up soured – a point to which I shall return
later.

Delighting the customer

Some companies these days talk not just about serving or
satisfying the customer but delighting the customer. It suggests an attitude of going out of their way to help, of being
proactive in volunteering ideas for improving the service.
There is a clear hint of this in Hiram's response. Solomon
had only asked for cedar, but Hiram offers cypress as well: 'I
will fulfil all your needs in the matter of cedar and cypress
timber' (v.8). He makes a positive proposal about how the
wood should be transported. Avoiding the difficult and hilly
route overland, he says: 'My servants shall bring it down to
the sea from the Lebanon; I will make it into rafts to go by
sea to the place you indicate. I will have them broken up
there for you to take away' (v.9). Hiram is doing his best to

please. Yet he's no softie. He demands an additional recompense in return for this service: 'And you shall meet my needs by providing food for my household' (v.9). Solomon in turn accedes to the request: he gives Hiram 'twenty thousand cors of wheat as food for his household, and twenty cors of fine oil' (v.11).

Win/Win

What we see in 1 Kings 5 is a genuine win/win situation. There is evidence of both parties seeking mutual benefit. Both Solomon and Hiram promote their own interests, and are robust in the way they make demands on the other, but each shows a genuine concern for their partners' interests as well. The success of the deal is based on trust, the high emotional bank account (to use Covey's phrase) that Solomon's father, David, had played a part in building up.

Power and Discipline

There are also important lessons to be learnt from a broader biblical theme, the story of God's covenant with his people Israel. In his contribution to the seminar, Chris Sunderland suggested three requirements for systems of trust to develop: *good memories, stable relationships*, and *effective discipline*. (He has developed this thinking further in his book *In a Glass Darkly: Seeking Vision for Public Life*). These requirements are all evident in the Old Testament. Good memories comprise a history of trustworthy behaviour, described as faithfulness, and often epitomised by memorable incidents. Israel could look back on a number of episodes when God had come to the rescue. Stable relationships have been tried and tested over time, resulting in good mutual knowledge and understanding. We see the outworking of this too in the Japanese system described by Womack, Jones and Roos. Effective discipline is the crucial third component, and should not be overlooked. When the Israelite nation behaved badly, there were unpleasant consequences. The dominant thrust is of a God who forgives his people and longs to restore the relationship, but they have to submit to his discipline.

Sunderland juxtaposed the twin realities of the synergy of established relationships and the necessary disciplines of competition. These two may seem to be in tension, but it can be a tension that is creative and healthy. The concept of discipline is relevant in two ways.

First, there is the discipline of the market, or if you like economic survival. Consider the episode in 1999 when with little or no warning (allegedly), Marks & Spencer abandoned its 30-year-old commercial 'partnership' with the British clothing manufacturer Baird. Baird felt betrayed. Marks & Spencer saw no option but to terminate the relationship because profit margins were under severe pressure and they needed to find a cheaper supplier overseas. There was an established relationship, but it had to bow before the reality – effectively the discipline – of competition. These relationships cannot be perpetuated indefinitely if they fly in the face of market response or economic sense.

Nevertheless, one has some sympathy for Baird, especially if – as has been alleged about many of its traditional suppliers – Marks & Spencer had made Baird unduly dependent upon it as the dominant customer. Then there would be a severe imbalance of power. Such a position naturally leaves suppliers dangerously vulnerable. Another example is the grave danger that closure of Rover presents to many small West Midlands engineering firms. It is estimated if Rover closes it will cost 45,000 jobs, not just in the workforce but in all the supplier firms, their suppliers, and the shops and services that support the suppliers' local communities. In contrast, a seminar delegate told of his construction firm's experience with Hewlett Packard. There is an ongoing relationship, but Hewlett Packard actively discourages the firm from being overly dependent on its custom. Wise suppliers should avoid putting too many eggs in one basket.

Second, the concept of discipline is relevant as an antidote to the sort of 'cosy' business relationship that can lead to complacency. It is precisely this prospect that causes some people to attack the partnership approach. They point to the danger of suppliers exploiting the goodwill of the customer. The possibility of the customer changing supplier keeps performance up to the mark. Stanley Kalms, the chairman of Dixons, is forthright about this: 'There are no guarantees. If the supplier stays competitive and wide awake, he's got my business for ever more. But he has to accept that if there's someone else down the road offering something better or cheaper, then he'll be shoved aside. Otherwise, what's his incentive to invest and keep state of the art if he's got an assured outlet? And how does a man making a new widget get rid of the man making the old widget?' ('Raising the Stakes', *Marketing Business*, p.30).

These are fair challenges, but a partnership approach should not be too easily equated with an attitude that is soft or oozing in tolerance. This is not what the MIT researchers found in the Japanese car industry. Suppliers faced constant pressure to improve their performance. *The Machine that Changed the World* gives an example of what effective discipline might mean in a loyal customer-supplier relationship.

In the Japanese system, when a supplier falls short on quality or reliability, an assembler like Toyota does not dismiss the company – the typical response in the West. Instead, the assembler shifts a small but significant fraction of the business from that supplier to its other source of that part for a given period of time as a penalty. (Assemblers usually divide their parts order between two members of the supplier group.) Because costs and profits margins have been very carefully calculated on an assumed standard volume, shifting part of the volume away can have a serious effect on the profitability of the underperforming supplier. Toyota and other companies have found that this form of punishment is highly effective in keeping everyone on their toes, while sustaining the long-term relationship essential to the system. Lean producers do occasionally fire suppliers, but not 'capriciously'. 'Suppliers are never kept in the dark about their performance' (*Machine*, p.154). The assembler regularly 'scores' their performance, and they only lose a repeat order if they show no evidence of a willingness or capacity to improve. This is an apt example of the juxtaposition between Sunderland's twin realities: the synergy of established relationships and the necessary disciplines of competition.

The Legal Dimension

Where does Britain stand in this tug-of-war between the two approaches? According to the testimony of most of the delegates to our seminar, as well as many others, the adversarial approach remains deeply embedded in much of British business culture. Some people in business positively revel in it. One delegate spoke of the traditional buyer who knows only two tools: the screwdriver to screw the price down and the hammer to force the contract home. Another related his dealings with a privatised utility where the contracts manager had no intrinsic concern about the efficacy of the supplier's product: 'Personally, I don't care whether your compressor ever pumps gas.' His only concern was for the contract and discovering an excuse to find fault with the supplier on the basis of it – a perverse approach if ever there was one!

Even where the partnership approach is being adopted, at least in name, the take up often seems to be half-hearted or uneven. The more powerful company may talk the language of partnership to bully its smaller counterpart into being co-operative and not complaining. Or there may be a genuine attempt to initiate a more 'trustful' approach that breaks down at the first sign of something going wrong, especially behaviour which is perceived as distrustful.

The adversarial approach is often reinforced by the involvement of lawyers, admits solicitor Jane Gunn. Once lawyers get involved in a commercial dispute conducted according to the adversarial model, they tend to take control of the process. It proves an emotionally draining experience for both litigant and defendant. Often people are reduced to tears and suffer loss of sleep. The process is slow and cumbersome, costly – because of high legal fees and expenses – and has an adverse effect on all the companies involved, through negative publicity, a decline in the share price, and the considerable demands on management time. The adversarial legal process drives parties further apart, making resumption of a commercial relationship unlikely in the extreme. The winners and losers in a court case are usually the solicitors and expert witnesses rather than the plaintiffs and defendants.

Gunn sits on a commercial mediation panel that is pioneering a different approach, Early Dispute Resolution (EDR) as opposed to Advanced Dispute Resolution (ADR). Using a neutral third party with special training, mediation is quick, simple and inexpensive – usually the cost of a couple of days of the mediator's time rather than weeks of court costs. It is based on cooperation between two parties who seek a resolution that accommodates both their interests. For it to work, the parties need to own the solution and not have one imposed upon them. Mediation deals in facts and seeks (often by encouraging confidential discussion) to identify the underlying issues that have created difficulties.

The aim of EDR, Gunn says, is to catch *conflict* before it becomes *dispute*. Conflict is a process of expressing dissatisfaction, whereas dispute is a possible outcome of the conflict process. Conflict can be a positive force but it also threatens to become destructive. EDR offers parties maximum choice in finding the best way to resolve their dispute for mutual benefit, at minimum cost in terms of time, money and relationships. In the USA, General Electric has introduced a process based around EDR to manage disputes on a company-wide basis. It has been a huge success, saving millions of dollars. It involves a more holistic approach, whereby disputes are viewed as business and human problems rather than legal ones. Mediation facilities are used both internally and externally. EDR is one example of a more conciliatory approach to customer-supplier relationships. It may not yet be the dominant one in British business, but is making definite inroads into the adversarial way of doing things.

David's Story

The seminar was fortunate to have a very experienced owner-businessman, David Runton, who has lived with the tension between the two approaches throughout his career. Runton's Yorkshire firm, FTL, supplies flexible all-metal high-pressure connection hoses to many leading British companies. At the time of the seminar, 30 companies represented 90% of FTL's sales with the top five accounting for 50% and FTL being sole supplier.

David said there had been a major change in the way his customers perceived his business as he consciously sought to change his attitude from reactive to proactive. This marks out FTL from other suppliers. The company seeks to discuss a customer's business development issues, even asking questions about what the customer's customers are doing. With this extra knowledge FTL is able to anticipate the customer's needs and provide a better service. The relationship with customers is developed in both a formal and an informal way (depending on the customer) and across the range of corporate positions. A 'batting order' is worked out in which people at the level of sales, operations, middle and senior management all know who their corresponding number is in the other company.

FTL has a Customer Service Charter that promises how it will behave. This consists of commitments on:

- Delivery Performance (within a known capacity will guarantee 100% delivery on time)
- Quality Performance (zero defect)
- Communication
- Problem Solving (customer service manager will respond immediately to customer reactions)
- Product Development
- Cost Reduction.

Just as FTL submits itself to being scored by its customers, so it keeps scores on them. Companies are marked according to positive and negative characteristics. From a supplier's perspective, these include whether there is a single sourcing agreement, whether orders are placed regularly or fluctuate wildly, whether the customer is open to new ideas and whether he is praise- or blame-oriented in his attitude.

Since winning a lifetime customer does not happen overnight, FTL has drawn up a *creeping commitment process*. This identifies 23 stages, starting with 'No – but keep calling' and graduating to winning an order (11), confronting the inevitable problems (Stage 16 is called suffering!) through to the final stage of customer satisfaction and the mature relationship. This brings repeated challenges for business development and has highlighted the need to select customers carefully. Where the decision is made to go ahead with a relationship despite unsatisfactory aspects, there needs to be a strategy to try to change what needs changing.

There was a strong sense in the seminar of the supplier going out of his or her way to please the customer. There is a complementary process in which the supplier has to earn the customer's favour. The parable of the persistent widow (Lk. 18:2-8) was cited, along with Jesus' saying about going the second mile (Mt. 5:41) – though it may turn out to be the third, fourth or fifth mile. The disappointment can be excruciating when a supplier has made every possible effort to satisfy a customer, but the order goes to someone else. Runton could also point to examples of customers who had stood by FTL through good times and bad. In a long-standing relationship, a trust bank of goodwill can be built up – a case of Covey's emotional bank account being borne out in practice.

Among many fascinating stories told by David Runton, one stood out. It concerned a customer back in the mid-1980s that bullied FTL, in a 'we win, you lose' culture, by constantly rejecting deliveries and alleging they were 'not to specification'. David became so disenchanted that he was prepared to terminate the relationship. He drove to the head office and told the customer he'd had enough. A short while later, the relationship did resume when the customer came back, 'dragging its tail,' and agreed a less harsh regime and a price increase. There was an improvement in the relationship for several years, until a change in customer ownership was followed not long afterwards by a further barrage of complaints. This time, David realised, FTL was to blame. The company was going through a difficult spell, and their quality of service was not what it had been. He got in his car again and visited the customer's head office, but this time to apologise and discuss how FTL could serve its customer better. This had a transforming effect, to the point where FTL received a letter saying it was the customer's most improved supplier of the year. David surely deserves credit for his courage on both occasions, first for confronting the customer company when FTL was *not* at fault and second for saying sorry when it *was* at fault. In each case, the initiative he took was unusual, but in each case, it led to very positive outcomes.

Honest Confrontation

I suspect that hidden in this episode lies the essence of an authentically Christian approach to handling relationships in the supply chain. This essence is surely looking for growth in working relationships, and for a more satisfactory, higher quality provision of products and services. Where problems occur Christians should lead the way in tackling them, rather than pretending they don't exist. An honest confrontation with an issue and with business partners may take different forms on different occasions. Sometimes the problem will lie with us and we should admit it. As people who regularly experience saying sorry and being forgiven, Christians ought to be able to set an example in that respect. At other times, we may be victims of unacceptable behaviour. When that happens, faithfulness to Christian values should not mean being a soft touch. Jesus displayed anger on occasion, in a controlled and targeted way. Consider his expulsion of the money-changers from the temple, on the grounds that God's house was meant to be a place of prayer, but they – by their dishonest practice – had made it a 'den of thieves' (Mk. 11:11,15-19). Jesus' self-control and premeditation are evident – he had viewed what was going on in the temple the previous day, and presumably reflected on it overnight. There is a time and place to express righteous anger in the face of injustice.

The trend towards a partnership approach in customer-supplier relationships is greatly to be welcomed, but it need not exclude discipline as and when needed. A theology that teaches both that human beings have great potential and are seriously fallen saves us from the twin perils of naivety and despair about those with whom we do business. It fits well with a commitment to cooperation, laced with a competitive edge.

5

CAN PARTNERSHIP REALLY WORK?:
ESTABLISHING TRUST IN THE CONSTRUCTION INDUSTRY

Barry, a practising Christian, told me how he ran up against sharp practice when he was in charge of the commercial aspects of a large project. He was a quantity surveyor with a contractor that was managing the project on behalf of a big infrastructure company. Almost all construction projects end up costing more than originally agreed, for reasons as varied as design changes, bad weather, and supply problems. Quantity surveyors are used to assess, negotiate and establish a final cost for the project, and fair payments to the subcontractors.

The main project comprised about 100 smaller projects, one of which was completed well over budget and several months late. Barry's conscientious investigation found that the cause of the delay, disruption and vast increase in costs was a decision made by a senior manager of the infrastructure company, and that the man had taken the decision against the advice of his colleagues and those employed to manage the project on his company's behalf.

The work had been carried out by a small contractor with about fifty employees who sent in a large claim for the effects of delay and disruption. On completion of his review, Barry reported to his managing director that he believed a valid claim existed for approximately £200,000. It was clear, Barry told me, that the contractor needed an early resolution to avoid bankruptcy due to the general effects of recession in the industry.

The next day, the storm broke. The managing director summoned Barry into his office and said he had been advised in no uncertain terms that if they paid so much as a single penny to the contractor they would never manage another project for the infrastructure company. Furthermore, Barry should bear in mind that 'redundancies are always necessary in this difficult market'.

The choice was stark, Barry explained. He was torn between two painful options. He could stand by his report, lose his job, and risk ending a relationship between his company and the infrastructure company worth over £50 million a year in turnover. Or he could deny justice, lie, rewrite his report to recommend no payment to the contractor, and argue the case doggedly in the expectation that the contractor would soon be out of business.

Barry was in a dilemma. He turned to several company directors in his church for advice and was saddened that each gave the same advice: Be pragmatic, look after your own company and safeguard your job. Where was justice in all this, he wondered? The minister of his church took a more principled view and urged him to do the right thing, putting his trust in God. After much prayer and reflection, Barry decided to stick by his report and face the consequences. It was a difficult decision.

What happened to Barry? Turn to page 115 to find out.

Not a Pretty Picture

There is an overwhelmingly negative feeling about the construction industry among those who work in it that tells of something gone seriously awry. Delegates to a consultation on *Establishing Trust in the Construction Industry* were asked how they saw the industry in which they worked. Their pictures of the industry are:

- A clock which has passed its deadline
- Several people pulling a building block on different directions
- A man at the bottom of a hole, pushed there by others
- Different groups separated by brick walls
- A wheel with some spokes broken or missing

We saw in Chapter 4 how the practices of partnering and lean production are gradually infiltrating British industry. There is still a long way to go, but both the manufacturing and service sectors have experienced changes in attitude and increases in efficiency that would have been unthinkable in the 1980s. Construction is a much more difficult nut to crack.

A Troubled History

The construction industry has long had a tarnished reputation. This is not a reflection on its technical capabilities. Its best work is excellent and of outstanding quality, and the industry can be proud of its many formidable engineering feats. It is the unevenness of that work and the high level of client dissatisfaction, especially in the commercial sector, that causes the dissatisfaction. A few years ago, a property developer conducted a comparative survey of the car and construction industries, assessing their relative success in meeting the wishes of their customers. There were nine criteria:

- value for money
- pleasing to look at
- free from faults
- delivered on time
- fit for the purpose
- supported by worthwhile guarantees
- reasonable running costs
- satisfactory durability
- customer delight.

The construction industry scored worse on eight points – being particularly low in the areas of 'free from fault' and 'supported by worthwhile guarantees' – Sir Michael Latham wrote in his 1994 report *Constructing the Team* (known as *The Latham Report*, pp.11-12). This low level of satisfaction reflects the process by which buildings get constructed and the poor relationships that often bedevil it. Historically, the industry has been highly adversarial for several reasons.

Construction is a highly complex process, involving interaction between a wide range of disparate parties. I became aware of this when I spent a fascinating day on a building site in Leicester, watching the erection of a shopping centre. The client, a firm of property developers, was working with:

- a major construction company, responsible for overall site management
- a firm of architects, who had designed the centre
- an engineering firm, providing the centre's essential structure
- surveyors, checking the state of the foundations
- numerous subcontractors, carrying out specialist tasks
- retailers, large and small, to whom shop units were being let.

Each segment of the construction industry has a distinctive culture and a favoured way of operating. A gulf often exists between the 'professionals' and the rest – essentially those who do the manual work of construction. Adding to the complexity, there is no standard pattern that determines what professionals should do which jobs. A project manager may turn out to be an architect, an engineer, a quantity surveyor, a main contractor, a consultant, or someone employed by the client. This often results in confusion about who has final authority.

The industry is highly fragmented. Of nearly 200,000 registered firms in the UK, about half are one-person outfits. Only 12,000 firms employ more than seven people. It is extraordinarily easy to set up in construction: hence the problem of so-called 'cowboy builders'. Many small firms are specialist contractors, who 30 years ago would have been directly employed by large contractors. The tension that simmered then was born of the mutual suspicion between employer and employee, managers and the managed. The formal relationship has changed: contractors have trimmed their workforces and now outsource much of the work. But the mutual suspicion remains.

Most disputes are between main contractors and subcontractors. There is even dispute over the term subcontractor. 'Specialist contractor' tends to be preferred by those who practise a distinctive trade, but 'subcontractor' – or worse, the disparaging 'subbie', as in 'screw the subbie' – is how they are described by the big firms. Main contractors frequently complain about the 'unreliability' of specialist contractors, who in turn protest about 'onerous conditions', 'contractual abuse' or even 'contractual mugging' by the main contractors. The most common complaints are over failure to pay on time and looking for excuses not to pay. Specialist contractors take strong exception to the now illegal practice of 'pay-when-paid', the condition which many contractors write into contracts to say they will only pay when paid themselves.

Various problems originate with the client. The clients who receive most satisfaction tend to be the regulars. They include BAA (British Airports Authority), major retailers such as Sainsbury's and Tesco, and hotel/restaurant groups such as Whitbread. These clients have developed a clear idea of what they want, generally use standard designs, and look to use the same 'team' of firms on a regular basis. They have an enviable record of procuring good quality buildings on time and on budget. Many clients, however, only want a new building very occasionally – every ten years, or maybe less often.

Lack of experience is problematic for two main reasons. Inexperienced clients may make the naïve assumption that best value can be equated with lowest price. This is not necessarily the case at all. An unrealistically low price never turns out to be the final price: all manner of reasons are found for adjusting it upwards. On the other hand, they may be taken for a ride. A lack of familiarity with the construction process leaves clients vulnerable to exploitation by unscrupulous operators. Occasional clients are probably less sure of what they want from a building. They may change their minds during construction. This is likely to be a particular problem for voluntary or charitable organisations if they have a difficulty in raising sufficient money for the original plan. Changing the design and specification after the construction process has begun causes considerable frustration and delay for the practitioners. The fact that many parties in the process (especially the specialist contractors) relate only to the next link in the contractual chain also contributes to a situation where little thought is given to what the client actually wants or needs. The specialist may not even know who the client is.

Short of Capital

Construction is under-capitalised compared with other sectors of British industry. The City is inclined to regard construction as unpredictable and a poor investment, and recession hits it harder than other sectors of the economy. Between 1989 and 1994, almost half a million jobs were lost and over 35,000 construction firms went bankrupt. The squeeze on profit margins has created high levels of corporate insecurity. When everyone is struggling for survival, the prevailing atmosphere is more cut-throat and relationships are less likely to be characterised by trust. Stephen Covey may commend a win/win approach based on an abundance mentality, but the different parties in the construction industry have often found it difficult to believe 'there can be plenty for everyone'. The low rates of profitability have a serious side-effect. Construction invests very little in either training, or research and development. This does not augur well for the future of the industry.

'If the economy is weak, the industry will suffer, and its participants will try to alleviate that suffering at the expense of others (including clients). It is not easy to create teamwork in construction when everyone is struggling to avoid losses ...

[The industry] cannot create its core activities out of nothing. If there is more work around, there may be more money for efficient firms. If there is more money, there may be more trust. This is not a "begging bowl" approach, or a lack of a "can/do" attitude. It is a simple statement of commercial reality. It pervades virtually every decision taken every day by every participant in the construction process' (*Latham Report*, p.9).

In the circumstances, it's unsurprising that the construction industry is characterised by sharp practice. Exploiting the weaknesses of rival firms is often seen as the only way to ensure corporate survival. Cooperation in a joint endeavour is marred from an early stage by acrimony and adversarial attitudes. Additional costs are caused by mishaps, avoidable delays, disputes over who is to blame, and resulting litigation. That shopping centre in Leicester ended up in a messy and expensive legal dispute. It is astonishing and ridiculous, but at the same time understandable, that the construction industry spends more on litigation than it does on research and development. No wonder many clients are left feeling very dissatisfied.

The Latham Report

It is not all bad news. There have always been examples of good practice, satisfying projects completed successfully, on time and with a minimum of hassle. And in the last decade, the mood has been growing that the construction industry must find a better way of doing things. In his 1994 report, jointly commissioned by the industry and the last government, Latham drew on this feeling and produced a host of recommendations for changing industry practice and ethos. These include:

- Creation of a Construction Clients Forum, bringing together regular private clients to share and promote best practice
- Encouragement to government, as the foremost public sector client, to adopt best practice

- Use of a 'complete family' of interlocking documents, embracing all the contracts entailed in a project, along the lines of the New Engineering Contract
- Introduction of a Construction Contracts Bill to give statutory backing to newly amended standard forms
- Making adjudication the normal method of dispute resolution
- Clearer definition of the role and duties of a project manager
- Evaluation of tenders according to quality as well as price
- The setting up of a productivity target of 30% real cost reduction by the year 2000.

Latham's recommendations provoked lively debate and were welcomed by many in the industry. Several were implemented – at least in part. Four years later, in March 1998, the Ridley Hall Foundation brought together a 'think tank' of 25 people representing clients, main contractors, specialist contractors, suppliers, consulting engineers, quantity surveyors, architects, procurement consultants, trainers and academics with a special interest in the industry for a consultation on *Establishing Trust in the Construction Industry*. They expressed their views frankly, listened carefully and pooled their ideas for a positive way forward. The hope was to give impetus to beneficial developments and consider how to overcome obstacles to progress.

Building in the Bible

Building is a prominent theme in the Bible. There are descriptions of the planning and construction of many notable buildings, including Solomon's Temple (1 Kgs. 5-9) and the city walls of Jerusalem (Neh. 1-6). Building also features strongly on a symbolic and metaphorical level. For instance, Jesus is described as the cornerstone that the builders rejected (1 Pet. 2:4-8). Paul describes his role in 'growing' the church in terms of a 'skilled master builder' (the Greek word is *architekton*, from which we derive the word architect). In the early chapters of Genesis, the Tower of Babel is seen as the hallmark of human aggrandisement: humanity wanting to reach up to the heavens, 'make a name for ourselves' and be like God (Gen. 11:1-9). In the final chapters of Revelation, the ultimate experience of salvation is described not only in terms of a 'new heaven and a new earth' but also as 'the Holy City, the new Jerusalem', whose walls are made out of precious jewels (Rev. 21).

Just as the books of Kings provide a positive example of customer-supplier relations (see pp.84-5), so they furnish us with a fascinating snapshot of a trustworthy construction industry. Set over a century later than Solomon, in the reign of Jehoash, this describes the belated carrying out of repairs to the temple.

> *Jehoiada the priest took a chest and bored a hole in its lid. He placed it beside the altar, on the right side as one enters the temple of the Lord. The priests who guarded the entrance put into the chest all the money that was brought to the temple of the Lord. Whenever they saw that there was a large amount of money in the chest, the royal secretary and the high priest came, counted the money that had been brought into the temple of the Lord and put it into bags. When the amount had been determined they gave the money to the men appointed to supervise the work on the temple. With it they paid those who worked on the temple of the Lord – the carpenters and builders, the masons and stonecutters. They purchased timber and dressed stone for the repair of the temple of the Lord, and met all the other expenses of restoring the temple.*
>
> *The money brought into the temple was not spent for making silver basins, work trimmers, sprinkling bowls, trumpets or any other articles of gold or silver for the temple of the Lord; it was paid to the workmen, who used it to repair the temple. They did not require an accounting from those to whom they gave the money to pay the workers, because they acted with complete honesty.* (2 Kgs. 12:9-15, NIV)

Two things stand out. First, priority is given to paying the workers rather than making fancy additions to the temple. This is an exercise in restoration, not embellishment. Second, the works supervisors are trusted to spend money properly to the extent that they do not even have to give a financial accounting. Their impeccable reputation for honesty rendered it unnecessary.

Establishing Trust

Trust is the factor which is largely absent from the British construction industry. Delegates at the consultation saw trust as consisting – essentially – of confidence that others will do what they say they will do, and not act contrary to one's own interests. This confidence will be based partly on the perceived competence of another party (e.g. do they have the resources to deliver on time?) but also on a judgment about their perceived intentions (e.g. are they trying to pull the wool over my eyes?).

Insights stemming from the two metaphors about trust used by Fukuyama and Covey struck chords. Some people had experiences that resonated strongly with what Fukuyama says about low-trust cultures, and the difficulty of moving out of such a culture. One delegate said: 'Low trust is in the nature of the industry.' Another said: 'The culture assumes there will be confrontation from the start.' A third said: 'Trust can be destroyed very quickly by something going wrong.'

Some delegates questioned the relevance of Covey's concept of an Emotional Bank Account, saying they felt it applied only to relationships between persons, not relationships between organisations. Others argued that the key to good relationships between organisations is warm personal relationships, especially between people at the top. Some had tried the win/win approach and found that it worked. However, they did recognise that trust involves risk. Someone has to be prepared to take the initiative in displaying trust, sharing information, and disclosing difficulties and concerns. Others could use that to their own benefit, disadvantaging the person who took the risk. It is a brave person who makes the crucial first move.

Much of the consultation was taken up by presentations on the different perspectives of client, main contractor, specialist contractor, consulting engineer and professional. Important insights emerged.

The Client's Perspective

Clients feel marginalised in the construction process. Historically, they have been excluded from discussions about reform of the industry. Sir Michael broke new ground when he ensured that clients were involved in his review and insisted that change of the industry should be client-led.

Central and local government are a critical force for change, being responsible for 30-40% of new buildings, according to Stuart Humby, a former chairman of the Construction Clients Forum. It can be as hard for government to change its way of doing things as for any other sector. Stuart advocated more enlightened professional training, total supply chain thinking, the development of client networks, and learning from best practice in other areas of business.

A discussion group listed the characteristics of a good client, meaning someone who was likely both to be satisfied with the end product and satisfying to work with. The list included:

- using the building as occupiers, for their own purpose
- clear about what they want
- both attuned to immediate needs and far-sighted
- sensitive to safety considerations
- practical about what can be delivered
- aware of best practice
- fully exchanges all relevant information
- well advised about the procurement process
- has a single point of reference for making authoritative decisions
- aware of their legal responsibilities
- in receipt of genuine care from the other parties
- judges on more than financial criteria – and is therefore ready to pay more than the lowest tendered price in order to get value for money.

The Main Contractor's Perspective

The key to trust is a greatly improved process for executing projects focused *exclusively* on providing value for money for clients, according to Geoffrey Wort, then director of External Services at John Laing, one of Britain's largest construction firms. He said a good process can minimise the amount of risk, and that in an industry with a troubled history this creates more trust: the more risk there is involved in a project, the less trust there is. The converse is also true. He mentioned 'risk hygiene' factors that he would like to become intrinsic to the construction process:

- predictability – producing a consistent standard of performance
- measurement – 'we're only practising if we're not scoring'
- transparency – open communication between all parties
- repeatability – in process and participants
- risk management techniques – for identifying, assessing, quantifying, responding to and reviewing areas of risk

In discussion, a contractor suggested the focus should be on improving relationships with people rather than getting the process right. On the whole, most delegates felt both were important. Contractors manage 'frail coalitions' where attention to people *and* process is crucial. Most of the group with experience of partnering were enthusiastic about the concept and three aspects for making this successful were emphasised.

First, *bring the key parties together at the design stage* for an honest discussion of project plans and costs. Specialist contractors or suppliers are rarely incorporated into the process, yet they have much to contribute – both in terms of providing innovative ideas and giving realistic estimates about costs. All too often, they are brought in too late. A consulting engineer reported that his attempts to involve specialists at the design stage had met with a disappointing response. Perhaps those viewed as being at the far end of the chain have an us-and-them mentality, and are suspicious of any attempt to move away from this.

Second, *have an agreed disputes procedure*. Obviously it is best to avoid disputes, and emphasising partnership and team-work undoubtedly has this effect. Nevertheless, conflict may arise despite everyone's best intentions. Sir Michael said he favoured contracts with a built-in process for speedy adjudi-cation of disputes, and this – though itself the subject of dispute – has now been embodied in legislation. The impor-tant point, delegates agreed, is that partnering should be realistic. Disputes should be allowed for rather than ignored.

Third, *understand that good performance is likely to lead to repeat orders*, and so a partnership is potentially long-term. The conventional process of tendering militates against this. It assumes that clients benefit from bringing together a new team of designers, constructors and specialists for every fresh project. This inhibits learning from experience, and pre-vents the building up of skilled and experienced teams who know each other well and develop trust in each other. Whitbread has slashed the number of main contractors it uses from thirty to five. It shares its five-year business plan with its partners, so they can contribute proactively to Whitbread's objectives and plan their own businesses with greater foresight.

The criticism of long-term partnerships, as we saw in the previous chapter, is that they can become too cosy. This is why a commitment to continuous improvement is so impor-tant. Tesco reduced the capital cost of its stores by 40 per cent between 1991 and 1998 by reducing its supply base and developing long-term relationships, and through cutting waste and inefficiency out of the process. They are aiming for further substantial reductions in both costs and time. There is mounting evidence that long-term relationships facilitate the capacity to learn from experience and improve on performance.

The Specialist Contractor's Perspective

On the whole, specialist contractors were encouraged by the Latham developments. They felt that Sir Michael had listened to their concerns and that legislative changes moved in the right direction, although some recommendations got watered down in the process of becoming law. The Construction Act provides an objective benchmark against which to measure a contractor's in-house contract documents, and the Confederation of Construction Specialists uses this to carry out detailed analyses that expose the many ways in which specific companies fall short. Each issue of the confederation's bi-monthly newsletter features a well-documented case of an 'onerous subcontract'. The consultation revealed a feeling of there still being a long way to go in terms of changes in fundamental attitude.

On the vexed question of the timing of payment (an area where the small firm is most vulnerable) there was a wide spread of opinion, ranging from full payment at the beginning to full payment at the end; but there was most support for 'milestone payments' to ensure a reasonable cash-flow. It was recognised that inadequate cash-flow is a major problem in an under-capitalised industry.

Respect for the specialist contractor should also mean provision of decent site conditions. Too often people are expected to work in exceedingly cramped situations, without sufficient attention to safety or to provision of facilities (clothing, canteens, showers, etc.) that would be taken for granted in most industries. The conditions in which workers are expected to do their job is a reflection of the way they are valued.

There is no doubt that specialist contractors feel that they are the main victims of sharp practice in the industry. As a result, they take more convincing than most of a genuine change of heart and practice by others. Where fine words are not matched by actions, the response from specialist contractors is liable to be disillusionment and a hardening of suspicion.

The Professional's Perspective
Two aspects of the divide between the so-called professionals and those who actually do the building came to the fore during the consultation.

First, it is tempting for the professionals to think that in an industry with a 'macho' image, people can only understand a macho approach. A consulting engineer told how many of his colleagues working as project managers sought to ensure that contractors 'knew their place' by using tough, no-nonsense talk with a few carefully chosen expletives to communicate the most pressing concerns. His experience was that this approach was counter-productive. He prefers to establish genuine two-way communication, listening to the contractor's point of view before deciding action. He said he avoids inflammatory language, sticks to the facts, and reserves a display of anger for really serious incidents. Every construction project throws up awkward and idiosyncratic characters, and there is a need for managers who enjoy the challenge they represent and can respond positively and flexibly to them.

Second, there is a limited move in the industry towards using professionals as specialists (i.e. purely as architects, engineers or quantity surveyors) and less as consultants or project managers. Not surprisingly, the professions are resisting this and something of a power struggle between them and the main contractors is evident. The contractors said they thought it made sense for them to be overall coordinators, reducing the number of interfaces, while the professionals concentrated on the areas of their particular skills as true team members. The clients said they would judge which was the better distribution of roles and functions by results. They wanted to know which configuration of parties would supply the best quality of advice and, at the end of the day, best value for money.

One Body, Many Members

Cooperation makes more commercial sense than confrontation. Sir Michael, responding on the final day of the consultation, said his strategy was to persuade people to do good things for hard business reasons. He tells them that partnering is to their commercial advantage, while an adversarial approach is not. This can feel threatening, and there are deeply entrenched attitudes that cause people to say things such as 'I've always done things differently' 'It's not an approach that comes naturally to me', and 'There's nothing new in this – I've always done things this way' (though that's not usually how others perceive their way of working).

If more clients understood the difference between a typical tender price and a typical outcome price, Sir Michael thinks they would go for partnering every time. Partnering makes the whole team part of solving problems: there is gain share and pain share. But whole companies (not just the people at the top) need to be committed to this approach if it is to work.

By avoiding disputes and delays, he said, costs in the industry could be reduced by 30 per cent without hurting profit margins. The cuts would come in items which add no value, such as the expensive business of litigation. Sir Michael said progress in the industry since his report had been 'better than I expected but not as good as I had hoped' as people gradually come to see there are different and better ways of doing things. Where legislative recommendations had not been implemented, this was because the industry and clients couldn't reach agreement on a way forward and the government had been unwilling to impose a solution.

Sir Michael, a reader (lay preacher) in the Church of England, quoted St Paul on the importance of teamwork. In 1 Cor. 12:12-28 Paul expounds his understanding of the Christian church by analogy with the human body:

'The body does not consist of one member but of many. If the foot were to say, "Because I am not a hand, I do not belong to the body", that would not make it any less a part of the body. And if the ear were to say, "Because I am not an eye, I do not belong to the body", that would not make it any less a part of the body ... The eye cannot say to the hand, "I have no need of you", nor again the head to the feet, "I have no need of you"... If one members suffers, all suffer together; if one member is honoured, all rejoice together with it.' (NRSV)

Although this is teaching about the church, Sir Michael is surely right in thinking that the principle of mutual interdependence has a practical relevance in the wider world. Healthy attitudes for Christians are healthy attitudes for human beings in general. You may protest that applying Paul's notion of 'one body, many members' to the construction industry makes the mistake of seeing the supply chain as a dispersed firm: after all, each company is a significant power base within its own right, and has its own interests to protect. But from the client's point of view, the project is a united concept, with each firm having a contribution to make towards the whole. Clients find it difficult to understand why partnership should be so recent an innovation or (to some) so alien an idea. For partnership to work, 1 Corinthians 12 holds good. It is crucial that everyone involved in the complex process of construction appreciates the contributions made by each other. Sir Michael said this points towards the desirability of integrating specialists at an early stage of the design and planning process; and of clearly defining who is responsible for what.

Pursuing the body analogy, one person asked whether the different parts of the body are arranged in the right way. Sir Michael agreed they might not be, but said he thought different shapes were appropriate to different projects. There is no one right answer as to which party should be responsible for overall project management. The crucial requirement is for everyone to see themselves as integral members of a team.

Our group did not agree on all matters of detail, but delegates were united in seeing co-operative rather than confrontational relationships as the way forward for the industry. In particular, they supported partnership arrangements that combine:

- bringing all key parties together at the design stage
- real shared benefits (the 'win/win approach')
- agreed procedures for resolving disputes
- continuous improvement.

The aim is to give clients excellent value for money.

Rethinking Construction, the report of the Construction Task Force as a follow-up to Latham published later in 1998, takes a very similar approach. The Task Force was chaired by Sir John Egan, chief executive of BAA, and included Professor Daniel Jones, co-author of *The Machine that Changed the World* and director of the Lean Enterprise Centre at Cardiff Business School. It recommends that much of the philosophy and many of the techniques of lean enterprise be applied to the construction industry, through an 'integrated project process'. Noting that solid data on company and project performance in terms of efficiency and quality is currently hard to come by, it urges that clear targets be set for substantial improvement in relation to a wide range of criteria:

- capital cost   10% reduction
- construction time   10% reduction
- predictability   20% increase
- defects   20% reduction
- accidents   20% reduction
- productivity   10% increase
- turnover and products   10% increase

It would be a massive contribution to social welfare, a fillip not just for the construction industry but for the country as a whole, if those targets could be reached by 2005.

Postscript: the fragmentation of British Rail

Broken Rails: How Privatisation Wrecked Britain's Railways, by Christian Wolmar, is a salutary read. It is a reminder that while some industries may be hesitantly moving away from an adversarial culture towards a partnership model, Britain's railway system has moved in precisely the opposite direction.

British Rail, though far from perfect, was in the early 1990s growing more efficient. In particular, its safety record was improving. In a publicly owned, integrated system, lessons were learnt from accidents; who was responsible for what was clearly understood; and there was a basic willingness to co-operate for the common good. In the mid-1990s, the railways were privatised and broken up, on grounds whose coherence was never properly established and which can only be described as ideological. British Rail fragmented into operating companies, rolling stock companies, Railtrack (which owned the track, bridges, tunnels and stations), and track maintenance and renewal companies, to whom Railtrack effectively delegated the responsibility of keeping the system up to standard. All these companies expected, and were expected, to make a profit. Some made handsome profits. Ironically, the amount of taxpayers' money spent on the railways has increased since privatisation. Substantial public subsidies proved necessary – initially to make the new companies attractive to investors, and then to remedy major problems that ensued.

The contrived structure that has characterised the rail system since 1996 is a recipe for confusion and disaster. The rail companies relate to each other on a contractual basis, which means they inevitably jockey for the most advantageous terms and seek to exploit each other's weakness. This has dramatic implications for the travelling public, whom these companies are meant to be serving. Wolmar convincingly shows how the accidents at Southall, Ladbroke Grove and Hatfield, in which a total of 42 people died, were caused not just by individual errors but systemic failure rooted in the break-up of British Rail. (The name of Potters Bar can be added to this catalogue of disaster since *Broken Rails* was published.) There is a slipshod attitude to public safety and a sense of key responsibilities slipping between various corporate nets.

The Cullen inquiry on the Ladbroke Grove disaster revealed clearly that the way people worked together in the industry had changed. Three examples from the inquiry hearing demonstrate how a culture of trust and cooperation turned into one of deliberately stimulated antagonism:

'We were given on several occasions evidence that if track workers from Scotland had been sent down to York, for example, to work on a bit of track that was unfamiliar to them, they find themselves working with other employees from a different contractor. Their instinct is to ask the local people about the nature of the track. The local people may have been told by their employer, "Don't talk to these persons because they are employed by the opposition". In other words, there are actual obstacles put in the way of this pooling of both site knowledge and hazards knowledge. ...

'But, more worryingly, it used to be the case that signallers would probably know the personnel that were appearing in the stretch of track under their jurisdiction and when track maintenance was done on a more geographical basis. Now they have people requesting possession of track and they have no real idea of what their competence is or what their track awareness is or what their knowledge of the track layout is. ...

'Privatisation has created a big cultural change. There is now little inter-linking of culture from one company to another. There has been a loss of comradeship between drivers, signalmen, cleaners, etc. There is no longer a sense of working together. Questions of delay and attribution of blame strengthen the divide. This has led to a loss of confidence in others. No one is encouraged to discuss someone else's problem, or volunteers, or shares information. There has been a loss of learning and this leads to poor communication.' (Ladbroke Grove inquiry evidence, cited in *Broken Rails*, pp.180-181)

The importance of establishing trust in a fractured industry – or, in this case, of re-establishing trust – could not be demonstrated more starkly.

Barry's Story

In contrast to all expectations, and much to Barry's amazement and delight, there is a happy ending to this story. Within hours of Barry taking his stand, the infrastructure manager was promoted to a position away from the project. His successor, who was no admirer of the individual he followed, supported Barry's report and a fair conclusion was reached. Payment of the subcontractor's claim helped him to stay in business.

6

THE CHANGING FACES OF LOYALTY:
RESHAPING THE EMPLOYEE RELATIONSHIP

Peter Curran entered into two contracts the day he started work, one legal and one psychological.

The first specified that he would work 7.25 hours a day, have four weeks annual leave, and give one month's notice if he wanted to resign. The other was hinted at in his interview when someone said: 'This is a good company to work for. They look after you.' The message was that the company offered good career prospects, interesting work, a sense of belonging and job security, and treated employees fairly and with respect.

The corollary was that the company expected much of Peter in return: a high degree of competence, unflagging commitment, a readiness to put in extra hours when the pressure was on, and loyalty in the face of alternative offers. This was a psychological contract, and it went deeper and wider than the formal contract. As Peter learned, an employment relationship is more than words on a piece of paper.

His experience reflects the fact that twenty to thirty years ago Britain had relatively stable work structures. Either explicitly or implicitly, many of the larger organisations promised a job for life to people who joined them at eighteen or twenty-one. The assumption was that the firm was here to stay and no major forces of disruption were anticipated. If you did your job con-sistently and conscientiously, doing as you were told and sometimes going the extra mile, then you could expect to progress through the ranks with gradually increasing rewards. Curran rose to become a senior manager in the energy industry.

Admittedly, work was not all it might be. Many people were stuck in boring and repetitive jobs, their abilities latent and unfulfilled within them. Organisational structures were hierarchical and unwieldy. Workers on the traditional assem-bly line, where thousands of people repeated the same actions over and over again, were scarcely realising their potential. In addition, though they often saw ways to organise the work better they were inhibited from offering suggestions because they didn't see it as their place.

Empowerment

An important force in the changes revolutionising the work-place is empowerment, a movement that was fashionable for a while in the mid-1990s. Companies were suddenly keen to empower their workforce. This did not just mean delegation, passing more work on to people lower down the line, though doubtless this is all it amounted to in some organisations. Nor did it mean the dismantling of all authority systems. For all the talk of people empowering themselves, the fact is that lim-its were almost always imposed. It was comparatively rare for power actually to be given away. In reality empowerment was a trend towards encouraging and allowing individuals and teams to exercise greater initiative and assume increased responsibility. This was intended to contribute to:

- their own personal and group development
- the successful performance of tasks
- the good of the organisation as a whole.

In one sense, empowerment was nothing new. It clearly evolved from the ideas of work theorists in earlier decades, such as job enrichment (the 1960s), semi-autonomous work groups (the 1970s) and quality circles (the 1980s). Each of these sought to bring greater variety into working practices, tapping employees for good ideas and developing a momentum of continuous improvement. Empowerment can be said to have brought these loosely connected ideas into a creative synthesis, and neatly summarised them in one word.

In some companies, empowerment clearly brought four benefits:

It released people's creativity

Organisations had often said that people were their greatest asset, but empowerment gave them the opportunity to put that bold assertion into action. Employees proved they had abilities they or their bosses had only dimly suspected. Shop-floor workers came up with imaginative money-saving improvements they had not previously been motivated to suggest.

It provided greater job satisfaction

Jobs were made more varied, more interesting and more challenging. On assembly lines, responsibility for a connected sequence of tasks often replaced a single function, with teams rotating who did what. More workers had the satisfaction of taking responsibility for an end result, of seeing a process or project through to completion.

It produced better customer service

A key aspect of empowerment was giving employees freedom to do whatever they deemed necessary to satisfy a customer's needs better. For instance, Lufthansa and BA empowered ground staff to make on-the-spot decisions about compensating disgruntled customers. The emphasis was on responding to the customer swiftly.

It released managers for a different role

By empowering staff, managers implicitly put more trust in them. To some extent they abandoned their traditional functions of organising and controlling. Managers were thereby released to spend their time in other, arguably more creative ways: strategic thinking, coaching, and winning new customers. Perhaps unsurprisingly, there is evidence that empowerment comes more easily to women managers than to men.

For every positive experience there is another less encouraging. There is a reverse side to most of the benefits: eradication of routine unskilled jobs, inconsistency in customer treatment, managers uncomfortable with their new role. The biggest problem with many empowerment initiatives, however, was the climate in which they took place. The early and mid-1990s were a period of massive corporate uncertainty.

Bernard Taylor, a professor at Henley Management College, is blunt: 'When I hear the word empowerment, I reach for my gun!

'People aren't fools. They need some vision of the future and some reassurance that the job will still be there in a few years. This requires some commitment to develop the business. At the moment, however, companies have got a major problem in motivating their employees and persuading them to commit themselves. This has come about because the unions have been disempowered, a massive amount of restructuring has led to large job losses, companies are traded like commodities, and managers and employees do not know from one minute to the next if they have a job. Empowerment is often introduced in the context of a siege mentality.' (quoted by David Clutterbuck in *The Power of Empowerment*, p.19)

The discomfort empowerment caused managers went beyond requiring them to rethink their roles. In many cases, it threatened their jobs altogether. Empowerment came in as a vast amount of de-layering was taking place. Taylor claims that typically two layers of management were taken out and employees were then 'empowered' to do three times the amount of work. He questions the motivation for empowering. Is it the necessary corollary of a cost-cutting exercise?

Clutterbuck poses the conundrum of what came first: 'Does de-layering make empowerment possible, by freeing up the structure, or does empowerment make de-layering possible by getting staff to take on management responsibilities? Companies are cutting back on middle management ranks to cut costs, while empowering their subordinates to take up the decision-making slack. All of which begs the question: which came first? Are we sacking managers because staff are more empowered, or empowering staff because we need someone to do the work?' (*The Power of Empowerment*, p.67).

It doubtless varies from case to case, but many suspect the second answer is true more often than the first. Certainly, in my discussions with people in business I have found widespread disillusionment with the empowerment movement. In too many cases extra responsibility has just meant additional stress and hassle. It may even entail being exposed to extra risk: 'More rope to hang yourself by.'

The Corrosion of Character

A pessimistic view of life under 'new capitalism' pervades sociologist Richard Sennett's provocative book *The Corrosion of Character*. Sennett says flexibility is the hallmark of today's organisation. Investors and stock markets exert pressure for short-term results. People in teams work on short-term projects, often competing with other teams in the same company. There is radical insecurity: people feel their job is at risk, because it is at risk. The Protestant work ethic, which nurtured the capacity to delay gratification, now appears misplaced and irrelevant. In a 'get there quick, get there first' economy people know delay is fatal.

What makes Sennett's book so interesting is that he explores the personal consequences of work in the new capitalism. He defines character as 'the ethical value we place on our own desires and on our relation to others' (*The Corrosion of Character*, p.10) and says enduring connections with people and organisations produce enduring character. The new, flexible economic order, with its lack of long-term commitment, undermines the depth and continuity of connections on which character depends. Sennett illustrates this with a series of vivid, real-life scenarios set in the United States; but it would be easy to find parallel examples in Britain.

Sennett describes an airport meeting with the son of a blue-collar worker he had interviewed for another book 25 years earlier. Enrico, the father, spent his whole working life as a janitor. His work had a single and durable purpose, the service of his family. Sennett says: 'He carved out a clear story for himself in which his experience accumulated materially and psychically; his life thus made sense to him as a linear narrative' (p.16). Enrico had self-respect. His son, Rico, had gone into business and displayed all the trappings of upward mobility. Whereas Enrico had an income in the bottom quarter of the wage scale, Rico was in the top 5 per cent. Yet as their conversation on the flight revealed, 'this is not an entirely happy story for Rico' (p.18).

Having worked for several IT firms, Rico now runs his own consultancy. His wife, Jeanette, manages a big team of accountants. They have moved home several times. Rico feels a lack of control in his life, a striking contrast to the experience of his father. Friendships and immersion in local communities tend to be transitory and superficial. Above all, Rico worries about the quality of his family life: '"We get home at seven, do dinner, try to find an hour for the kids' homework, and then deal with our own paperwork." When things get tough for months at a time in his consulting firm, "it's like I don't know who my kids are." He worries about the frequent anarchy into which his family plunges, and about neglecting his children, whose needs can't be programmed to fit into the demands of his job' (p.21).

Rico wants to set his children an example of resolution and purpose, to demonstrate constancy of character in action. He has discovered that the conditions of working life militate against that. The message he repeatedly hears through his work – indeed, propagates through his work – is 'no long-term'. But this is not the philosophy he wants to teach his children. 'Transposed to the family realm, "no long-term" means keep moving, don't commit yourself, and don't sacrifice. Rico suddenly erupted on the plane, "You can't

imagine how stupid I feel when I talk to my kids about commitment."' (p.25). The underlying trend at the root of Rico's
concern is the corrosion of character.

When the Ridley Hall Foundation laid on a seminar exploring these complex and disturbing workplace trends in 2001, the
concept of loyalty was central. What used to be a straightforward idea in the organisational world is now considered a
thoroughly outdated concept by some, while others believe it is
a malleable concept that can be reshaped to meet the needs of
today's employment climate. The seminar, *The Changing Faces
of Loyalty*, focused on the changing nature of the employer-
employee relationship, though attention was also paid to other
stakeholder relationships where loyalty is an important issue.

Some memorable epigrams about loyalty were expressed
by speakers and delegates, and I have grouped my further
reflections on the subject around these.

'Loyalty is a Devalued Currency'

Peter Curran described how his first ten years working for a
multinational company were fairly stable. Changes took place,
but nothing dramatic. The second ten were anything but stable.
During the last decade he has changed job and location at least
six times, had ten different bosses, and experienced three near
redundancies. It was a roller-coaster ride for the company too as
it went through de-layering, downsizing, rightsizing, re-engin-
eering, and restructuring – all the major euphemisms for
uncomfortable corporate change that the 1990s threw up. The
company expanded and took over other oil companies, increasing employee insecurity by trimming jobs in the wake of every
merger or takeover. In Peter's company and others there are
several interrelated factors driving change at a frantic pace,
notably:

- New technology – particularly the computer revolution
- Increasing deregulation – resulting in competition in previously restricted markets

- The shift from manufacturing to service – affecting the industrialised countries most
- Increasing global competition – forcing organisations to streamline and cut costs
- Greater answerability to the markets for the company's financial performance
- Increasing answerability to NGOs for ethical, social and environmental performance.

The impact of these changes is that companies have had to be more efficient and usually leaner, but also more flexible to man up or down depending on circumstances and demand.

In the process, the psychological contract has changed in most sizeable organisations. There used to be a delicately weighted see-saw with the organisation's expectations balanced on one end and the individual's on the other. In more stable times, there was a reasonable equilibrium. This see-saw has now taken a decisive tilt (see diagram).

How the psychological contract is changing

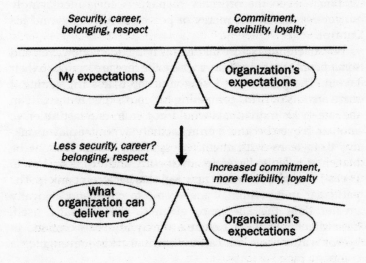

Organisations deliver far less by way of career prospects and job security but still expect a high degree of commitment, flexibility and loyalty from employees. Research shows that employees think they are keeping their side of the psychological contract while management is reneging on theirs. No wonder we get comments such as 'loyalty is a devalued currency' and 'I've delivered my side: why don't you deliver yours?' Loyalty now looks distinctly one-sided.

This is not necessarily because hard-hearted employers are deliberately exploiting their employees. It is partly that managers now have much less capacity to control the external environment, as illustrated by events at Vauxhall's Luton plant in recent years. In 1998 workers on the Vectra assembly line made financial sacrifices in a deal on pay and working conditions that they believed promised them long-term job security. Three years later General Motors went back on the agreement, and over the head of Vauxhall Managing Director Nick Reilly took manufacture of the Vectra's successor away from Luton. The Luton situation is symptomatic of a world in which the ordinary worker – even the ordinary manager – feels increasingly powerless and at the mercy of powerful forces beyond his control.

Not all employees are taking this lying down, however, and some people work in sectors where the dice are loaded in their favour. The prospect of losing your job is less frightening if there are lots of firms competing for your skills. In the City in the late 1990s individuals would hop from one institution to another. It even became a group activity: with star players taking their team with them. (A sporting parallel might be Manchester United's entire midfield transferring *en bloc* to Leeds.) This gives a whole new feel to what a company is. The particular units within it may come to command a loyalty greater than the allegiance given to the company itself. Disenchantment with a company may also be expressed in pettier ways. There are various ways of taking revenge on a company by:

- stealing time – unwarranted absenteeism
- stealing money – embezzlement
- stealing goods – pilfering.

Again, it's symptomatic of a corporate world where loyalty is breaking down.

One response to the situation is to accept that loyalty is a thing of the past. If companies don't show loyalty any more, then employees are absolved of any responsibility to be loyal. Each party therefore makes use of the other for their own purposes, milking the relationship for what it's worth. The company gets as much work and as many hours out of the employee as it possibly can. The employee pitches their salary demands high, looks for special perks, utilises training opportunities and strives to construct an impressive CV to snare the next job. Employment is much less like a long-term partnership and more a short-term liaison, with both parties in it for what they can get out of it. Indeed, if this is clearly understood on both sides, it may be asked, is there anything fundamentally wrong with such an attitude? Perhaps we are reaching a state of equilibrium where the psychological contract collapses and the concept of loyalty is buried.

I have discovered, both at seminars and in talking to people more widely, that there is a major difference in attitude along lines of age. People over forty resent the changes that have taken place and lament the passing of the good old days of corporate loyalty. People under forty have adjusted more easily. They no longer wish to stay with a company indefinitely and are beginning to embrace this foot-loose and fancy-free culture enthusiastically.

'Loyalty is Not a Stand Alone Concept'

We live in transitional times. Loyalty has not become an outdated concept in every organisational setting. Peter Curran's loyalty was bent, but it did not break. There was a residual commitment to and affection for his employer. When employees leave a company it is common for some sense of loyalty to remain, often finding its expression in the car they drive, the petrol they buy, or the supermarket they shop in.

Curran has sought to rethink the psychological contract by drawing on the biblical concept of covenant in a book, titled *All the Hours God Sends? Practical and Biblical Help in Meeting the Demands of Work*. A covenant goes deeper than a contract. It expresses and affirms the relationship behind the formal agreement between two parties. Whereas contracts are pre-occupied with stipulating obligations, and with the terms and conditions of service, covenants focus on the quality of the underlying relationship. They are a commitment to stay in relationship, even when difficulties occur and one side has disappointed the other. The covenant relationship between God and Israel vividly illustrates that; so does the wording of the marriage service. In order to work, a covenant requires the presence of certain qualities: faithfulness, consistency, trust, even forgiveness. This serves to emphasise that loyalty does not stand alone. Loyalty requires these closely associated attitudes if it is to have any chance of taking root, flourishing and growing.

Does covenant have any relevance to the corporate world? It may well be said that with contracts breaking down so easily there is little hope for something more demanding. Yet Curran convincingly demonstrates that faithfulness, consistency, trust and forgiveness all play a part in making companies healthier. They have an enduring relevance. Redemptive trust, standing by someone when it is costly, is no doubt the rarest variety. Curran tells of an employee who made a serious mistake, costing his company thousands of pounds, and expected to lose his job. 'His boss, however, responded, "Having just spent £10,000 on your training, you don't expect me to let you go now, do you?"' (*All the Hours God Sends?*, p.129). Curran says the story is apocryphal, but it has a certain plausibility: one can imagine companies where it might happen.

Some companies do genuinely care about their employees. Yes, it's harder for the George Cadburys of this world to maintain companies with a distinctive caring ethos – especially when they're answerable to investment analysts in the City. But it's not impossible. Corporate cultures vary enormously. A recent *The Sunday Times 100 Best Companies to Work For in the UK* survey makes impressive reading. There really are companies where:

- mothers who return to work after maternity leave receive a 25% pay rise
- you can order groceries online and have them delivered to the company car park by 4 pm
- you can take a free one-week holiday at cottages provided in Devon, Yorkshire and Scotland
- 10p is donated to the NSPCC if staff leave promptly at 5.30 pm, to discourage a long-hours culture
- enormous efforts are made either to avoid involuntary redundancies or to cushion the blow as much as possible when they occur.

Treating employees well pays off, by and large. A contented, happy staff is a productive one. These 100 companies have not been immune from difficulty, but over a five-year period their share and dividend returns grew 25%, four times the average All-Share index. Companies that are being generous to their employees may be doing it for ulterior motives. Exceptional perks – holidays, pensions, share schemes and private health insurance – are a not-so-subtle way of attracting and keeping the best talent. Employees' evaluations were not, however, simply about remuneration. The company that came top in 2001, food retailer Asda, pays many of its part-time employees less than £9,000 a year. A friendly, warm, appreciative environment where people thank and encourage each other may be just as important. One of the most telling revelations in the *Sunday Times* survey was how managers react to employees whose lives have come adrift, especially through illness or tragedy. Bosses who unquestioningly rallied round always earned the fiercest loyalty of all.

If what looks like the old-fashioned paternalist spirit is alive and well in corporate Britain, has anything fundamental changed? Yes; companies clearly cannot make the unguarded promises they used to. Indeed, those that did make unqualified commitments ('you'll never be made redundant') were probably guilty of hubris, imagining their dominant market position to be unassailable. No company should imagine itself to be invincible. When the next serious downturn comes, it may have no option but to make deep cuts to survive. As Curran says, psychological contracts need reshaping. Only thus can organisations demonstrate the sort of honesty that inspires trust. There is still a place for making commitments, but organisations – just like individuals – should limit themselves to those that are realistic. That way disappointment, distrust and a sense of betrayal are less likely to ensue.

Another speaker at our seminar was Willie Coupar, the director of the Involvement & Participation Association. As an example of the more sophisticated understanding that is developing between employers and employees, he cited the way cement company Blue Circle now talks about employment security. With the agreement of the unions, Blue Circle produced a statement

- affirming the employees' concern for job security
- supporting personal development through training and improvement of skills
- recognising the possibility of a 'cataclysmic' or employment-endangering event
- committing the company to a process of management and unions together deciding what measures should be taken in such an event.

This pledge was tested in September 1998, when Blue Circle announced that two of its smaller works, at Plymouth and near Ipswich, would close in May 1999. It asked the Company-Wide Action Team (CWAT) to develop ways of lessening the impact on the 250 employees at those works.

Derek Warren, the senior AEEU steward and Way Ahead facilitator, told *IPA Magazine*: 'Meetings were held at both sites to allow employees to raise their concerns, and a programme was developed to accommodate those who wanted to remain with Blue Circle. Training was stepped up to allow all employees to develop computer skills and update their qualifications. An allowance of £300 could be used for any training the company itself could not provide.

'These efforts were supplemented by a generous relocation package, financial advice, and a programme for those unable to relocate. Local companies were invited to see for themselves the skills and experience that Blue Circle employees had to offer, backed by job fairs, advertising and a video. Finally, consultants were engaged to help with CVs and interviewing skills.

'This comprehensive package meant that only 13 out of 250 people affected signed on as unemployed when the works closed at the end of May. A total of 76 people and their families were relocated to other works at a cost of £2.5m. Both sites maintained their safety record and full production until closure, with absenteeism virtually zero. Both works had their Investors in People accreditation renewed in January 1999, and all of their 1,000 customer sites remained with Blue Circle.

'Certainly, the closures were a blow, but we understood the economic rationale: ultimately, those two plants were never going to produce cement at anything like competitive costs. And in what is effectively a stagnant UK market, the importance of competition and productivity is clear.

'Only by working together in partnership can we boost the strength and profitability of the company – with long-term benefits for all the partners. Driving the business forward enables us to keep faith with our shareholders and investors, and to plan for future growth. Our partnership agreement is based on security of employment rather than jobs for life.' (*IPA Magazine*, November 1999, pp.14-15)

These events suggest that the commitment made by Blue Circle really counted for something and was not empty rhetoric.

'Loyalty is Nearly Always Divided'

Warren used the word partnership in the IPA article. Just as this word is making inroads into thinking about company-supplier relationships, so it is permeating the world of employers and employees. But here too it is controversial. It strikes a new note in industries that have been built on adversarial attitudes, on an assumption that management and workers can expect to be at loggerheads. Some think partnership belies the reality of clashing interests and class conflict.

Suspicion of partnership comes from both ends of the political spectrum. Sir Clive Thompson, chairman of Rentokil and the Confederation of British Industry (CBI), typifies the right-wing response. He fears the unions are using the language of partnership to regain power and warns that it is a trap to think that partnership must mean an agreement with unions. That would amount to companies giving away hard-won ground, and returning to the unions the excessive influence they enjoyed in the 1960s and 1970s, with disastrous results for business.

Equally forthright is the criticism of partnership from left-wing trade unionists and lecturers in industrial relations. John Kelly, from the London School of Economics, believes the unions are selling out. Far from strengthening the position of the union, he argues, partnership co-opts them into management, providing a pretext for companies to legitimise job cuts and erode terms and conditions. For all the talk of cooperation and consent, employers in partnership companies do not hesitate to use coercion when it suits them. In Kelly's view, partnership is part of a cunning plot by companies to emasculate workers and get their own way.

The assumption behind both the right-wing and left-wing reactions is that partnership cuts across the natural order of things – the management-worker divide. Chris Darke, general secretary of the airline pilots union BALPA, questioned this assumption at the seminar. Bosses often see trade unions as rivals for the loyalty of employees, and there may be times when that's true, but most of the time it is possible to maintain a dual loyalty to union and company. Chris believes that people's natural inclination is to want an advocate, and advocacy is essentially what unions provide. If management cultivates a good relationship with the advocate – consulting rather than coercing – partnership can contribute to corporate growth. In the airline industry, however, as in other industries, there have been times when it was necessary to stand up and fight for union members in order to reach the position where they are treated with respect, he said. What helped the pilots is that they are unusually powerful employees. Consider both the power and the responsibility entailed in flying a plane. They have a responsibility not only to their employers but to air traffic regulators, and can therefore resist illicit pressures that could be brought to bear on the grounds that they might jeopardise both public safety and their licence.

Other workers are clearly much less powerful, performing low-paid jobs in anti-social conditions with a minimum of job security. Delegates on the seminar expressed particular concern about the treatment of the considerable numbers of people who staff call centres – increasingly all round the clock. Not much bargaining power is evident there. A Christian concern for the poor and the vulnerable runs right through all strands of biblical literature: the law, the prophets, the wisdom literature, the gospels and epistles. The plight of such workers cannot therefore be a matter of indifference. The seminar warmed to Darke's understanding of the union as an advocate, a word with thoroughly biblical overtones. An advocate is one who pleads for another. He speaks for those who have difficulty in speaking for themselves.

Advocacy

In the Old Testament, taking care of the weaker members of society is seen as the responsibility of the powerful. Job, speaking of a time when he was a very rich landowner, says:

'I was eyes to the blind and feet to the lame. I was a father to the needy, and I championed the cause of the stranger.' (Job 29:15-16, NRSV)

The mother of King Lemuel, a non-Israelite king, warns him against abusing power in a drunken way and exhorts him to:

'Speak out for those who cannot speak, for the rights of all the destitute. Speak out, judge righteously, defend the rights of the poor and needy.' (Prov. 31:8-9, NRSV)

All too often, however, those in power trampled roughshod over the concerns of the underprivileged. King Solomon's magnificent building feats came at a major social cost. By the time his reign came to an end, the nation had had its fill of being conscripted into forced labour (1 Kgs. 5:13). The labourers found a spokesman in Jeroboam, and complained to Solomon's son Rehoboam: 'Your father made our yoke heavy. Now therefore lighten the hard service of your father and his heavy yoke that he placed on us, and we will serve you' (1 Kgs. 12: 4). Rehoboam refused to listen to them; indeed, he threatened to make their working conditions harder. Rebellion ensued, and the nation tragically divided into two.

In both parts of the divided kingdom, Israel and Judah, that oft-repeated pattern of the rich gorging themselves while the poor suffer is seen over and over again. The poor often lacked effective advocacy, but the prophets spoke out stridently on their behalf. We see this both in a prophet who held official court status, Isaiah:

'Wash yourselves; make yourselves clean; remove the evil of your doings from before my eyes; cease to do evil; learn to do good; seek justice, rescue the oppressed, defend the orphan, plead for the widow.' (Is. 1:16-17, NRSV)

And in one who was a humble herdsman and dresser of sycamore trees, Amos, a complete social outsider:

'You trample on the poor and force him to give you grain. Therefore, though you have built stone mansions, you will not live in them; though you have planted lush vineyards, you will not drink their wine. For I know how many are your offences and how great are your sins. You oppress the righteous and take bribes and you deprive the poor of justice in the courts.' (Amos 5:11-12, NIV)

The prophetic role was nothing like as organised and representative as a shop steward, but it almost always includes the advocate dimension.

In Jesus' activity, too, we see that willingness to speak up on behalf of the poor. Jesus' complaint is not so much about their exploitation by the rich as about a widespread social tendency to despise them and consider them of little account. He goes out of his way to convince the poor and the marginalised that theirs is the kingdom of God; they really are the recipients of God's loving mercy. The apparently trivial incident of the widow's mite (Mk. 12:41-44) actually speaks volumes about the thrust of Jesus' ministry. He speaks up for a woman who would doubtless otherwise have been completely ignored. He shows how generosity is not to be measured in terms of size of the cheque, but in relation to how much (or how little) of it a person has.

How interesting and appropriate, then, that Jesus uses the word *advocate* of the third person of the Trinity, the Holy Spirit. The Greek word *parakletos* appears in:

'And I will ask the Father, and he will give you another Advocate, to be with you for ever.' (Jn. 14:16)

'But the Advocate, the Holy Spirit, whom the Father will send in my name, will teach you everything, and remind you of all that I have said to you.' (Jn. 14:26)

'It is to your advantage that I go away, for if I do not go away, the Advocate will not come to you.' (Jn. 16:7)

Parakletos has a twofold meaning. On the one hand it can mean encourage, console or comfort: hence the translation 'comforter' in some versions. But it also refers to a friend who stands by the accused in a law-court. Elsewhere in the gospels, Jesus assures the disciples that they can rely on the help of the Spirit when they are hauled before Jewish and Gentile authorities (see Mt. 10:16-20; Mk. 13:11; Lk. 12:11-12). A crucial dimension of the Spirit's activity is helping people to stick up for themselves when the dice are loaded against them.

Trade union membership in Britain is roughly half what it was 20 years ago – about six and a half million – yet it is still the dominant means of representation in certain industries. Collective bargaining exerts a strong hold in, for instance, the public sector and the car industry. Unions are not a necessity in business life today. Some organisations can operate quite satisfactorily without them, so long as employers   listen carefully to employees' concerns and treat them fairly and with respect. There are a variety of ways in which the workforce can organise itself, and ensure that its interests are articulated and heard. What is important – and what Christians should be concerned about – is that there is a corporate readiness to let this process takes place. Employers who stifle workers' attempts to organise themselves into a representative forum are open to the suspicion of operating a 'divide and conquer' philosophy. The need for vigilance, for people with the foresight, wisdom and courage to take up the role of advocate, remains. These will include some who are union leaders.

'Managers Produce less Loyalty than Leaders'

Jill Garrett, the managing director of Gallup, frequently speaks on the extensive research her organisation has carried out on leadership. She concurs with a widely (though not universally) accepted distinction between management and leadership, which sees managers as being concerned with planning, organising, controlling and evaluating, whereas leaders provide protection, direction, inspiration and vision. I explore this distinction in more detail in my book *Transforming Leadership*. A major figure in popularising the distinction was the American leadership guru Warren Bennis, famous for snappy aphorisms such as 'managers are people who do things right; leaders are people who do the right thing' (Warren Bennis and Burt Nanus, *Leaders*, p.21). The two categories, however, are not watertight. Both management and leadership are important functions, and in many individuals they overlap.

Jill presented a startling statistic to the seminar – 70% of people who leave their job say it is because of problems in their relationship with their manager. Even if these people have a simplistic understanding of what is going in, it points to a significant trend. The *personal* dimension in corporate loyalty is not to be underestimated. An individual manager is not always representative of a company and there will always be personality clashes where different types of people simply don't get on. Alternatively, management style or direction may be dictated from above, and dissatisfaction then gets focused on a particular individual within the system. There is evidence that the more managers take on the character of leaders, the more they are able to enthuse staff into working together for a shared vision, and the more likely they are to evoke loyalty in response. Gallup's research shows that, interestingly, what is most likely to provoke loss of confidence in a leader is an ethical deficit: a perceived lack of integrity. Liz's story illustrates this.

Liz's Story

Liz, a single mother in her late thirties with two children, is head of a clinical trials unit. She has extensive experience of the pharmaceutical industry and was instrumental in developing the subsidiary's highly respected reputation. The drug industry has its share of controversial research, in particular research that lacks a serious scientific basis and is more of a marketing exercise than a clinical trial. The parent firm, a contract research company, had always supported her selective stand. But now the company faces stronger competition, and Liz is coming under pressure to compromise and cut corners. She is unwilling to jeopardise her unit's high reputation and her own professional standards.

The company's new attitude is typified by its appointment as marketing manager of a man with no experience of the industry and an undiscriminating approach to drug development. He returns from a trip to southern Europe with drug trial proposals that don't even clarify what disease the drug is meant to treat. Liz asks for more information, but is told to submit a quotation. Then she comes under pressure to cut costs by reducing the size of her trial sample. She objects to this, because she has no wish at all to see evidence she produces being used to support medical claims that cannot be justified.

Liz's growing unhappiness with the parent company comes
to a head during contract negotiations with a respectable client
that has a slow-moving legal department. Her practice is to
never start a trial with patients before a contract has been
finalised, but the board of directors, anxious to keep work
moving as fast as possible, tells her to make an exception. Liz
objects, appealing to the managing director. They have an
agreeable relationship, but over the phone she gets the frosty
response and he snaps: 'You will do as you are told!' She asks
for a face-to-face discussion, which takes place a week later.
The managing director hardly gives her a chance to speak. He
tells her that the parent company is in trouble, and her scruples are a luxury it cannot afford. He repeats: 'You will do as
you are told!' Liz hears those words resound in her ears again
and again.

What Liz has encountered is a lack of moral leadership. At a
time when the parent company is in trouble and under pressure, then more than ever it needs leadership that will hold its
nerve and, as Bennis says, do the right thing. Liz had hoped,
based on previous experience, that the managing director had
such qualities but at the time of testing she finds them signally
lacking. Not surprisingly, Liz starts to wonder if she has a
future with the clinical trials unit. She begins to consider other
employment options. The managing director is on the verge of
losing an outstanding employee because he lacks moral bottle.

'Loyalty is not Inertia'

Is loyalty relevant in the way we customers relate to companies? Should we reward firms that provide us with good
service by giving them repeat custom? Significant long-term
relationships can build up over a period of time, as I found
after I had been a member of the RAC for 25 years. They have
consistently given me good service, but for the last few years I
have received advertising from the AA offering a reduced
membership fee for new joiners. I was tempted by the short-
term cash advantage. I suspect too the AA's standard of

service is comparable with the RAC's. In the end, I stuck with the RAC because deep down I felt: 'They have never let me down; why should I leave them now?' I had some sense of a long-term relationship. You may think me foolishly sentimental, but I suspect most of us make similar customer choices.

Discussion at the seminar brought out the fact that people's purchasing habits display loyalty at many different levels. We worked out a spectrum that looks like this:

Repeat	Tit for	Brand	National	Moral
Behaviour	tat	loyalty	loyalty	principles

- Repeat behaviour: This may mean only that the customer is stuck in a rut, making the same purchases out of habit or inertia. Lots of people stay with the same gas or electricity supplier even when they know it is financially disadvantageous. They feel it's just too much hassle to change
- Tit for tat: This is where there's some reward for loyalty – price reductions, special offers, etc. Supermarket loyalty cards are an obvious example
- Brand loyalty: Attachment to a product that is linked to something distinctive, like a fashionable image or a reputation for high quality. There is some tangible explanation for loyalty, but it may not be entirely rational and to the extent that it is it works to personal benefit
- National loyalty: A patriotic commitment to buy products made in a country to which one has a strong emotional tie. The motive may be to safeguard people's jobs and welfare
- Moral principles: These may include national loyalty, but our group had in mind more universal considerations. These might entail a commitment to fair trade, a cleaner environment or sustainable development.

We realised that the further you move along that spectrum, the more likely your purchasing decision is to involve cost and sacrifice. Indeed it could be argued that where loyalty does not involve some self-sacrificial element, it isn't really loyalty at all. It's more a matter of convenience. Loyalty is not just about sticking with a particular company. It involves commitment to concepts that are bigger than companies, and provide a yardstick for their performance.

'Loyalty to the Big Idea'

The concept of loyalty to the big idea applies not only to how we think and act as customers, but also as employees. What are the big ideas that drive our organisations, and do we identify with them? One delegate made the point that loyalty is often seen as falling in with the prevailing culture, but it may also be seen in challenging that culture when, and where, it needs challenging. A counter-cultural challenge demands courage. One would hope that Christians, who claim to find their ultimate security in something other than the company they work for, would be among the first to demonstrate courage. In his teaching, Jesus doesn't abolish existing loyalties (to family, group and organisation) but he does *relativise* them. He says that loyalties are subordinate to being his faithful disciple; and being his faithful disciple may involve taking a costly stand.

In a similar way, one delegate suggested that a criterion of quality leadership is to put people's work in the context of a much bigger picture. Good leaders show where the detailed bits fit within the larger whole. Employees can then make a realistic assessment of their role, and some fruitful questioning and heart-searching might result.

7

FUELLING THE CONSUMER SOCIETY:
THE ETHICS OF MARKETING

'Perhaps 20% to 50% of what we now produce has little or no real value to humanity. We'd often be better off without cigarettes, alcohol, fast food, weapons, drugs, media dross, technically fast, but slow on the road cars, advertising, cosmetics, sugar drinks, security systems, lotteries, and many other things which sell. Rather than being goods, they are bads, indifferents or mere rubbish, and our degraded values merely make us poorer. ...'

'Let us reflect for a while on this conflict between the ideology of freedom and choice and the commitment to consumer captivity and slavery. With some products, the captivity drive is overwhelming. Coca-Cola started out as an addictive cocaine product and since then has just been a brown liquid marketed through gimmicks to gullible behaviour addicts. Others seem a more straightforward choice, like buying tomatoes. But now, because we like tomatoes that are red, big, firm and last a long time, they are uniformly produced, or genetically modified, to look like this. We have a lavish choice of new cars, many almost identical, but almost none of them small city runabouts, which would be cheap and economical, if less profitable to produce. The choices offered are often bogus – twenty different brands of baked beans – and focused on what the marketing people decide we want. The consequence is extensive captivity. We are

food junkies, fashion addicts, computer game epileptics, choco-
holics, shoe fetishists, alcoholics, TV addicts, drug dependents,
sports-gear obsessives. Companies win multinational wars
bringing consumers into captivity. This has only been done
with heavy manipulative intent over the last twenty years, and
adults have readily succumbed. Children, who have been
exposed nearly from birth, will be a pushover.' (Alan Storkey,
'Postmodernism is Consumption', Christ and Consumerism,
pp.103 and 112)

Alan Storkey pulls no punches. He makes a full-scale
frontal assault on the ethics of marketing which fuels the consumer society, and in the process raises serious questions
about the value of much that business does.

This type of critique is not unusual among Christian sociologists. Os Guinness calls advertising the handmaiden of
consumerism. It is the 'key shaping institution in the western
world,' creating an unrelenting desire for a materially
enhanced life. Guinness says: 'Advertising is unique as a primary national institution with no moral purpose, no social
responsibility, and no idealistic objectives' (*Fit Bodies, Fat
Minds*, pp.85-86). It determines public taste, and Guinness dis-
likes the flavour intensely.

The Identity Industry

An attack on advertising is part and parcel of a searching
analysis of postmodern society. David Lyon says consumerism
– lifestyles and cultures structured around consumption – is a
defining feature of the postmodern society. 'On a personal level,
identities are constructed through consuming,' he argues.
'Forget the idea that who we are is given by God or achieved
through hard work in a calling or a career; we shape our malleable image by what we buy – our clothing, our kitchens, and
our cars tell the story of who we are [becoming]. It is no accident
that the world of fashion is seen as an "identity industry"; the
idea is that self-esteem and our recognition by others may be
purchased over the counter' (*Jesus in Disneyland*, p.12).

'Where once Westerners might have found their identity, their social togetherness and the ongoing life of their society in the area of production, these are increasingly found through consumption,' he writes in another article. 'It's not that companies are producing less, or that people no longer work. Rather, the meaning of these activities has altered. We are what we buy. We relate to others who consume the same way that we do' ('Memory and the Millennium', p.284).

In the same vein, sociologist Zygmunt Bauman speaks of the main focus of social participation as 'a shopping mall overflowing with goods whose major use is the joy of purchasing them; and existence that feels like a lifelong commitment to the shopping mall' (*Intimations of Postmodernity*, p.vii). The readiness with which British society has taken to stores being open on Sundays is symptomatic of this. Graham Cray, former principal of Ridley Hall and a leading expert on postmodernity, is fond of using the phrase *Tesco ergo sum* to describe contemporary culture. Has Britain's foremost retailer given a final twist to Descartes' famous saying, *cogito ergo sum* (I think therefore I am)?

Preachers often join in the sociologists' tirade. They frequently deplore the fact that we live in a consumer society, spending so much time, money and energy on the pursuit of material goods. And there does seem some biblical justification for this. Didn't Jesus live a simple, itinerant lifestyle, often having 'nowhere to lay his head' (Lk. 9:58)? Didn't he exhort his followers to lay up treasure in heaven rather than on earth (Mt. 6:19-20)? His contemporaries recognised this as part of the cost of being his disciple. For the rich young ruler, the call to sell his possessions was too much to stomach: he went away with a heavy heart because he was unable to take so radical a step (Mk. 10:17-30). In another case, the change was dramatic: the crooked tax collector, Zacchaeus, reimbursed all whom he had cheated, with compensation thrown in (Lk. 19:1-10). The implication seems to be that Christians should live austere, self-sacrificial lifestyles, resisting the blandishments of the advertisers and giving generously to the poor. They should 'live simply' so others can 'simply live', to quote a popular phrase from a book written by Bishop John Taylor in 1975.

In Defence of the Material

While there is no mistaking the challenge of these Gospel passages, the jump from there to disparaging material goods and those who sell them is made too easily. It should be resisted. Storkey and Guinness use very blunt instruments to assault targets that are not sufficiently differentiated. Their attacks have a hollow ring, for several reasons.

First, it is not supported by the way most Christians live. They have lifestyles similar to most of their neighbours. They aspire to the same sorts of homes, holidays and leisure pursuits. They see value in a video recorder that lets them watch a programme aired while they were out because they have recorded it; in a CD player with better sound quality and greater flexibility in choice of tracks in a more compact form than previous musical recording devices; in a dishwasher that cleans dishes better than washing by hand and releases time for constructive activities. Perhaps the majority of Christians have been sucked into contemporary culture's seductive sidestream. That they value such things is no guarantee that they are thinking straight. Alternatively, perhaps they are showing a proper appreciation for things that are useful, beautiful or enjoyable. Many Christians are involved in making these goods, and so know their value from the inside. Many products – including heavily marketed products – can enhance the quality of our lives, so long as we keep a sense of perspective about them.

Second, Christianity is not – fundamentally – an anti-material religion. God created the material world, and at the end of the process he surveyed what he had made and pronounced it 'very good' (Gen. 1:31). With its stress on the incarnation (God assuming human flesh in the person of Jesus) and its endowment of earthly elements like water, bread and wine with sacramental significance (as in baptism and the Eucharist),

Christianity has even been described as the most materialist of them all – notably by Archbishop William Temple. Certainly the Jewish heritage we find in the Old Testament supports a positive and uninhibited enjoyment of the good things of creation. The lure of the promised land is that it is 'flowing with milk and honey' (Deut. 6:3). An adman couldn't have come up with a better strapline. Former advertising executive Mark Greene complains: 'Guinness et al. strike a dour note when they scowl at the crescendo of praise for material goods that soars through the ether. What precisely is wrong with enthusiasm for the material? An ice-cold Cola *is*, after all, a many-splendoured drink on a hot afternoon' ('Jingle Hell', p.10). For the Old Testament writers the issue was not whether plenteous possessions were to be enjoyed, but how. There were two key provisos: God should always be acknowledged as the ultimate giver of all good gifts; and wealth should not be hoarded for oneself but shared generously so that the whole people could share in God's bounty.

Third, the implications for other people if we adopt an ascetic lifestyle need to be thought through carefully. Christians need to be able to say no to the material pleasures that marketers dangle before our eyes. In all our lives there ought to be some element of asceticism – of going without – for our own self-discipline and spiritual welfare as much as the good of others. But if Western societies were to spend substantially less on material things, the large numbers of people currently making them would lose their jobs. Habits of mass consumption stimulate the economy. If the economy collapses, it creates massive deflation. Living more simply yourself does not necessarily result in others simply living. If all money saved were released for charitable giving it would have some effect on poverty in the South, but the effect would be marginal. Trade, not aid, offers the best hope of substantial long-term change. Producers in the South won't benefit from consumers purchasing less, but from them buying more at higher prices. This is an argument for alternative sourcing of consumption, for a strategy that sees poor nations not as receivers of handouts but as creators of goods whose value is properly recognised.

Fourth, today's global economy has a legitimate place for marketing in general and advertising in particular. The American Marketing Association defines marketing as 'the process of planning and executing the conception, pricing, promotion and distribution of ideas, goods and services to create exchanges which satisfy individual and organisational objectives.' At a Ridley Hall seminar on *The Ethics of Marketing* in March 1996, marketing was described more succinctly as: 'Selling goods which don't come back to customers who do.' Doesn't marketing deserve some credit for its insistent focus on who the company is trying to reach? The nature of marketing is customer orientation and its goal is customer satisfaction. The marketing mix reflects the range of means it has at its disposal to achieve this. Marketing people in any organisation are its 'ears and eyes': they look outward, listen and observe. This distinguishes them from one-off selling which is not inherently a marketing activity. You don't win repeat business if you foist products on people against their will or better judgment. Only by finding out what they want do you stand a chance of ensuring their satisfaction.

Marketing, then, can be a mutual exercise for the benefit of both buyer and seller. It is an exercise in mass communications, which is the only efficient way to bridge the gap between the things people consume and the places where they are made when operating on a large scale. Marketing has a crucial role to play in helping the public make informed choices, in responding to their needs and wants, and in developing new and improved products. This is not to deny the more questionable aspects of marketing as it is currently practised, but it is important to stake a claim for the legitimacy of the marketing function before we come on to these.

Advertising's Many Hues

Advertising is the aspect of marketing with the strongest impact on the public consciousness, because it confronts the public most vividly. Jane Campbell Garratt, a vice-chairman at the leading advertising firm Ogilvy & Mather, drew the seminar's attention to the variety of roles played by advertising. They include:

1. The basic impartation of information, e.g. announcing an event that is soon to take place.
2. Creating awareness of a product, service or organisation that was hitherto unknown.
3. Education of the public about a side of an organisation's activities that may be little known or understood.
4. Reminding people to use a product they may already have but easily forget about, e.g. the Bird's Custard left at the back of the cupboard.
5. Reappraisal, whereby advertisers seek to change the image associated with a product. A good example of this is Lucozade, which used to be associated with illness and recuperation. In the mid-1970s its position in the market was that of a glucose-based restorative that was especially good for convalescing children. Due to a major advertising campaign, Lucozade was successfully repositioned as an energy-aid popular with healthy sportspeople of all ages.
6. Comparison of what is on offer from different companies, to the advantage of one and detriment of the other or others. If the primary emphasis is on the limitation of the rival company's products, this is often known as negative advertising.
7. Campaigning, which seeks to persuade people to support a worthy cause or to boycott an unworthy one. In the mid-1990s there was a campaign to say 'No' to French nuclear testing by saying 'No' to French wine.
8. Warning the public against risks to their health. A particularly blunt hoarding seen frequently on Australian roads proclaims: 'If you drink and drive, you're a bloody idiot!' (sometimes reduced to four words: 'drink, drive, bloody idiot'). There is a positive version of this that says: 'If you don't drink and drive, you're a bloody good mate!'

When described in this multidimensional way advertising appears fairly innocuous. All these functions of advertising seem

legitimate and coherent, and the public often derive considerable benefit from them. We know, however, that the substantial
criticisms of advertising demand to be taken seriously. I shall
concentrate on one major objection, the intent and effect of
advertising to *deceive*. This is a complex charge so I shall separate
it into three distinct if inter-related issues: exaggeration, manip-
ulation and promotion of image.

Exaggeration

Advertising may be said to be deceptive because it exag-
gerates the benefits of particular goods and services. It
encourages the public to buy things that aren't as good as they
sound. In short, it resorts to puffery and I have first-hand
experience of it.

I took my family on a camping holiday at La Tranche, in
the Vendée area of France. We camped with a tour operator
that specialises in luxury beach holidays because we were
attracted by their brochure, which made their campsites
sound a cut above the average. The brochure conveyed the
'feel' that the site we were interested in was small and
select, an impression that was reinforced when we rang to
check on the size of the site. We were told there were 22
tents and 110 mobile homes. What we were not told – and
only discovered when we reached our destination – was
that the firm was just one of many operators on a large site,
containing 1,200 pitches and about 6,000 people. The sight
of tents crammed almost on top of each other, the huge
numbers of people, and the stalls selling greasy food at the
entrance were a dreadful shock when we arrived. We were
one of about a dozen families we spoke to who said their
first reaction on arrival was to want to turn round and drive
home.

Like the others, we stayed. Further disappointments were
in store. The 8-berth tent was really a 6-berth with extra beds
crammed into space which scarcely existed. The toilet blocks
were dirty and it turned out to be a 2-star campsite. We made
the best of things as the campsite was next to a lovely beach.
The children made some good friends and the sun shone most

of the time, so it wasn't too depressing, but we came away feeling we had been conned by clever advertising. Re-reading the brochure, there was nothing I could put my finger on as definitely untrue. But the selective use of pictures, the things left unsaid as much as was said, the overall impression, all combined to leave us feeling we had been misled.

There is a thin line between advertising that is acceptable and advertising that isn't. We can hardly object to a marketing strategy that emphasises a product's good points, rather than the bad. Advertising puts things in the best light. We do the same every time we send off a CV or dress smartly for an interview. We accept the legitimacy of rigorous questions designed to search out our weak points at the interview, but do not feel obliged to draw attention to our limitations. The principle of *caveat emptor* (let the buyer beware) suggests I should have queried the tour operator more thoroughly or examined the aerial photographs of the French campsite more closely.

Hyperbole is acceptable. Jesus often employed hyperbole, using exaggerated language to make a point. 'If your right eye causes you to sin, tear it out and throw it away; it is better for you to lose one of your members than for your whole body to be thrown into hell.' (Mt. 5:29) His call to self-mutilation is not to be taken literally, but it serves to underline the message that avoiding temptation may involve severe self-discipline. 'Whoever comes to me and does not hate father and mother, wife and children, brothers and sisters, yes, and even life itself, cannot be my disciple.' (Lk. 14:26) Jesus doesn't actually want his disciples to hate their relatives; he's saying that in a situation of competing loyalties he should come first. At other times, he uses hyperbole for comic effect, telling of a shepherd who – with apparent irresponsibility but great compassion – leaves 99 sheep to rescue one that is lost (Lk. 15:1-7). Christians should beware of being po-faced and lacking humour when they criticise advertising.

We need to recognise the part hyperbole plays in making advertisements entertaining. So long as the audience understands its role, hyperbole is harmless. Nobody seriously believes that Heineken reaches parts of the body other beers can't. But if a claim is false and the audience *might* take it seriously – such as that a particular car is technologically superior when it is only average or inferior – this cannot be construed as acceptable exaggeration. It is untruth with an intent to deceive. It is misleading to emphasise a product's good points when they are palpably outweighed by its bad points.

Manipulation

Advertising may be said to deceive when it manipulates people by getting behind their mental and emotional defences. They are unaware they are being influenced, or *how* they are being influenced. The accusation is of underhand activity.

China prohibits cigarette advertising – they cannot be displayed or mentioned – but not brand names. American multinational Philip Morris, maker of Marlboro cigarettes, has exploited this loophole to the full. A Marlboro-sponsored music programme plays a theme song every ten minutes accompanied by the sounds of cattle, horses and shouting cowboys. Then the announcer says in Chinese: 'Jump and fly a thousand miles. Raise the whip so the horse will run faster. This is the world of Marlboro. Ride through the rivers and mountains with courage. Be called a hero throughout the thousand miles. This is the world of Marlboro.' Shanghai's phone booths are covered on three sides with red and white Marlboro logos, and with pictures of a cigarette-free Marlboro cowboy sitting on his horse or walking with a saddle slung over his shoulder. The message being conveyed by association is highly subversive: Smoking Marlboro cigarettes is the stuff of courage, heroism and the outdoor life. Ironically, one of the models who posed as Marlboro man died of lung cancer (Jeffrey Robinson, *The Manipulators*, p.67).

Another clever way to keep a cigarette brand in the public eye and circumvent restrictions on advertising is to put the logo on other products. Tobacco companies are buying up travel, clothing and restaurant companies for this purpose. Philip Morris offers black leather backpacks, biker jackets, sunglasses, vests and skirts in its Virginia Slims 'V-Wear' line.

This is a brand particularly targeted at women, a vast and as yet relatively untapped market in South East Asia. The name Virginia Slims is significant as 'slim' cigarettes are associated with attractive physique. In Japan, advertising for Virginia Slims cigarettes emphasises personal authenticity: 'I'm going the right way – keeping the rule of the society, but at the same time I am honest with my own feelings. So I don't care if I behave against the so-called rules as long as I really want to.' In the background, a slim glamorous woman of indeterminate Asian nationality embraces a fair-haired man. The tag line for the campaign is 'Be You.' Tobacco companies also sponsor disco dances and beauty pageants, and use young women, often in cowgirl outfits, to give away free samples at such events.

Campaigns that work by association thrive on lack of education. Since there is no explicit advertising of cigarettes in China, there is no explicit advertising of the health risks either. The public is being sold a deadly drug through the manipulative combination of a well-known logo and a falsely glamorous image. Philip Morris is handsomely compensated for the decline of cigarette sales in the West (where the message that 'smoking kills' has made some impact, and manufacturers have been hit with expensive litigation) with rocketing trade elsewhere.

Cigarette profits in the USA increased 16% in the 1990s, while overseas profits soared 256%. Asia consumes about half the world's cigarettes. The smoking rates of men in China, Vietnam and Cambodia are 66%, 73% and 65% respectively. Lung cancer deaths are expected to rise sharply over the next twenty years in consequence. Young people are being sucked into the smoking habit in particularly large numbers. Some are used as vendors, like the 13-year-old 'jump boys' who sell cigarettes to drivers when the traffic lights turn red in cities such as Manila. Since the jump boys usually end up smoking themselves, it could be said that they are victims of a double exploitation; as an unofficial workforce and as imbibers of a noxious substance. Here is the less attractive side of the world of international marketing.

Movies exhibit a form of brand promotion that is widespread in the West, but rarely recognised as such. When actors and actresses drive cars, drink beers or use mobile phones, they don't just do so in a generic sense. They are very specific cars, beers and phones, with their logos shown clearly and often referred to by name – BMW, Fosters, Nokia. Jeffrey Robinson reports that in the film *Home Alone*, 31 different brand names are mentioned. We're probably unaware of the dealing and bargaining to decide what products feature. Kraft General Foods had the script of *Home Alone* changed so that, instead of turkey, Macaulay Culkin ate Kraft macaroni and cheese for Christmas dinner (*The Manipulators*, p.238). Even if watchers weren't led to change their choice of menu for Christmas dinner, they may have been influenced into eating Kraft foods at other times. When Tom Cruise made his first hit, *Risky Business*, Ray-Ban had him wear their latest Wayfarer model sunglasses. This led to a dramatic increase in sales. Apparently within 30 days of the film's release, Ray-Ban sold 18,000 pairs, more than they'd sold in the previous three years. The key corporate concern is to get the right person or people in the film using your product.

Manufacturers and film executives both play down how much money changes hands for 'product placement'. Clearly many companies regard it as a potentially lucrative form of covert advertising – all taking place with the audience largely unaware of what's happening. It is becoming more important with the advent of digital VCRs that are capable of automatically editing out commercials. If people are going to watch a film on tape and fast-forward past the ads, the obvious answer is to get the ad inside the film so that it can't be edited out.

Promotion of Image

Outside the USA, Marlboro is probably much better known than Philip Morris. In her presentation, Jane Campbell Garratt drew attention to the significance of the *brand*. Ogilvy & Mather's mission statement actually speaks in terms of serving brands rather than customers: 'Products are made in a factory; brands are bought by customers'. People buy into the image that is linked with a brand, whether that's sophistication, glamour, confidence, security, excitement, freedom or sex appeal. Many other desirable associations could be listed. To be the possessor of a fashionable brand can do wonders for an individual's prestige and public standing: it says something about you.

'At the very top of the market the ads just have to look extraordinary,' Robinson says. 'The glossiest magazines run the most powerful photos with the most beautiful models in the most exotic settings and with the fewest words. Often the only word on the page is the designer's name. Some people see that message as, "If you don't know what we're talking about, you're not our kind of customer". In reality, it's closer to, "All you have to do to join these people who do understand, and make everyone else think you understand too, is buy this". Hermes, for example, doesn't have to say anything more than Hermes because years of hard work have successfully burned that brand and the image of a certain quality into our minds' (*The Manipulators*, p.215).

Something irrational is happening here. Whether or not a product conveys the right image has become more important than whether it provides intrinsic satisfaction. Mark Greene relates how when Sainsbury's launched its new 'own label' cola, blind tests among consumers suggested that it compared well with the two major brands. But despite a taste preference for Sainsbury's and competitive pricing, it hasn't really caught on. One teenager summed up why: 'I wouldn't drink Sainsbury's, it's naff.' By this he meant not that Sainsbury's was naff on performance grounds but in terms of image. He risked losing face with his contemporaries if he was caught drinking it.

The Cola Wars

Coca-Cola and Pepsi have had their share of the drinks market sewn up for several decades now, and are unlikely to be disrupted. The two colas are virtually undistinguishable (when regular users taste the two brands 'blind' they often get them wrong) but that does not prevent consumers strongly favouring one over the other. Pepsi is the long-standing number two, but has made serious inroads into Coca-Cola's dominant position from time to time. In the 1960s it did so through adverts featuring the 'Pepsi Generation'. This was the first advertising that made no claim at all about the quality of the product. It simply exalted the type of people who used it. The Pepsi Generation communicated the message that Pepsi was drunk by trendy people, the coming generation; Coca-Cola by implication was old-fashioned and fuddy-duddy. The taste was irrelevant. This was underlined by another fleeting victory for Pepsi in the mid-1980s, when Coca-Cola – rattled by Pepsi's effective use of pop star Michael Jackson in advertising – changed to a sweeter taste. Pepsi leapt on this with glee, saying that the change pointed to a flaw in the original product. Coca-Cola quickly realised that their traditional customers favoured the original product, and went back to 'the real thing' with Coke Classic. Few advertising wars can have had so little substance to them, yet significant changes in allocation of market share have taken place and enormous sums of money have shifted hands as a result.

Fashion, mediated through peer pressure, wields formidable power in many societies. In making our purchases, we follow the lead of others. Seen from this perspective, the consumer is 'a weak and malleable creature, easily manipulated, dependent, passive and foolish' (Yiannis Gabriel and Tim Lang, *The Unmanageable Consumer*). Ten years ago there was a craze for Teenage Mutant Ninja Turtles. Michelangelo, Leonardo, Raphael and Donatello were transformed from great Renaissance painters to gaily coloured turtles, heroic resistance fighters who adorned mugs and pencil cases. For several months, any child who failed to sport some turtle merchandise could be described as culturally deprived. But the fad passed and before long these treasures became objects of derision. It takes a brave child to buck a trend.

It would be unfair to put all the blame for this obsession with image on the shoulders of advertisers. Social groups have always shown a tendency to attach meaning to objects, and label their wearers or consumers 'in' or 'out'. Drinking beer creates social bonding among men; wearing jewellery generates mutual admiration among women. Advertising latches on to something that is already happening. Products are made to match an aspiration that is already there, deep inside us. Several seminar delegates expressed concern that it reinforces an unhelpful and unhealthy trend. Advertising fastens on the anxiety many feel about their social image, and bids them find the answer in material goods. This may be a short-term solution to individual insecurities, but is unlikely to offer lasting satisfaction.

If Christians are right to be concerned about marketing, it is here that they should target their objections. The Christian view is that a true understanding of our identity is to be found through our relationship with God. Our value as human beings is based, fundamentally, on the fact that we are made in the image of God, created by him, sustained by him, redeemed by him, and offered the prospect of spending eternity with him. The New Testament urges us to be conformed to the image of Christ, who was himself the perfect image of God (Rom. 8:29; Col. 1:15). The problem with advertising is that it often encourages people to base their identity on something ephemeral, and leads them down false paths.

Mark Greene points to the relevance of the prophet Jeremiah's words in this context: 'My people have committed two sins: They have forsaken me, the spring of living water, and have dug their own cisterns, broken cisterns that cannot hold water.' (Jer. 2:13) I think he is justified in saying: 'In our society, one of our broken cisterns is brands. The brand is required to be the sign of a value that it cannot truthfully carry' ('Ads 'R' Us', *eg*, pp.7-8). The products cannot fulfil the implicit or explicit claims made for them in terms of providing personal meaning and security.

On the whole, the advertising industry does not seem particularly bothered about its contribution to this process. Seminar delegates said their experience is that the industry

largely lacks a sense of wider social responsibility. The adver-
tiser is client-centred rather than community-oriented. Firms
are concerned to help their clients sell products. To do that
they will identify the relevant market, and develop approaches in tune with its attitudes. Public taste provides the
yardstick for what is acceptable copy, though from time to
time there will be a 'daring' pushing of the boundaries when
it accords with the relevant social mood. Ogilvy & Mather
came over as an advertising agency with high ethical standards (they run workshops for employees to discuss values,
and have ethical checkpoints before material goes to regulators like the Advertising Standards Authority), but this was
felt to be unusual. Advertising needs to be seen within the
overall business context, which also tends to be guided by
social acceptability when it comes to establishing an ethical
framework. Advertising is one tool used by companies as
part of a broader marketing strategy. Responsibility for the
character of advertising is shared by the clients who commission it.

Marketing as Productive of Health

Our seminar ended with a plenary discussion, which came up
with a positive model for marketing ethically. Fundamental to
this was the potential for marketing to contribute to personal
and social health or wellbeing. This requires asking deeper
questions than usual about marketing. The following recommendations may be a bit vague at certain points, but they
provide a valuable checklist:

Marketing should promote not only the product, brand,
image, etc. but also:
- health in the community
- health in the individual psychologically
- health in the individual physically
- health in the organisation commercially
- health in terms of relationships.

Marketing should achieve:
- the development of new and improved products
- humble and respectful market/customer research
- informed choice
- values that go beyond profit
- customer satisfaction (preferably delight)
- satisfaction for all the various stakeholders.

For marketing to do this, the organisation must build an infrastructure that encourages people to act ethically: a culture visibly supported by top management where:
- people are aware of ethical best practice
- ethical issues get on the corporate agenda
- ethics are seen as a benefit (internally and externally)
- systems are in place to identify, modify and change dubious practices
- people are aware of the risks and think through the implications of alternative marketing strategies.

Failure to implement these practices will open the door to:
- exploitation of weak and vulnerable groups in society by the strong
- exploitation of the workforce
- dishonesty
- failure to live up to customer expectations
- depersonalisation of the customer and disintegration of society.

Fair Trade, Excellent Coffee

Putting a model like this into practice need not result in dull, half-hearted or heavily diluted marketing. On the contrary, I believe it is compatible with colourful, enthusiastic and persuasive marketing. But the call for greater honesty entails an essential congruity between the product, the claims made for it, and the way it is advertised. Where advertising consists of a sincere appreciation and affirmation of the product's benefits, then it displays integrity. A good example is the CaféDirect campaign that transformed the image of 'fair trade' coffee in the mid 1990s. What makes some coffee 'fair' is a combination of four factors:

- the coffee is bought directly from growers' co-operatives, not from middlemen
- the price is never less than an agreed minimum, however low the world price falls
- when the world price is above this minimum, CaféDirect pays an extra 10% social premium
- pre-payments, regular market price updates and a business development programme help growers to consistently improve their business and negotiate better terms for all their coffee.

There used to be a problem. Many of the people who thought fair trade coffee was ideologically worthy, didn't like the taste. In the early 1990s, it was widely regarded as being of inferior quality. This limited sales. Market research showed that you cannot sell coffee on charity alone.

The taste of fair trade coffee has slowly improved, but it takes time for customer perceptions to change. (The same can be said of Skoda cars.) Market research commissioned by CaféDirect shows that a few consumers (about 2%) are highly 'ethical' and would buy the coffee whatever it tasted like, but there is a much larger category of 'semi-ethical' consumers. For them to be lured, they needed a more sophisticated approach that appeals both to their conscience and their physical senses.

The advertising company used by CaféDirect came up with a simple but effective formula based on two propositions: help the world and enjoy good coffee. They launched a mainly poster campaign with a clever strapline: 'FAIR TRADE, EXCELLENT COFFEE – Richer, mellower and distinctly less bitter'.

Less bitter is a clear *double entendre*, referring both to the taste of the coffee and the terms and conditions with which the coffee growers work. The words were accompanied by images of a South American farmer and the steamy swirls from an appetising cup of coffee. Looking at the poster, you could imagine the coffee smell.

The advertising campaign was successful, if not spectacularly so. It led to a substantial increase in the sales of fair trade coffee. Perceptions of the quality of the coffee were changed. Of course, advertising by itself could not achieve this. It only worked because the coffee was of a standard at least comparable with other coffee. The advertising was a genuinely sincere appreciation and affirmation of the product's benefits.

8

TACKLING INTERNATIONAL CORRUPTION:
DOING BUSINESS WITHOUT BRIBES

In an episode of *Yes Minister*, the famous BBC comedy about the British civil service popular during the 1980s, minister Jim Hacker and his permanent secretary, Sir Humphrey Appleby, have just returned from signing a major contract in the Middle East when Hacker starts to suspect that corruption was involved. The conversation goes like this:

Hacker: The contract was won by bribery?

Appleby: Oh Minister, I do wish you wouldn't use words like bribery.

Hacker: Well, what would you like me to say – slush funds, sweeteners, brown envelopes?

Appleby: These are extremely crude and unworthy expressions for what is no more than creative negotiation. It is the general practice…

Hacker: I announced a British success won in a fair fight.

Appleby: Yes, I did wonder about that.

Hacker: Now you're telling me that it was got by bribery.

Appleby: That is not what I said.

Hacker: What did you say?

Appleby: I said I am not telling you it was not got by bribery.

Hacker: Well how would you describe these payments?

Appleby: How does the contract describe them? That's really quite simple – retainers, personal donations, special discounts, miscellaneous outgoings, agents' fees, political contributions, management expenses.

Hacker: And how are these payments made?

Appleby: Well, anything from a numbered account in a Swiss bank to a fistful of used oncers slipped under the door of the gents.

Hacker: Do you realise how shocking this is?

Appleby: Oh Minister, that's a narrow and parochial view. In other parts of the world they see things quite differently.

A few minutes later:

Hacker: Are you saying that winking at corruption is government policy?

Appleby: No, no, minister, it could never be government policy – that is unthinkable – only government practice... This contract means thousands of British jobs, millions of export dollars. Surely you're not going to throw all that away because of some small technical irregularity?

Compare that fictional account with comments made by Lord Young on the BBC programme *Talking Politics* in April 1994. Young, a former secretary of state for trade and industry, was then chairman of Cable & Wireless plc. Mark Mardell, the presenter, asked him: 'What happens if our competitors are paying bribes? Would business see any moral problem about a level playing field of kickbacks?'

'The moral problem to me is simply jobs,' Young replied. 'Now when you're talking about kickbacks, you're talking about something that's illegal in this country, and that, of course, you wouldn't dream of doing. I haven't even heard of one case in all my business life of anybody in this country doing things like that. But there are parts of the world I've been to where we all know it happens. And if you want to be in business you have to – not something that is morally wrong because in some parts of the world... .

'For example, I went to a Middle East country back in the 1970s and the first thing I saw was a legal agreement, drawn up by an English firm of solicitors, in which a relation of the ruler got a percentage off the top of every government contract. Now that is the accepted standard practice in that particular country; and in many countries in the world it's the only way in which money trickles down from the head of the country, who owns everything, to the people. Now that's not immoral or corrupt. It is very different from our practice and would be totally wrong in our environment but it wasn't wrong in their environment; and what we must be very careful of is not to insist that our practices are followed everywhere in the world.'

What strikes me is the similarity in thinking of the fictional and real characters. The satirical character Sir Humphrey and real-life politician and businessman Lord Young say much the same things. First, they appeal to cultural relativism. Other countries follow different practices and we have no option but to fall in with them. When in Rome, do as the Romans do. Second, they appeal to business necessity. If we're not prepared to pay bribes our competitors will. That will lead to the loss of substantial contracts, which in turn will imperil our companies and throw our people out of work. Third, notwithstanding these two arguments, they exhibit discomfort with the practice. Both Appleby and Young reveal a certain amount of shame about what they're doing. They resort to euphemisms, attempting to wriggle round the plain words of bribery and corruption with glaring *non sequiturs*. We shall return to these themes in due course.

The Worldwide Problem

At a consultation in 1999 hosted by Ridley Hall, 18 senior people from business, charities, NGOs, academia and the church considered the topic *Tackling Corruption in Business*.

The fight against corruption is a crucial matter, exercising the minds of many people in business and politics.

Corruption, best defined as 'the misuse of public or corporate position or power for private gain', is one of those besetting human temptations that will always be with us. Fresh allegations of corruption, affecting a wide variety of countries and international institutions, surface in the media regularly. As I arrived in Australia on study leave in September 2000 I was confronted by two topical prominent cases. In the Cash for Comment Affair, Sydney radio personalities John Laws and Alan Jones were paid to make positive comments about companies. In the Secret Tickets for the Rich Affair, the general public was deceived by the Sydney Olympic Committee into thinking that the majority of tickets were available for purchase whereas many had been set aside for the wealthy.

Corruption is found all over the world, Britain included, despite Lord Young's claim to have never found it on home territory. It is important not to cultivate an air of white Western moral superiority. Nevertheless, corruption is not equally prevalent everywhere. The global anti-corruption coalition Transparency International publishes the Corruption Perceptions Index, an annual survey of how corrupt countries are perceived to be by a mix of nationalities who regularly do business with them. The latest index is available at the Transparency International website www.transparency.org. Although there are small variations from year to year, certain countries (Finland, Denmark and Sweden) consistently score best, i.e. they are considered the least corrupt. Others, such as Cameroon, Nigeria, Paraguay and Indonesia, consistently score worst. In some countries corruption is the exception, arousing deep indignation when it is exposed partly because it is unusual. In others it is endemic and so deeply institutionalised that publicising it produces little shock.

The particular trend in international trade that was the focus of the consultation and is the theme of this chapter is the way companies based in the North win contracts in the South. The evidence I have gleaned, both documented and anecdotal, is that in most commercial contexts operating across the North-South boundary it is very difficult to secure business without making special payments to powerful people who decide the fate of contracts. Abundant evidence that the scale of the problem has increased considerably over the last thirty or more years is well marshalled by George Moody-Stuart, a former chairman of Transparency International and a delegate at the consultation, in his book *Grand Corruption*. Why this is so is keenly debated. Has the impetus come from the supply side or the demand side? The answer is surely a mixture of the two, though the responsibility is difficult to quantify with any accuracy – and doubtless varies from country to country.

On the supply side (companies from the North offering bribes) there is reason to believe that as markets have opened up and global competition has increased, smaller companies trying to outfox their larger competitors have been less scrupulous about resorting to financial inducements to win business. These offers were doubtless gratefully received and before long the traditional companies, anxious to defend their market share, went with the flow.

On the demand side (government ministers and public officials requesting bribes) there is reason to believe that there was a decline in standards following decolonisation and the failure of many Southern countries to make the hoped for economic progress. These politicians and civil servants are often poorly paid, lacking in pension provision and, in Moody-Stuart's words, liable 'to be dismissed at the whim of a leader who has enriched himself to an extent beyond their contemplation' (*Grand Corruption*, p.9). The temptation to make money on the side while they can – especially if everybody else is doing it – is entirely understandable. In many countries, especially Asian ones, the primary obligation is often seen as looking after oneself and one's family, rather than commitment to a disinterested ideal of public service.

Motives on both the supply and demand side, which can be variously described as unmitigated greed or protecting one's interests (and are actually a combination of the two), have therefore merged to create a situation where contracts often carry a 'commission' that may be anything from 5 to 20% of the contract's value.

Bribery Rules, OK?

Is this trend so well established there is no alternative to learning to live with it – in other words, however reluctantly, adopting the practice? This is the conclusion reached by Sir Humphrey and Lord Young. Does bribery rule? Is it OK? We need to take seriously the arguments used by Appleby, quite elegantly, and Young, less coherently, as they are the ones most often used for accepting this 'way of the world' and for *not* regarding corruption as a serious moral problem.

There is the *cultural relativism* argument. We must avoid the insensitivities of our colonial past and not impose our standards on other nations. We live in a postmodern world where few absolutes transcend all cultures, and it is hard to make a case for bribery as one of them. In addition, we should be wary of using the word 'bribe' too readily. What is considered a bribe in one culture is a gift in another, viewed as a mark of friendship or sign of social respect.

Then there is the *practical necessity* argument. Clearly it is a very tall order to eradicate bribery from many cultures. Not paying bribes will lead to the loss of business to competitors. For many companies, this is the crucial argument. They don't wish to pay bribes, they haven't initiated the practice, but if it's going on all around them and they wish to stay in potentially profitable markets, what else can they do but follow suit? Furthermore, if the necessity of paying bribes is understood, is the practice actually unfair? Can't one have a level playing field that includes such payments as a rule of the game?

Subsidiary arguments can be summed up in the phrase *economic mobility*. Bribes, it is said, can be an antidote to rigid over-centralised bureaucracies. Where inaction is the order of the day, they have the effect of getting things moving. They can be a means of augmenting the income of poorly paid government officials. Just as tips are seen as a legitimate supplement to a waiter's wages, 'commissions' (note the subtle change of language) can be viewed in a similar way. In addition, corruption and economic growth are not necessarily incompatible. Some countries that tolerate bribery have made significant economic progress, notably in South East Asia.

A Brief History of Bribery

If these arguments are to be resisted and we are to insist that bribery is a serious moral issue about which action needs to be taken, what are the moral grounds for doing so? Clarity in this area is very important. Some of the arguments put forward by those opposed to bribery are lamentably weak, and fail to get to the nub of the problem. For instance, two criteria I often hear businesspeople use for detecting a bribe are:

- the sleep-well factor – does reflection about it in the middle of the night cause unease?
- the newspaper factor – would the nature of the payment cause embarrassment if revealed on the front page of a newspaper?

These may be useful supportive indicators but are very far from being sufficient or decisive. The ability to sleep well is highly subjective and variable. How the media portray our actions should not be determinative for our moral judgments.

Anyone seriously interested in evaluating the morality of bribery needs to look at its history. For this I recommend without hesitation John T. Noonan Jr..'s outstanding book *Bribes*. The American scholar helpfully defines a bribe as 'an inducement improperly influencing the performance of a public function meant to be gratuitously exercised' (*Bribes*, p.xi). He demonstrates that down the centuries the core meaning of the word has remained constant, though the specific constituent elements (e.g. exactly what is meant by 'inducement' or 'improperly') have changed from culture to culture. He observes that bribes come openly and covertly, in all shapes and sizes, as sex, commodities, appointments or cash.

'In the shape of sex, bribes have been both male and female, a slave, a wife, a noble boy. As commodities, they have included bedspreads, cups, dogs, fruit, furniture, furs, golf balls, jewels, livestock, peacocks, pork, sturgeon, travel, wine – the gamut of enjoyable goods' (*Bribes*, p.xxi). A bribe these days may often consist of securing a relative a key position in a prestigious organisation or university in a developed country. The essence of bribery lies not in the nature of the inducement (what acts as an inducement varies among individuals) but in whether it has the power to distort a person's judgment.

Noonan highlights the paradox at the heart of bribery's history, a sort of double thinking. He says that although bribes have been widely condemned in most times and places, the conviction that bribery is wrong has had a 'precarious hold' because it runs 'counter to normal expectations in approaching a powerful stranger' (*Bribes*, p.xx). Giving something to make someone favourably disposed towards you seems natural, almost an instinctive thing to do. Society's double thinking about bribes is apparent in the linguistic ambiguity (e.g. phrases like 'graft' and 'tea money') we have already noted, and in the widespread reluctance to punish the offence severely – often because those responsible for upholding the law are themselves involved in bribery.

Furthermore, our Judaeo-Christian heritage has profoundly influenced the West's understanding of bribery. This fact is less well known that it ought to be. It is therefore well worth examining the basis for an anti-bribery ethic in the Old and New Testaments. Here is a fairly comprehensive list of texts relating to the practice, set out within the categories of different type of literature:

References to Bribery and Corruption in the Old Testament

Law
- Exodus 18:21
  '... select capable men from all the people – men who fear God, trustworthy men who hate dishonest gain – and appoint them as officials...'

- Exodus 23:8
  'Do not accept a bribe, for a bribe blinds those who see and twists the words of the righteous.'
- Leviticus 19:15
  'Do not pervert justice; do not show partiality to the poor or favouritism to the great, but judge your neighbour fairly.'
- Deuteronomy 10:17
  'For the Lord your God is God of gods and Lord of lords, the great God, mighty and awesome, who shows no partiality and accepts no bribes.'
- Deuteronomy 16:19
  'Do not pervert justice or show partiality. Do not accept a bribe, for a bribe blinds the eyes of the wise and twists the words of the righteous. Follow justice and justice alone, so that you may live and possess the land the Lord your God is giving you.'
- Deuteronomy 27:25
  'Cursed is the man who accepts a bribe to kill an innocent person.'

Historical Narrative

- 1 Samuel 8:3
  '[Samuel's] sons did not walk in his ways. They turned aside after dishonest gain and accepted bribes and perverted justice.'
- 1 Samuel 12:3
  '... From whose hand have I accepted a bribe to make me shut my eyes?'

Wisdom Literature

- Job 15:34
  'For the company of the godless will be barren, and fire will consume the tents of those who love bribes.'
- Job 36:18
  'Be careful that no-one entices you by riches; do not let a large bribe turn you aside.'
- Psalm 15:5
  '(Lord, who may dwell in your sanctuary? Who may live on

your holy hill? He...) who lends his money without usury and does not accept a bribe against the innocent.'

- Psalm 26:10

'...in whose hands are wicked schemes, whose right hands are full of bribes.'

- Proverbs 6:35

(Of a wronged husband.) 'He will not accept any compensation; he will refuse the bribe, however great it is.'

- Proverbs 15:27

'A greedy man brings trouble to his family, but he who hates bribes will live.'

- Proverbs 17:8

'A bribe is a charm to the one who gives it; wherever he turns, he succeeds.'

- Proverbs 17:23

'A wicked man accepts a bribe in secret to pervert the course of justice.'

- Proverbs 18:16

'A gift opens the way for the giver and ushers him into the presence of the great.'

- Proverbs 21:14

'A gift given in secret soothes anger, and a bribe concealed in the cloak pacifies great wrath.'

- Proverbs 22:16

'He who oppresses the poor to increase his wealth and he who gives gifts to the rich – both come to poverty.'

- Ecclesiastes 7:7

'Extortion turns a wise man into a fool, and a bribe corrupts the heart.'

Prophecy

- Isaiah 1:23

'Your rulers are rebels, companions of thieves; they all love bribes and chase after gifts. They do not defend the cause of the fatherless; the widow's case does not come before them.'

- Isaiah 5:22-23

'Woe to those ... who acquit the guilty for a bribe, but deny justice to the innocent.'

- Isaiah 33:15
  'He who walks righteously and speaks what is right, who rejects gain from extortion and keeps his hand from accepting bribes ... this is the man who will dwell on the heights, whose refuge will be the mountain fortress.'
- Ezekiel 22:12
  'In you (the city of bloodshed) men accept bribes to shed blood ... you have forgotten me, declares the Sovereign Lord.'
- Amos 5:12
  'For I know how many are your offences and how great your sins. You oppress the righteous and take bribes and you deprive the poor of justice in the courts.'
- Micah 3:11
  '[Israel's] leaders judge for a bribe, her priests teach for a price, and her prophets tell fortunes for money.'
- Micah 7:3
  'Both hands are skilled in doing evil; the ruler demands gifts, the judge accepts bribes, the powerful dictate what they desire – they all conspire together.'   (All NIV)

Even a cursory glance at this list reveals that references to bribery and corruption abound in all sections of the Old Testament: historical narrative, law, prophecy and wisdom literature. These references are overwhelmingly negative, though there are three verses in Proverbs (17:8, 18:16, 21:14) where the message is more ambivalent, recognising that a 'gift' can have a desired effect. These should be taken as descriptive rather then prescriptive. The overall theme is that the giving and taking of bribes is a serious affront both to God and society.

Bribery is never mentioned in the New Testament, but there are several references to money being used as a lure to dishonest or otherwise wrong behaviour. John the Baptist tells tax collectors to 'Collect no more than the amount prescribed for you' and soldiers not to 'extort money from anyone by threats or false accusation' (Lk. 3:13-14). Judas' betrayal of Jesus for thirty pieces of silver is notorious (Mt. 26:14-15). On the island of Cyprus, the local magician Simon is sternly rebuked by the apostle Peter when he offers money for the gift of the Holy Spirit which came through apostles laying their hands on newly converted Christians (Acts 8:18-20). The implication of the story is that there are some things that are beyond monetary value and should not be for sale. When Paul was a Roman prisoner in Caesarea, the corrupt governor, Felix, frequently met with him because he hoped that Paul would give him money, presumably to secure his release (Acts 24:26).

There is also anti-bribery teaching in Islam. The Koran says: 'Do not devour one another's property by unjust means, nor bribe the judges with it, in order that you may wrongfully and knowingly usurp the possessions of other people.' The sayings of the Prophet include this pronouncement: 'Allah curses the giver of bribes and the receiver of bribes and the person who paves the way for both parties.' It is interesting that the middleman was already a factor in dubious transactions in the Middle East. I shall return to the part he plays later.

Greek and Roman legal thought joined with biblical teaching to establish a Christian repudiation of bribery in the West. Human nature being what it is, the practice persisted. In the waves of reform that swept the church from the eleventh century onwards, the protests nearly always included a cry against corruption, both in ecclesiastical appointments and the law courts. This anti-bribery ethic gained momentum in the wake of the Reformation. Despite, or perhaps because of, its religious roots it proved durable, carrying over into the secular ideas of morality that developed following the Enlightenment. The ethic was part of the moral package spread by the British Empire, though inevitably some colonial governors were poor exponents of it. It is only during the last 200 years that the primary application of the anti-bribery ethic has shifted to the commercial scene.

Bribes are Wrong Because...

In the light of this heritage we are in a position to set out the arguments for regarding bribery as a serious moral problem.

In doing so I will also pay attention to consequential factors – observations that can be made about the effects of corruption in countries where it is rife.

Perversion of judgment

This is the primary reason bribery is wrong. The lure of personal gain sways decisions that should be made on objective, impartial grounds. If it doesn't sway the decision, there is a very grave danger of its doing so. Bribery is therefore a violation of high standards of public service. It is a betrayal of trust.

The biblical material is more relevant here than it might seem at first sight. Most of the references in the Old Testament are judicial, concerning the administration of justice. The prophets were concerned that acceptance of a bribe would pervert a judge's judgment, so that the guilty were acquitted or the innocent convicted. The judge's capacity to weigh the evidence objectively would be jeopardised: he should show no partiality. Is this relevant to a business context 2,500 years later? It is.

In the case of a government minister or civil servant assessing the merits of rival bids, deciding which company it is in his country's interest to grant business to, there is a similar need for cool impartiality. Decisions should be decided by criteria pertaining to the contract such as quality, cost and timing – in short, value for public money. They should not be decided by how much money is going into the individual's private bank account, or whatever else serves as an inducement. Moody-Stuart says: 'When personal gain becomes a factor, it rapidly becomes the main factor and others pale into insignificance' (*Grand Corruption*, p.42). The company that deserves to supply the goods and services – the one that would serve the needs of the developing country best – is less likely to win the contract in a bribe-ridden climate.

Distortion of the market system

Bribery is a buying of preferential treatment by those who can afford it. It carries with it a tendency to create a monopoly situation. Resources are diverted from worthy enterprises

– those that provide 'best value' goods and services – to those that may simply be well connected. Bribery therefore distorts the market system in an unhelpful direction.

Financial cost

In *East and West*, his fascinating reflection on experiences in Asia as the last governor of Hong Kong, Chris Patten describes corruption as a 'heavy tax on economic activity'. The financial cost is considerable, and it extends in several different directions. There is cost to:

- the companies, in terms of bribes paid (which may be anything up to 20% of a contract, though 10-15% would be more common)
- customers, with compensating increases in price that are likely to be built in
- governments, in terms of lost taxation on undeclared transactions
- whole societies, as a disincentive to legitimate trade and investment, and in money spent on unnecessary goods and services.

This last point is very important, and is related to the initial objection about the tendency for judgment to be perverted. Again it is confirmed by Patten. Many a country in the South has expended money on vast capital projects, such as power stations or military hardware, when there was a more pressing need for the construction of schools or hospitals – but it is the big projects that yield the big pay-offs. Corruption is often a contributory factor to the making of poor choices about public priorities.

Threat to security

Where bribes are paid, there is the temptation to bypass regulations on product quality and safety. A blind eye is turned to matters that could imperil the general public. In some particularly lawless societies, refusal to pay a bribe may result in threats of physical violence. Holding people to ransom is the most deplorable form of bribery, though precisely because of the gravity of the situation it is harsh to criticise desperate relatives who give in to the threat and pay for the release of their loved one.

Effect on individuals and society
Our consultation included people from countries of the South who have seen the insidious effect of corruption and lament it. Each act of bribery contributes to a further degrading of the public environment. Corruption breeds disloyalty and laziness among employees, and cynicism and despair among the general public. What is the point of working hard when the quickest route to personal wealth is extortion? When such a mentality holds sway, institutional corruption becomes deeply embedded. The poor, as is usually the case, are the hardest hit.

Emerging moral consensus
Even in countries where bribery is widespread, it is rare for it to be practised completely openly. Prabhu Guptara, who works for UBS Warburg, is an expert on doing business across cultures and a Hindu follower of Jesus the Lord. He believes that the reason for this is *shame* – a feeling that is indicative of a moral unease that most people feel deep down. The converse of this is moral protest. Even in countries where corruption is notorious, protests about the corrupt practices of politicians increasingly feature in elections. There is some evidence of an emerging moral consensus about the issue, whatever the cultural relativists say.

When is a Bribe Not a Bribe?

The view of the delegates at the consultation was that the arguments for regarding bribery as a serious moral issue eclipse those for not doing so. For some, the Christian contribution to the debate weighed heavily in the argument; for others, it was more pragmatic considerations. However, corruption is a complex issue, and it is important to consider some of its more delicate and controversial aspects. In a nut-shell, when is a bribe not a bribe? Although one must beware the linguistic subterfuge that surrounds this issue, the tendency to beat around the bush and indulge in self-deceit, there are meaningful distinctions to be made between bribes and three other categories of payment:

(i) *Gifts*
Gifts are:

- expressions of friendship and goodwill, intended to further the relationship
- usually made openly and directly
- often reciprocal – gifts are exchanged
- not intended to create an obligation to provide special treatment.

In some cultures, notably Japan, the giving and receiving of gifts is of great social significance, and one jeopardises progress in the development of a relationship by ignoring this.

On the other hand, care is needed in this area. Gifts may not always be understood the same way on both sides. The more attractive the gift or act of hospitality in the mind of the recipient, the more likely it is to create a sense of obligation. The more I enjoy the beautiful painting or the holiday in an exotic location or the round of golf followed by a superb meal, the greater the possibility it will undermine my capacity for coolly assessing the business proposition that follows.

(ii) *Facilitation payments (or, as the Americans call them, 'Grease')*
These:

- expedite the performance of routine business or procedures
- are usually small payments to low-level government officials (e.g. customs clerks or immigration officials, to get goods cleared)

- persuade officials to do what they should be doing rather than what they shouldn't.

Most companies with a public position of avoiding bribes to win contracts are prepared to make – and defend – this sort of payment. In Moody-Stuart's phrase, this is at worst 'petty corruption' rather than 'grand corruption'.

On the other hand, such payments acquiesce in what can only be described as an unsatisfactory system. They also have a cumulative effect, possibly weakening moral resistance to more serious forms of corruption. Some officials charge a differential price according to ability to pay, with those who pay the most receiving the best service. Where this happens, the distinction between a 'customary' and 'special' payment starts to break down. For such reasons a few companies, notably Shell, are seeking as a matter of policy to avoid paying them altogether.

(iii) *Payments to agents*
This is a crucial aspect of the corruption issue. It is comparatively rare for bribes to be solicited and paid directly. In many cultures, agents or representatives play a vital role as middle men. A third party in itself need not create a moral problem: we use estate agents to buy and sell houses without having moral qualms about it. In doing commercial business with countries of the South, using someone who knows the language, the local law, the relevant institutions, the government departments and the cultural niceties of the situation makes eminent good sense. Because he performs a crucial role as a middle man, there is nothing wrong in principle with paying him a percentage of the contract's value as a reward for services performed. Or is there?

Ray's Story

Ray is the managing director of a company trying to win a contract in a developing African country. He has a telephone conversation with an agent who has been recommended to him as a well-connected local businessman.

Ray: I gather you have had preliminary conversations with the head of state.

Agent: Indeed I have. His excellency is keen to press ahead with the project subject to satisfactory finalisation of the financial details.

Ray: You know the terms of our tender. We estimate the project will cost $80 million. Then of course we would expect to pay for your services and expenses. Would I be right in thinking that would be about 6%?

Agent: I'm afraid not. The current rate for such services is 12%. The expenses involved are considerable.

Ray: That is much more than I expected. Are there special circumstances in your country which are contributing to that?

Agent: Indeed there are. I need to explain the climate in which we are operating. The president faces an election in a few weeks time. He urgently needs to bolster his campaign fund. I can assure you that his continuing in office is crucial for the stability of this country and the prospect of continued international trade in this country. One of your competitors is also seeking to win this contract. I have learnt confidentially that they have indicated they are willing to make a substantial donation to the president's campaign fund.

Ray: I'm very sorry to hear this. I am afraid that making payments for political purposes is contrary to our company policy.

Agent: I assure you that it need not be regarded as such. The president asks only that a significant sum be made available for him to donate to a worthy cause. Without your paying 12%, it will be difficult for me to give him the necessary assurance.

Ray has uncovered a hornet's nest. What looked like a straightforward deal turns out to be fraught with complications. The agent has not said directly what he will do with his commission, but there is a clear implication that he will use it to win what is effectively a bribe auction, with potential for changing the political future of the country.

Often, the issue that remains murky is what the agent does with the money paid to him. Some of it may be passed along to the relevant minister, effectively securing the contract. In many cases this is almost certainly what happens, but the agent rarely reports it explicitly. He will talk about expenses and commission, and the managing director or finance director will swallow hard and refrain from asking questions when these payments turn out to be surprisingly high. So it is that many companies from the North bury their heads in the sand and convince themselves that they have never (directly) bribed anyone, when it is probably the case that they have done so indirectly and without knowing the full details of what has gone on. In other cases, it may be that the agent has done nothing shady at all. It is the middlemen who make getting a handle on the corruption issue such a difficult matter, to the extent that the involvement of many Northern companies in corrupt practice is hard to quantify even for the companies themselves. The accountants they employ also become well versed in the art of not asking too many awkward questions.

A few companies state in their corporate code that agents should operate according to the company's standards, i.e. that they should not pay bribes. The key issue then becomes how closely they monitor this. There are some clear pointers that ought to alert a company's suspicions:

- the fee or commission being asked for is excessive, i.e. not commensurate with the work being asked of the agent
- the agent stipulates that his commission be paid offshore and a disproportionate part must be paid on signing of the contract
- the agent starts talking in an allusive, elusive or frankly underhand manner.

Thus far, the consultation had agreed on two main findings. First: corruption is a widespread practice and difficult to eradicate. Second: corruption is sufficiently serious to be well worth the effort to eradicate it. In the final stage of the consultation, we were able to share several examples of things that can be, and are being, done about it. These give ground for some cautious optimism.

The Global Fight against Corruption

There are many current anti-corruption initiatives worldwide, but three are singled out here: the OECD Convention, the World Bank and Transparency International.

The OECD Convention

For 20 years the USA stood alone in having a Foreign Corrupt Practices Act. Passed in 1977, it made criminal the payment of a bribe to a foreign official. The prohibition included payment through a local representative, but not the payment of facilitation fees. Americans complained that the Act put them at a competitive disadvantage with countries from the North that were able to pay bribes without infringing national legislation – though whether by fair means or foul, the USA did not seem to do badly in keeping its share of global trade during this period. Companies in many European countries were able legally to classify offshore bribes as legitimate business expenses, which are not tax deductible.

However, that situation changed in 1997. Pressure from the USA, allied with moral concern in other countries, bore fruit in December 1997 when all 29 members of the Organisation for Economic Cooperation and Development (OECD) plus five non-members signed the OECD Convention on Combating Bribery of Foreign Public Officials in International Business Transactions. This required the signatories to make it a crime to bribe any foreign public official to win or retain business or for any other 'improper advantage'. The onus was then on signatory governments to adopt and ratify the convention. It took effect on 15 February 1999, following ratification by sufficient number of countries. If this legislation is adopted and enforced rigorously (and that is a big if), it should produce a more level playing field and in time reduce the scale of international corruption. For companies to say they cannot make such payments 'because they infringe our criminal law' should make saying no to temptation easier; and the OECD members carry sufficient economic weight that it is difficult to imagine countries of the South excluding them from those they do business with.

The UK was one of the 29 OECD signatories. Parliament ratified the convention in 1998. Sadly, the government was deplorably slow preparing the legislation required. The OECD monitoring team castigated the UK in no uncertain terms for its lack of action. In March 2001 the House of Commons Select Committee on International Development issued a report in which it stated forcefully: 'The current legislation on corruption, which is over ninety years old, is inadequate to meet our responsibilities under the OECD Convention ... . New legislation is urgently needed to meet our international obligations but, incredibly, has yet to be introduced.' Eventually, the events of 11 September 2001 proved the trigger for action and the anti-bribery stipulations were included in the 2001 Anti-Terrorism Crime and Security Act.

The World Bank

For many years the World Bank seemed relatively indifferent to international bribery in its lending policy. Since 1996, under the presidency of James Wolfensohn, there has been a clear change of policy. Wolfensohn has described corruption as a 'cancer' that diverts resources from the poor to the rich. The World Bank has imposed standards for borrowing its funds and auditing their use, and has tightened its procurement rules to include 'no bribery' pledges. Increasingly it is going to 'grass roots' level to check the delivery of its funds to specified projects. Examples of the bank's tougher stance include the cutting of loans to Kenya and Nigeria. Uganda meanwhile has suggested a link between good governance or clean finance and debt relief. In 1994 President Museveni asked the World Bank to write off Uganda's debt progressively if he allowed an independent team of accountants to supervise the country's finances. This 'transparency' offer appears to have stood the country in good stead. In 1998 Uganda became the first country to be declared eligible and to benefit from the Heavily Indebted Poor Countries (HIPC) Debt Initiative, ensuring some $700 million in debt relief, of which about 50% was from the World Bank. The World Bank Institute has a major ongoing initiative on corruption in partnership with the government of Uganda. The problem has certainly not been eradicated from the country, but some progress is being made.

Transparency International

Transparency International has grown rapidly in influence and reputation since its foundation as an international anti-corruption NGO in 1993. It now has over eighty national 'chapters' developing a variety of strategies to combat corruption, such as encouraging multinational companies working together in a particular part of the world to make an 'anti-corruption pact'. TI is best known for its Corruption Perceptions Index. Among countries ranked lower than they would like, this is stimulating some measure of heart-searching and internal reform. Clearly, for lasting progress to be made, there needs to be a convergence between the countries of the North and the South in terms of moral understanding – in particular a shared understanding of the responsibilities of good government. TI is actively involved in helpful, informal discussions going on at senior levels.

There are also worthwhile anti-corruption initiatives taking place on the corporate front. Part of what happened at the consultation could be described as a pooling of good practice. These initiatives relate to two main areas, the use of corporate codes and the training of staff.

Formulating and applying codes

There are differences of opinion about the value of company codes of ethics, but the advantages seem to outweigh the disadvantages as long as they are not used as public window-dressing. Codes define the limits of what constitutes acceptable or unacceptable behaviour, they have the potential to help employees think about ethical issues before they are faced with the realities of the situation, and they provide employees with the basis for refusing compliance with a proscribed action.

At the consultation we saw examples of how ten multi-national companies treat the area of bribes, inducements, hospitality and gifts in their codes. The codes which are most helpful:

- Make clear the company's position on facilitation fees (e.g. Caterpillar)
- Make clear that the company's standards also apply to the agents they use (e.g. BP)
- Include 'kickbacks' – retrospective rewards – in what is prohibited (e.g. Honeywell)
- Make clear that the danger in all these different forms of 'gift' is the distortion of commercial judgment (e.g. Standard Chartered Bank).

Two points were particularly emphasised.

First: It is vital that a code of ethics is given the attention and publicity that the gravity of its contents deserves. For this to happen, senior management must 'walk the talk'. Too many employees in too many companies are either only vaguely aware of a code's existence or give it token recognition. There are staff who say they've never seen a code, when they've actually signed a document that they've read and abide by it.

Second: By way of implementation, principles from the code should be written into employment contracts and linked with disciplinary procedures. References to the code could also be built into goal setting, appraisal, reward, remuneration and recognition systems within companies.

Staff training
There was a recognition that the pressures on companies and individuals to resort to bribery can be very strong. Three

multinationals represented at the consultation (Shell, ICI and SmithKline Beecham – now GlaxoSmithKline) are counteracting these pressures by:

- The development of training programmes that establish a clear corporate standard, backed up by appropriate discipline, but which also allow employees space to discuss difficult cases and exercise their own initiative. Codes of ethics are supplemented by imaginative training seminars. GlaxoSmithKline has a particularly good line in case study material. Shell has published a management primer, titled *Dealing with Bribery and Corruption*, that includes 15 detailed case studies.
- The use of target setting and record keeping to measure corporate progress. For instance, Shell keeps a register of requests for facilitation payments. This highlights parts of the world where it is a particular problem and it may be appropriate for senior management to raise the issue with public authorities. As mentioned in Chapter 2, *The Shell Report*, Shell's annual ethical self-audit, documents the number of cases in which bribes have been offered to, solicited and/or accepted by Shell employees.

An area where companies agree that more could be done is the celebration and reinforcement of examples of good practice, by praising or rewarding individuals who turn down 'unethical' business, or by publicising the cases of subsidiaries that have maintained their standards and still managed to flourish in generally corrupt environments. For instance, it was reported that ICI has done this in Pakistan through some excellent local leadership who have put fine words into action. The channelling of trade towards societies making genuine efforts to reform in this area also sends out important signals.

Costly Christlikeness

Clearly there are encouraging developments on the anticorruption front, but a word of caution is in order. Human beings are fallen and sinful. We can therefore expect a dragging of heels to slow down the measures being taken and a resort to devious means to get round them. The practice of demanding and receiving bribes is never going to be eradicated. This will remain an area that requires moral scrutiny and provides moral challenge.

The plain fact is that there are situations where a refusal to pay a bribe will lead to a loss of business. Business ethics are often commended on the grounds they are good for business. In other words, maintaining moral standards and acting with integrity in business gives a company a good reputation and contributes to its prosperity. In general, I believe this is true: doing the right thing usually does pay off in the long run. But it is one of those truisms that is only true about 90% of the time.

We need to be honest and acknowledge that sometimes doing the right thing is costly. It is at this point that the Christian faith has an important contribution to make. Christians believe in a Saviour whose life and death were grounded in the values of self-service and sacrifice, culminating in his death on the cross. This should give cause for inspiration. It ought to provide sustenance and encouragement in making those difficult decisions that involve an element of self-sacrifice – and which are genuinely costly. Actions that go against the stream and contribute to an improvement in the moral climate often have the character of *costly Christlikeness*.

I write these words with some hesitation, because I am aware of just how hard this can be in a corporate setting. It is one thing to make a sacrificial decision that brings suffering to oneself. It is much harder (and ethically speaking, much more complex) when it brings suffering to others – such as employees whose jobs are put at risk by the failure to win a substantial contract. It is also hard if your position in the organisation is such that you are expected to carry out orders from above, rather than having the freedom to decide independently.

Taking a strong moral stand on this issue – as I have suggested it is important to do – needs to be balanced with a spirit of sensitivity and charity. Significantly, most business-people at the consultation (who were largely united in having a strong anti-corruption commitment) had at some stage done things in this area of which they were ashamed. Very few people regularly involved in doing business across cultures can claim to have entirely clean hands. It is an area where practitioners need the support and understanding of their Christian colleagues, who can point to the profound forgiveness and enabling courage that comes from an ongoing relationship with a gracious God.

9

SAVING THE FUTURE OF THE PLANET:
BUSINESS AND SUSTAINABLE DEVELOPMENT

Mama Cash is a women's micro-credit and funding foundation, based in the Netherlands, that facilitates women-based companies by providing seed capital and grants. Its aim is to improve the position of women worldwide, especially those who run environmentally friendly businesses and are improving the status of women in their society. Mama Cash won the Triple Bottom Line Investing Award for 2001.

The Triple Bottom Line

Triple bottom line is an unfamiliar phrase that is gradually supplementing – or in some case replacing – use of stakeholder language in companies with a strong sense of corporate responsibility. It was coined by sustainable development campaigner John Elkington in 1994. It expresses the idea that returns to shareholders aren't the only bottom line; there are other yardsticks by which corporate performance should be measured. Alongside financial or economic sustainability, social (often described in terms of social equity or justice) and environmental sustainability are becoming equally important criteria. This is focusing the minds not only of organisations you are unlikely to have heard of, like Mama Cash, but of many big multinational companies that are household names. The triple bottom line is reflected, for instance, in the structure of the 2001 *Shell Report*, which – in the words of its title-page – 'documents the actions we have taken in 2001 to meet our economic, environmental and social responsibilities, and describes how we are striving to create value for the future.'

Environmental responsibilities affect every type of business. Under pressure from the green movement, the last decade saw the successful promotion of many environmentally favourable products, from ozone-friendly aerosols to cruelty-free cosmetics. Every company – indeed, every organisation or family – has a contribution to make towards a cleaner, greener world. But the onus is particularly heavy on companies that, like Shell, are involved in the energy industry. Energy was the main focus of a consultation on *Business and Sustainable Development* at Ridley Hall in May 2001. What sort of energy policy we need if the twenty-first century is going to finish without planet earth in irretrievably bad shape has become a crucial question, and ought to be prompting more concerted thought and urgent action than is currently the case.

The Environmental Challenge

The extent of the environmental challenge facing humanity was underlined at the consultation by Sir John Houghton, a co-chairman of the Intergovernmental Panel on Climate Change (IPCC) Scientific Assessment Working Group. The IPCC recognises that economic activities are significantly affecting the global climate and the latest scientific data leaves no doubt that the world is warming up. There has been a marked increase in average global temperature since 1975 and 1998 was the warmest year on record, with the first eight months each individually the warmest on record. Since the Industrial Revolution, the amount of carbon dioxide in the atmosphere has increased by a third and the amount of methane has doubled. If carbon dioxide emissions double during the next century (which will be hard to stop) then the average temperature could increase by 2.5 degrees Celsius.

The IPCC Working Group predicts an average temperature increase by 2100 ranging between 1.4 and 5.8 degrees. The range results from the complexity of the calculations and uncertainties concerning both natural controls within the ecosystem and whether we increase, stabilise or decrease the use of fossil fuels. This was reported by some elements in the press as a predicted increase of 6 degrees. Sir John said it was important not to present an over-alarmist picture, because when this is corrected it leads to complacency.

The likely effects of global warming include:

- the melting of glaciers, a rise in sea levels and the flooding of large areas of land
- greater extremes of climate, e.g. more heavy rainfall and less light rainfall – so more floods and more droughts
- environmental refugees – with Bangladesh, Egypt, China and India likely to be the worst hit countries.

The level of international concern over the environment has grown steadily during the last 50 years, and a considerable convergence of views has taken place. This can be charted through such landmark events as the 1972 UN Conference on the Human Environment, which produced the Stockholm Declaration, the development of a World Conservation Strategy in 1980, the 1987 Brundtland Report *Our Common Future* (significant for its influential definition of sustainable development as 'development that meets the needs of the present without compromising the ability of future genera-tions to meet their own needs'), through to the 1992 Earth Summit at Rio. This was attended by 25,000 delegates from 160 countries, including over 100 heads of state. Rio reaffirmed the Stockholm Declaration 'with the goal of establishing a new and equitable global partnership through the creation of new levels of cooperation among states, key sectors of society, and people'. Recognising 'the integral and interdependent nature of the Earth, our home', the nations committed themselves to working towards international agreements respecting the interests of all, and protecting the integrity of the global environmental and developmental system.

But for all the agreement on words, disappointingly little has happened in the way of an effective response to the environmental crisis. Sir Crispin Tickell, author of *Climatic Change and World Affairs*, says: 'Mostly we know what to do, but we lack the will to do it.' Paul said something similar in Romans 7:19: 'For I do not do the good I want, but the evil I do not want is what I do' – the evil in this case being that of sloth or apathy. A cynic might say that the highest level of recycling triggered by the environmental movement is in the production of worthy statements about the environment.

The Political and Business Response

One of the most practical and promising follow-ups to Rio was the 1997 Kyoto Protocol, an agreement achieved at the UN Convention on Climate Change that commits 38 developed nations to collectively reducing their emissions of greenhouse gases 5.2% by the year 2010 compared to 1990. Within this framework, each country stated its own target: 8% in the case of the European Union as a whole, 7% for the USA. The developing countries were not required to set limits, but have been given the option to comply and to receive technological and material aid in return. The protocol includes all the major greenhouse gases: carbon dioxide, methane, nitrous oxide, hydrofluorocarbons, perfluorocarbons, and sulphur hexafluoride. It also opened the way to a programme for international trading of certificates relating to the abatement of greenhouse gas emissions.

For the Kyoto Protocol to be effective, governments must ratify it. Even before US President George Bush took office, the Senate was showing a marked reluctance to do this unless developing countries were included in reductions. The sight of the leader of the nation that emits most greenhouse gases turning his back on Kyoto – with an energy plan for increased commitment to oil and gas development – is ominous. Some people at the consultation were deeply embarrassed that a leading politician who professes to be a Christian appears to be exhibiting national selfishness and disregarding expert opinion. With Canada and Australia also dragging their heels, there is little prospect of the 2010 targets being reached. Most countries in the European Union, however, remain committed to their individual targets within the EU 'umbrella'.

In the UK, the Emissions Trading Group has over 100 corporate members. Involvement in the scheme is voluntary, but financial incentives are offered to companies to take part. The essence of the system is that companies that exceed their targets for reducing carbon emissions can sell credits to companies that fail to meet their targets. It represents an innovative move in using market methods to try to improve the environment. Delegates were interested but questioned both the practice and principles:

- Will there be a balance in the units bought and sold, in order to ensure liquidity of the scheme? One person suggested that most companies would be motivated to meet or exceed their targets, the prospect of buying units being an unattractive one. This augurs well for the environment but not for the viability of the scheme, which could suffer from a lack of buyers
- This is a voluntary approach, and many of the worst business offenders will probably choose not to take part. It is likely that only the regulatory approach, rigorously enforced, will have an impact on such companies
- There is something morally odd about a scheme which makes poor performance acceptable – even if it carries a financial cost. It has the feel of companies purchasing an 'indulgence' and seems too complacent an approach when the environmental crisis is so serious.

BP and Shell

Two energy companies involved in the Emissions Trading Scheme are BP and Shell. They have both made a very positive response to Kyoto:

- BP has committed itself to reducing its 'in-house' global greenhouse gas emissions by 10% below its 1990 baseline levels by 2010 (nearly twice the rate of the Kyoto global target). These reductions will occur through broad-based efficiency gains, the development and application of new technology (e.g. with the Trans-Alaska pipeline) and the reduction of flaring (e.g. in the North Sea). BP operates its own internal emissions trading system across its global operations. It says it is on course to meet its 2010 commitment.
- Shell has committed itself to reducing its global greenhouse gas emissions by 10% below 1990 levels by the end of 2002. It too reports that it is on course to meet this target, despite the fact there was a 2% increase in emissions during the year 2000 – mainly due to increased production in Nigeria, where the company has committed itself to eliminating continuous flaring by 2008. Shell is also developing new technologies and cleaner fuels, and operates its own internal emissions trading system.

Without taking anything away from these laudable measures, three notes of caution are in order:

1. Although BP and Shell are increasing their level of investment and research in forms of renewable energy, this remains tiny compared with their continuing involvement in oil and gas. BP is a very long way from its stated aim of moving 'Beyond Petroleum'. In other words, a big question still remains about the main activity – extraction of fossil fuels – that is the core business of these massive multinationals.
2. Controversy attaches to particular projects that BP and Shell are involved in, notably BP in Alaska (and the threat to the Arctic National Wildlife Refuge) and Shell in Nigeria (and the environmental impact on Ogoniland and its people). Evaluating the pros and cons of the two companies' involvement in these environmentally and politically sensitive areas is an interesting exercise. Indeed, it is now possible for any member of the public to conduct this

exercise and reach an informed judgment by considering relevant material from the websites of both the companies and their prominent critics, such as Greenpeace and Friends of the Earth. It is particularly interesting how local communities are often divided in their response to energy companies, with some welcoming the employment they bring and others opposing their disruptive effect on culture, landscape and wildlife.

3. In terms of ethical standards and commitment to improving their environmental performance, BP and Shell are a long way ahead of most other companies in their field. It would be a mistake to take them as representative of the energy industry. All too many companies are lagging well behind the emissions targets set out at Kyoto.

James Wilsdon, then a senior policy advisor with Forum for the Future, reported a mixed response from business to issues of sustainable development. Forum combines the three elements of NGO, think tank and consultancy in pursuing a 'solutions agenda' with companies. On the plus side, Wilsdon said, there was an increasing sense of sustainability being a shared agenda, and positive initiatives were being taken by companies such as Dudley Stationery, where an ethos of integrity in all corporate relationships had produced a positive environmental stance. Some companies were prepared to accept the argument that sustainability makes good business sense in the long run. Businesspeople are often prepared to concede the importance of sustainability issues when transported from their normal working environment into a countryside setting. Jonathan Porritt, a director of Forum for the Future, says: 'Given half a chance, I am always amazed at the speed with which sober-suited business people will take off their shoes and start hugging trees.'

On the other hand, it is rare that the case for sustainability is made on moral and spiritual grounds in a corporate context. Yet Wilsdon said: 'Spiritual wellbeing is the cultural glue that makes a difference between a good company and a great company.' He suggested that a 'politics of reverence' needs to infuse the world of business, with the awe and concern that people feel at a personal level given space and voice in the boardroom. Not one to underestimate the corporate obstacles, Wilsdon noted that spirituality and power make uneasy bed-fellows and reverence might be hostile to the innovation and risk-taking necessary for making progress. Nor will it neces-sarily lead to better environmental understanding. The group felt that if significant improvement in corporate environmen-tal performance comes, it is likely to be from a variety of sources:

- Internal – because it is embedded in the values of the com-pany or a key individual. One delegate mentioned a Malaysian he'd known who took an environmental stand simply because it was the right thing to do
- Commercial – because customers have put pressure upon them to do so. Green customers have made a difference, but the impetus of the movement needs to be sustained
- Legislative – because regulation with 'teeth' requires it of them. This creates a level playing-field so that companies with a pro-active stand on the environment do not feel put at a disadvantage.

The Christian Response

There is an important link between spirituality and the envi-ronment, but what of Christianity? Professor Lynn White, a historian, is among those who say Christianity is at the historic roots of our ecological crisis. In a 1967 lecture, White said the mandate in Genesis 1:26 for man to 'have dominion' over the creation led to an anthropocentric view of the world, with human beings feeling 'superior to nature, contemptuous of it, willing to use it for our slightest whim.'

Christianity 'bears a huge burden of guilt' for science and technology having been blessed and given free rein, resulting in human beings ruthlessly exploiting nature with powers that are out of control, he said. White also recognised the alternative, largely suppressed, Christian approach to the natural world found in St Francis of Assisi. Francis' virtue was to seek to depose man from his monarchy over creation and to set up a democracy of all God's creatures. He spoke of Brother Ant and Sister Fire. White called for a revival of this tradition: 'Since the roots of our trouble are so largely religious, the remedy must also be essentially religious … I propose Francis as a patron saint for ecologists.'

Christian concern about the environment has developed steadily since then. The Church of England Doctrine Commission visited the subject in 1975. It said: 'Our nature as created in God's image and likeness and as destined to grow towards him involves responsible use of those godlike powers over the natural environment which God has put into our hands'. In 1991, the Board for Social Responsibility effectively 'Christianised' the new G7 Code of Environmental Practice by putting its talk of stewardship in terms of a responsibility to God as creator, redeemer and sustainer of the world. Pope John Paul II in 1993 said: 'Respect for the natural environment and the correct and modulated use of the resources of creation are a part of each individual's moral obligations … We must all learn to approach the environmental question with solid ethical convictions involving responsibility, self-control, justice and fraternal love. For believers, this outlook springs directly from their relationship to God, the creator of all that exists.'

In 1994, the Evangelical Environmental Network launched *An Evangelical Declaration on the Care of Creation*, which was endorsed by several hundred church leaders. IVP has published a commentary on the declaration, *The Care of Creation*, edited by Professor Sam Berry, a contributor to our consultation. The 1998 Lambeth Conference warned: 'Unless human beings take responsibility for caring for the earth, the consequences will be catastrophic'. It prayed in the spirit of Jesus Christ 'for widespread conversion and spiritual renewal in order that human beings will be restored to a relationship of harmony with the rest of creation'. During the last 20 years, Christian environmental organisations have mushroomed and now include:

- Christian Ecology Link (founded 1981)
- A Rocha Trust (1983)
- Environmental Issues Network (1990)
- John Ray Initiative (1997)
- EcoCongregation (2000).

In international discussions about the environment, Christians have often taken a prominent role. Other faiths have been involved, but there are significant differences of understanding. There is the notion of man as steward in the Koran, but little development in Islamic theology. Buddhists lack a doctrine of creation, but view the world as holy; for Christians it is not holy so much as worthy of respect as God's creation.

Sam Berry suggests that a sound Christian understanding of the environment can be summed up in three basic statements. The foundation for these is found in a variety of biblical passages.

Three Biblical Convictions about the Environment

1. *The earth belongs to God*

'In the beginning God created the heavens and the earth.' (Gen. 1:1, NIV)

'Yours, O Lord, are the greatness, the power, the glory, the victory, and the majesty; for all that is in the heavens and on the earth is yours...' (1 Chr. 29:11, NRSV)

'The earth is the Lord's and the fullness thereof, the world and those who dwell therein' (Ps. 24:1, RSV)

'For every beast of the forest is mine, the cattle on a thousand hills. I know all the birds of the air, and all that moves in the field is mine.' (Ps. 50:10-11, RSV)

2. *God has entrusted his creation to humanity*

'Then God said, "Let us make humankind in our image, according to our likeness; and let them have dominion over the fish of the sea, and over the birds of the air, and over the cattle, and over all the wild animals of the earth, and over every creeping thing that creeps upon the earth' (Gen. 1:26, NRSV)

'The Lord God took the man and put him in the garden of Eden to till it and keep it' (Gen. 2:15, NRSV)

'You have given them [human beings] dominion over the works of your hands; you have put all things under their feet, all sheep and oxen, and also the beasts of the field, the birds of the air, and the fish of the sea, whatever passes along the paths of the seas.' (Ps. 8:6-8, NRSV)

'The heavens are the Lord's heavens, but the earth he has given to human beings.' (Ps. 115:16, NRSV)

3. *We will be held accountable for our stewardship*
'He turned rivers into a desert, flowing springs into thirsty ground, and fruitful land into a salt waste, because of the wickedness of those who lived there.' (Ps. 107:33-34, NIV)

'The earth dries up and withers, the world languishes and withers; the heavens languish together with the earth. The earth lies polluted under its inhabitants; for they have transgressed laws, violated the statutes, broken the everlasting covenant. Therefore a curse devours the earth, and its inhabitants suffer for their guilt; therefore the inhabitants of the earth dwindled, and few people are left.' (Is. 24:4-6, NRSV)

'The nations raged, but your wrath has come, and the time for judging the dead, for rewarding your servants, the prophets and saints and all who fear your name, both small and great, and for destroying those who destroy the earth.' (Rev. 11:18, NRSV)

All delegates to the consultation agreed on these three theological premises, but that left considerable scope for debate on both the precise understanding of these statements and their practical outworking.

The Understanding of Stewardship

In an understandable desire to amend for faulty Christian understanding in the past, there is a danger of presenting too sanguine and harmonised a biblical picture. Genesis contains two creation stories, one starting at 1:1 and the other at 2:4. I think they reflect different theological emphases in the account they give of humanity's place in relation to the created order. In Genesis 1, men and women are told to 'have dominion' over living creatures and to 'subdue' the earth (v.28). The Hebrew words used are quite violent in tone; there is an implication that if nature is to satisfy human needs, considerable force may have to be exerted on it. In Genesis 2, the picture of man is much more suggestive of the caretaker. God gives Adam the twofold task of looking after the garden and naming the animals. The atmosphere is that of friendly benevolence, not the struggle for survival.

Rather than harmonise the two accounts too quickly, I believe we should acknowledge their distinctive nuances and see that each has something important to teach us. In other words, we should recognise a positive creative tension between them. It is sentimental nonsense to imagine that some element of subduing the earth is unnecessary. Pests have to be controlled, some wilderness has to be tamed, water has to be found. But that is not the whole story. In the role of gardener, humanity has the leisure and opportunity to cultivate and classify. The relationship with creation becomes more that of companion than master. As Sir John Houghton said, a garden is to be maintained as a place of beauty where human beings can be creative.

The concept of stewardship also needs teasing out carefully. It should not be assumed that everyone understands the same things by it. There are different aspects to being a steward. A good steward conserves, manages wisely and gives an account to the master. The aspect that is sometimes neglected is that of resource utilisation, adding to the store or, to use a fashionable phrase, adding value. Jesus praised two of the servants in the parable of the talents (Mt. 25:14-30) for doing precisely this: They doubled what they had been given, whereas the unworthy servant did nothing. There is a plausible theological rationale for manufacturing industry in terms of making the most of God-given resources. It takes raw materials that God has put within his creation and extracts, converts and refines them so they are useful to humanity. The duty of resource utilisation is surely intrinsic to a full understanding of stewardship, but it is precisely here that controversy creeps in. For in developing these resources we can do harm as well as good. We can destroy value as well as add value. In particular, the extraction of fossil fuels presents a mixed picture.

Professor John Twidell, a director of the AMSET Centre, put forward the interesting view that extraction of fossil fuels is against the natural order. Over a period of billions of years, most carbon was removed or sequestered from the atmosphere, going underground. (Atmospheric carbon dioxide composition was originally 99% and became 0.03%.) This made possible the conditions in which life could flourish. In the painstaking process of evolution it makes sense to detect the creative purposes of God. The logic of this natural theology is that returning carbon to the atmosphere by burning it is contradictory to the ecological processes that make life possible. It may even be seen as defiance of such purposes.

Other delegates were unconvinced by his arguments, believing that just because the resources are underground it doesn't mean they're not 'part of the going concern' and they could be useful in meeting the world's energy needs. However, there was overwhelming agreement that the world at present is far too dependent on fossil fuels, and the rate at which they are being used imperils the planet. While reliance on fossil fuels cannot be abandoned overnight, there is a need to be much more ambitious and to invest far more money in moving away from them.

Renewable Energy and Nuclear Energy

In considering the alternatives to fossil fuels, two clear camps emerged; those delegates who pinned their hopes on the development of renewable sources of energy, and those who felt far greater use should also be made of nuclear energy.

We heard the case for renewable, sustainable energy options. The amounts currently being invested in these from public funds are niggardly: in the year leading up to the consultation, £15 billion to improve the safety of the rail system following the Hatfield disaster compared with £150 million for investment in renewable energy, mainly to support 'off-shore wind' and 'energy crops'. Only 2% of total power output in the UK comes from renewables. The Germans are much more interested in energy efficiency and renewable energy than any other European nation.

Types of renewable energy:
- Solar: active, passive and photovoltaic
- Water: hydro, tidal, wave and current
- Wind: onshore and offshore
- Geothermal: geysers and hot rock
- Biomass and biofuels: timbermill waste, agricultural and arboricultural residues, straw burning, energy crops, meat and bone meal, poultry litter, livestock slurry, farm slurry.

'There is no shortage of renewable energy; the challenge is to develop, manufacture, and utilise the associated technology,' Twidell rightly says. The need is for effective markets, linked with ongoing research and development, which requires a deliberate shift in UK government policy. Many people, including some of the delegates at the consultation, are sceptical about the levels of electricity that could be generated from renewable energy sources but it certainly deserves to be given a chance. The sooner substantial solar and wind capacity is operating on grid systems, the sooner their advantages and limitations will become evident and their potential can be properly assessed.

The case for nuclear energy:
- Uranium is available in prolific quantities – in the words of one delegate, it is 'ubiquitous on the earth'
- Unlike fossil fuels, nuclear energy does not emit greenhouse gases or other damaging emissions

- The industry has an impressive safety record, Chernobyl excepted; about one-third of the cost of a typical reactor is spent on safety systems and structures
- Wastes, though problematic, are manageable and are generally well managed
- If we are to use substantially less oil, gas and coal, it is difficult to see an alternative to nuclear fission for continuous and reliable electricity supply on a large scale
- From a Christian perspective, it can be seen as part of God's abundant provision for us when our technological capacity has developed to take advantage of it.

Not all delegates were convinced of this case either. Some feared the leakage of discarded radioactive material into the biosphere. Others pointed to the link between nuclear energy and nuclear weapons, though the two uses can surely be separated. It is a stark illustration of the human capacity to use God-given resources both for good and evil. Current decommissioning of nuclear weapons means that a lot of uranium is now being used to generate electricity, with military plutonium set to follow.

Delegates from the nuclear industry commented on the irrational and ill-informed nature of much of the debate over nuclear power. Outside Cumbria, the home of British Nuclear Fuels' Sellafield plant, there is a widespread prejudice against the industry that inhibits politicians from going further down that route. Britain has moved on from the NIMBY (Not In My Back Yard) syndrome to BANANA (Build Absolutely Nothing Anywhere Near Anyone!) among the public and NIMTOO (Not In My Term Of Office!) among politicians. It takes eight years to build a nuclear power station, and there is no sign of any being commissioned. Public perception on issues of safety, waste and nuclear proliferation must change if we are to realise the huge potential of the nuclear industry to meet future energy needs.

Some favoured renewable energy and others nuclear energy, but all agreed that each have an important role – a case of both/and rather than either/or. The scale and intensity of demand for electricity ought to affect the choices we make. The merits of both positions certainly warrant further discussion. Christians should set an example in weighing the evidence calmly and objectively, acknowledging the advantages and disadvantages of every energy option. But this needs to be done alongside a prophetic call against the current balance of usage. It simply is unsustainable to continue a practice whereby nearly two-thirds of electricity worldwide comes from fossil fuels.

Changing the Climate of Opinion

It's hard to see how can we change the climate of opinion, which remains frighteningly indifferent to the gravity of the environmental crisis. The consultation did not come up with any easy answers, but pointed to three key areas that warrant serious attention.

Generating a sense of awe

At various points the words 'reverence', 'awe' and 'wonder' peppered the discussion. If these attitudes were more widespread, the way humans interact with the environment might be substantially different. When we asked ourselves how we generate a sense of awe, we found ourselves citing Proverbs 1:7: 'The fear of the Lord is the beginning of knowledge.' Both parts of the verse, the fear of the Lord and the beginning of knowledge, are well worth careful consideration.

Fearing God has become unfashionable. But both Old Testament and New Testament make clear that God's displeasure at wilful, sustained human wrongdoing is a fearful thing. We will be held accountable for our stewardship. The passages quoted above say we reap what we sow. Careless stewardship and pollution bring ecological disaster in their wake, and calamity for mankind. The fear of God should bring us to our senses.

The beginning of knowledge is crucial. In this area above all, ignorance is dangerous. Awe comes with in-depth

Questions of Business Life

immersion in God's world, both natural and technological. Journeying through a nature reserve is awesome, but so is seeing the fission of uranium. Art and science, travel and study can all contribute to kindling a deeper respect for the planet we live on. We must distance ourselves from the triviality of everyday existence and stop insulating ourselves from the wonders around us. The writer of Proverbs suggests that fear of God actually creates a thirst for knowledge and wisdom.

Nurturing responsibility for the future

Short-term thinking prevents the current generation taking the decisive, self-sacrificial steps necessary to safeguard the planet for future generations. The limited response to the Kyoto Protocol illustrates that only too clearly. Many organisations are now creating future scenarios: extrapolating how the world might look in say 2020, not liking aspects of what they see, and using the prognosis as a spur for change. The Old Testament prophets used the same technique. Forum for the Future aims to get that forward-looking thinking incorporated much more into companies' strategic planning.

One way to instil greater urgency is to personalise the future. Instead of talking in general terms about 'future generations' think of your grandchildren. What sort of world do we want them to live in? Grandparenting, like parenting, is both a privilege and a responsibility. There is a need both to set an example to children on environmental issues and to educate them to the best of our ability about these issues.

Although the agencies which can make the biggest difference to the environment are clearly international bodies, national governments, and multinational companies (especially those in the energy sector), there is a need for everyone to do what they can. Each individual or organisation can make a contribution to a cleaner environment, through regular practices such as:

- ensuring maximum energy efficiency and saving
- purchasing energy from renewable or other non-carbon sources

- using methods of transport other than the car
- reducing waste and re-using materials.

Edmund Burke is reputed to have said: 'It is necessary only for the good man to do nothing for evil to triumph.'

Opposing a spirit of fatalism

Some people throw up their hands in despair, because the environmental prognosis is so grave. One argument says fatal damage has already been done and it is impossible to reverse the decline. Even if we dramatically reduced our reliance on fossil fuels today, global warming would increase for several decades because of the impact of our activities during recent decades. There is also a version of Christian fundamentalism that is indifferent to this issue, saying there is no point investing a massive amount of energy in saving the world when God is going to wrap up the whole world order anyway – possibly quite soon.

It is very important to contest the view that this world isn't worth bothering about, or that it's a sinking ship that cannot be saved. However, there is no doubt that it is 'groaning', to use Paul's phrase in Romans 8:22. Phenomena like the hole in the ozone layer indicate something is seriously awry. But Paul uses the language of groaning within the context of hope – hope that 'the creation itself will be set free from its bondage to decay and will obtain the glorious freedom of the glory of the children of God.' (Rom. 8:21) God remains committed to his world, and the dramatic transformation the Bible predicts for its future is the creation of a 'new heavens and a new earth' (Is. 65:17, 2 Pet. 3:13, Rev. 21:1) rather than its consignment to oblivion. For Christians, that should be a solid ground for hope and a major spur for action.

But there are other reasons for optimism as well, cited by Sir John Houghton at our consultation. There is a high level of commitment in the scientific community, evident in the remarkable degree of international cooperation and agreement in the work of the Intergovernmental Panel on Climate Change. There is the availability of the necessary technology, which contains the potential to meet the world's foreseeable energy needs. There are also many keen minds in the business world who see the urgency of the situation, who may still be minority voices in their companies, or 'maverick' companies within their sector, but are putting the case for presenting sustainable development as a major business opportunity.

Curitiba's Story

Curitiba is not an individual, nor a company, but a city – though one particular individual *has* played a crucial role, and many companies have been constructively involved. Curitiba in south-eastern Brazil has a population of nearly 2 million people. It has grown enormously over the last half century, and continues to do so.

Most cities like Curitiba, throughout the world but especially in the South, are recipes for social problems with all the ingredients close at hand: poverty, unemployment, squalor, disease, illiteracy, congestion, pollution and corruption. They can easily drive their inhabitants to despair. Yet many residents of Curitiba think they live in the best city in the world, and lots of outsiders would agree. The city has 17 new parks, 90 miles of bike paths and trees everywhere. It has transportation and refuse systems that officials from other cities come to study.

'Though starting with the dismal economic profile typical of its region, in nearly three decades the city has achieved measurably better levels of education, health, human welfare, public safety, democratic participation, political integrity, environmental protection, and community spirit than its neighbours, and some would say than most cities in the United States' (Paul Hawken, Amory B. Lovins and L. Hunter Lovins, *Natural Capitalism*, p.288). One might add, better than most cities in western Europe.

The transformation of Curitiba began in the late 1960s with the development of a master plan for the city, formulated by a visionary group of young architects. Among them was Jaime

Lerner, who became mayor of Curitiba in 1971 at the age of thirty-three. Lerner served three terms of four years and therefore 12 years in all as mayor, alternating with three other mayors under Brazil's single-consecutive-term limit. In fact, his vision attracted broad consensus. There has been considerable continuity in the development and government of the city throughout the three decades since he first came to office.

Lerner's bold and successful initiatives have included:

Pedestrianisation of the city centre

His first move was to convert the central historic boulevard, the Rua Quinze de Novembro, into a pedestrian mall. The shopkeepers were initially opposed to this, but the move led to a massive increase in custom, so that other streets in the centre asked to be included in the scheme. The original boulevard was planted with thousands of flowers and is now called the Rua des Flores.

A revolutionary new bus system

The master plan entailed persuading Curitiba's citizens to travel by bus, rather than car. Concentric circles of local bus lines connect to five main lines that radiate from the city centre in a spider web pattern. On the radial lines, specially designed triple-compartment buses in their own traffic lanes carry up to 270 passengers each. These buses stop at tube-shaped stations which provide protection from the weather and facilitate fast bus entry and exit. About 1,250 buses make more than 12,500 trips a day, serving 1.3 million passengers.

The citizens of Curitiba have not abandoned their cars; indeed, the city has the second highest per capita car ownership in Brazil. Yet for most journeys they don't use them, because of near-universal satisfaction with the public transport system. Curitiba consequently enjoys Brazil's lowest rate of car drivership, uses one quarter less fuel per capita than other Brazilian cities, and has far cleaner air.

Curitiba's buses are privately owned by ten companies, which are managed by a quasi-public company. The bus companies receive no subsidies. Instead all the transit money collected goes into a central pool, and companies are then paid on a 'distance travelled' basis. Through this public-private collaboration, the city has combined public sector concerns about safety, accessibility and efficiency with private sector goals about low maintenance and operating costs. It is an astonishing achievement.

Diversion of water

Curitiba lies between two major rivers and contains five smaller ones. During the 1950s and 1960s flooding was a major problem, caused partly by migrants from rural areas settling in low-lying shanty towns. Lerner and his fellow-designers 'decided to switch from fighting flooding to exploiting the water, a gift of habitat' (*Natural Capitalism*, p.296). They diverted the water from lowlands into lakes, which became the central feature of new parks. Heavy rains no longer cause floods. Local residents say they just make the ducks float a metre higher on the lakes!

Planting of trees

'There is little in the architecture of a city that is more beautifully designed than a tree,' Lerner says. He provided 1,500 saplings for neighbourhoods to plant and look after. The city now has over 1,000 areas of woodland, one sixth of its total area. No one is allowed to cut down a tree without a permit. The trees play an invaluable role in keeping the air clean and reducing noise. They also provide a habitat for no less than 250 different types of bird in the city.

Recycling of waste

Curitiba's citizens separate their trash into two categories, organic and inorganic, for pick-up by two kinds of truck. Poor families in squatter settlements that are inaccessible by truck bring their garbage bags to neighbourhood centres. For each 60 kilograms of rubbish they earn 60 tickets, which can be exchanged for a month's food, bus tokens, school notebooks or whatever the family needs most. The rubbish goes to a plant, itself made of recycled materials, where marginalised people in society (e.g. the disabled, recent migrants and alcoholics) sort out the different types of waste. Materials that can be reused are then sold to local industries.

Even the buses, which occupy pride of place in Curitiba's transformation, are recycled. Some decommissioned buses are refitted and become mobile job-training centres. Others become clinics, classrooms, baby-sitting centres or soup kitchens.

Of course, Curitiba isn't perfect. No human city is. But most other cities on this planet could learn a lot from the way it has set about meeting its challenges – environmental challenges and related social challenges.

Let the last word on the subject rest with Lerner: 'There is no endeavour more noble than the attempt to achieve a collective dream. When a city accepts as a mandate its quality of life, when it respects the people who live in it, when it respects the environment, when it prepares for future generations, the people share the responsibility for that mandate, and this shared cause is the only way to achieve that collective dream.'

10

BUSINESS WITHOUT FRONTIERS:
THE GROWTH OF E-COMMERCE

Each day brings news of fresh developments with business on the internet, and Christians need to know how to respond. E-commerce (electronic commerce) is transforming relationships between companies, and between companies and customers.

While the term e-commerce refers to all online transactions, it's called B2B (business-to-business) when the customer is another company. B2C stands for business-to-customer and applies to any business or organization that sells its products or services to customers over the internet for their own use. When most people think of B2C e-commerce, they think of Amazon.com, the online bookseller. In addition to online retailers, B2C has grown to include services such as online banking, travel services, online auctions, health information and real estate sites.

E-commerce is also creating a three-way relationship among companies, suppliers and customers through the sharing of information in 'integrated value chains'. The growth of e-commerce promises, and delivers to some, astonishing wealth. It threatens the economic survival of others.

Mark of the Devil?

If, as I argue, the Bible has unexpected relevance to many aspects of business, from managing the supply chain to tackling corruption, what about the internet? Can veiled references be found within its pages? Mr A. Albert, a reader of *The Economist*, apparently thinks so. In a letter published on 22 January 2000, he suggests that the identity of the Antichrist in Revelation 13 has been revealed as the world wide web.

'The numeral six corresponds to the Hebrew letter "vav" or "waw", typically rendered as "w" in the Latin alphabet, so that www equals the Beast whose number is six hundred sixty and six,' he writes. The clincher for Albert is that the Beast 'causes all, both small and great, both rich and poor, both free and slave, to be marked on the right hand or the forehead; so that no one can buy or sell who does not have the mark, that is, the name of the beast or the number of its name' (Rev. 13:16-17). He says: 'The reference to a password to enter or purchase goods on the internet could not be more striking, and the unstoppable trend to trade on the net is starkly stated.'

Contemporary interpretations of the number 666 are rife. Here is one I found on the internet:

'The real name of Bill Gates is William Henry Gates III. By converting the letters of his current name to ASCII- values and adding his III, you get the following:

B	66
I	73
L	76
L	76
G	71
A	65
T	84
E	69
S	83
I	1
I	1
I	1

666

Is it any wonder that Bill Gates is so powerful?!'

I suspect that both Albert and the counter of the letters in Bill Gates' name make this connection with their tongues firmly in their cheeks. Even if they don't, I see little reason to take this line of interpretation seriously. Down the centuries, ingenious reasons have been put forward for identifying the beast of Revelation as numerous individuals, including Nero, Mohammed, various popes, Martin Luther and Napoleon to name just a few. All these personalised applications are almost certainly mistaken. The beast is best understood as false religion, anything that sets itself up in idolatry against God.

However, this merely opens up an important line of thinking about the internet. Some Christians would say the internet does have idolatrous pretensions – or, more precisely, that some of its enthusiastic champions make claims that come close to idolatry. There is mounting evidence that web surfing can be addictive. It threatens to become an all-consuming preoccupation, while alternative forms of consumption, entertainment or even doing business are seriously neglected. The internet has a seemingly infinite capacity, in the sense that there appears to be no physical limit to the number of websites that can exist in cyberspace. (I know there are currently problems with the availability of internet addresses, but that is not beyond the capacity of human ingenuity to solve.) Is there something alarming, sinister even, about this potential for indefinite expansion?

What is abundantly clear is that the internet has been the subject of a great deal of hype. It has been an arena for exaggerated claims, personal aggrandisement, and excitable behaviour. Nothing illustrates this better than the extraordinary way small internet companies, so-called 'dotcoms,' attracted such media attention and investor money for the best part of a year during 1999 and 2000.

A Hectic Dash for Riches

Peter Warburton, an economic researcher and forecaster, subjected this trend to a searching critique at a Ridley Hall

Foundation conference on *Business in Cyberspace* in June 2000. His paper was subsequently published as 'Golf courses on the Moon: is commercial investment in the internet doomed to disappoint?' in *Faith in Business Quarterly* (4:4, pp.3-8). I shall now reproduce the main lines of his argument, with adaptations of my own.

Originally conceived as a free public service, the internet has prompted a hectic dash for riches. This should not surprise us in the least. Throughout the course of history, human beings have sought to annex the rich endowment of the earth's resources for exclusive personal use and gain. Whether it be land, coastal access, fresh water, oil, gold, diamonds, uranium or timber, men have fought for control over valuable resources that cost them either nothing at all or merely the cost of collection or extraction.

Obviously, the internet is more like electricity than water in that it has taken a considerable research effort to develop the various hard and soft technologies underpinning its use. Most of this research was carried out by government-funded scientists and technologists. Access to the internet comes comparatively cheaply for those who benefit from their work. Warburton says: 'The internet is like a road bridge, originally funded by one group of taxpayers, that stretches across the globe. Every user must buy a roadworthy vehicle – a personal computer and a modem – but beyond this the financial costs are minimal' ('Golf courses', p.4). The marginal cost of access to the internet is the electricity used by the equipment and the rental cost of the communications access.

Along with the low cost of initial outlay, there are two main reasons why a massive diversion of financial resources to 'virtual' companies took place: the peculiar nature of the 'virtual' company and the changing nature of the capital markets.

The peculiar nature of the virtual company

There is nothing new under the sun. Long before the internet there were dreamers who persuaded others to back fanciful ideas or deliberate deceits with commitments of money. In a now-famous quote relating to the time of the South Sea Bubble

(1719-20), one new issue prospectus read: 'A company for carrying on an undertaking of great advantage, but nobody is to know what it is.' The intangibility of the internet presents an opportunity for the sale of false title that far exceeds that in the material world.

'In the physical world, there are mountains and valleys, wet places and dry places, river banks and estuaries, fertile plains and deserts, seams of valuable mineral deposits and so forth,' Warburton notes. With the physical world the potential for development can be objectively assessed. In cyberspace, there are no such distinguishing features: 'There is no landscape. Every place is like every other place. No pleasant streams, no fertile plains, no safe harbours – no locational benefits. Like the moon, only more so. This basic difference between the physical world and the virtual world is all-important for the capacity to establish a franchise and a corporate value. It opens up the opportunity for anyone to dream about building a golf course in cyberspace. There are no bad locations and no good ones. No one can lay hold of the best plot because there isn't a best plot. Cyberspace has infinite dimensions, therefore everyone can build their dream golf course without getting in each other's way' ('Golf courses', p.4).

A crucial question remains: Who will visit these courses and pay the full price of admission to play on them?

In the physical world, some locations clearly are better than others, like the shopping mall at the intersection of two major highways. It may be objected that something similar is possible in cyberspace, in the shape of hyperlinks and an internet company harbouring a close association with a popular brand. Well-known brands bring with them a comfort zone, a sense of familiarity, substance and quality. For a lesser known company, this might involve getting its trade name or logo on or near initial sign-on screens (e.g. Microsoft, Compuserve, AOL). This is rather like an advertising hoarding adjacent to a busy highway. Such advertising space is, however, likely to be expensive.

Nor are commercial secrets easily kept in cyberspace. Every website's construction is easily copied, and bright ideas stolen.

Ease of entry becomes a disadvantage if it gives rise to a host of competitors offering a similar product or service – too many, perhaps, for any to be successful.

Most dotcoms are intermediaries or distributors, combinations of a clearing-house and electronic mail-order system. They offer cheaper prices and have the effect of bypassing retailers or the middlemen on the ground, such as travel agents. The theory is that they can afford to do this because of their low overheads. If they attract sufficient business this will compensate for the discounts they are offering on price. The evidence so far is that they are failing to do so in sufficient volume. Although the public is doing an increasing amount of business online, most people are wedded to old-fashioned practices like seeing and handling the goods they wish to purchase, or having direct contact with an agent. At the time of writing the most successful internet company in terms of amassing market share, Amazon.com, is struggling to make a profit, even though it has over 18 million customers across 160 countries. Most virtual companies were set up on an assumption about changing market trends that was based more on hunch than solid market research.

The changing nature of the capital markets

Given the intangibility of virtual business, the obvious question is how internet companies found financial support so readily. The answer is four-fold.

First, investors seem to have been sucked into the belief that the internet is a revolutionary development, and that a brand new type of business with a different culture and corporate value system is required to capitalise on it. A new company that does this before a bigger company gets wise to the potential of e-commerce will provide rich rewards for the initial investors. And so they did, but only through buying and selling company shares as their value rocketed, not by making real profits.

Second, the hype surrounding the dotcoms had a curious effect. The financial tools used by analysts to value the condition and prospects of large profitable companies were jettisoned in the case of loss-making start-ups. For instance, the frequency of visits to a website became the arbiter of corporate success, rather than accounting profit or cash generated. 'Cut adrift from conventional measures of financial performance and value, internet investors are asked to believe in little more than a hypothesis about the future and the capability of the founders to secure a stake in it' ('Golf courses', p.6).

Third, the cultural upheaval in corporate fundraising opened a new door. Since the 1980s, commercial banks had lost their position as the dominant providers of loans to the corporate sector and been replaced by capital markets – bonds and equities. Instead of obtaining their initial borrowing from a bank or a venture capitalist, internet companies were financed by equity investors, principally through an Initial Public Offering (IPO) but sometimes through a private placing. This involves selling part of the equity owned by the founders of the company to a new group of investors, usually financial institutions or wealthy individuals. The cultural shift is significant for a number of reasons:

- the capital markets offer the opportunity for the founders to raise significant amounts of money from the sale of shares while retaining a majority shareholding
- the new shareholders will not have, and probably would not want, the closeness of relationship with the company's management that a bank or venture capital company would insist upon
- the degree of financial reporting and management accountability tends to be much less than if the company had borrowed from a bank.

Warburton makes a sharp contrast between traditional banking and today's commercial markets. 'The capital markets are to traditional banking what "free love" is to a faithful marriage. There is accountability in both, in the latter it is continuous and in the former discontinuous. The bank says: obey the rules; pay the interest and repay the loan when it falls due. Tell us if you have problems as soon as they occur; we'll try to work out a way to help. The capital market says: there are no rules. Pursue your business plan. Dream your dreams and be successful. Don't tell us your problems; we don't want to know. Just deliver on your business plan, or else' ('Golf courses', p.7).

Fourth, part of the answer lies in the way that institutional fund management has developed in recent years to favour stock market index-tracking. This is a passive style of investment that seeks only to follow an industry benchmark regardless of the merits of the constituent companies. A saying of Jesus comes readily to mind: '... If one blind person guides another, both will fall into a pit.' (Mt. 15:14)

The lack of attention to detail, of ongoing accountability and supervision is a key element in the successes and failures of the capital markets. They offer the freedom for creative talents to thrive and prosper, but also the potential for colossal errors of judgment to pass unnoticed. Of course, sooner or later, the errors are noticed and share prices can then rocket downwards as quickly as they spiralled upwards. This is what happened to many of the dotcoms in the second half of 2000.

What all this amounts to, in Warburton's analysis, is a situation where excitement for gain (greed), *plus* a lack of reliable information, *plus* a cultural shift in access to capital, *plus* slavish index-tracking behaviour by investors equals an ample supply of risk capital. At the height of dotcom mania in early 2000 this produced the absurd situation where the much-celebrated lastminute.com when it floated its shares was more highly valued than Whitbread plc, the pub and leisure company. This was despite the fact that Whitbread had a higher annual turnover in one of its pubs than the whole of lastminute.com.

The unseen cost of investment opportunities foregone

Some readers may say: why worry about all this? What happened was just a blip in the capital markets. The preoccupation with investing money in internet companies was only a short-lived craze, and investors soon realised their mistake and put their money – the public's money – elsewhere. They now realise it may never be possible to derive enough revenue to achieve commercial viability for more than a few select companies. Yet the episode remains one that arouses serious concern for two reasons.

First, for the best part of a year there was a major global reallocation of financial resources, particularly in the USA and UK. Both established and emerging companies, which harboured far more solid long-term prospects in comparison to the dotcoms, were starved of investment capital.

Warburton says: 'The cost of the internet investment mania lies in the opportunities foregone. The forced contraction of healthy businesses deemed to be offering too low a rate of return, together with the unnecessary shedding of jobs in these industries. The starvation of access to capital for offline businesses in need of replacement fixed assets' ('Golf courses', p.8). The internet companies borrowed real money; they used real resources for which profitable uses existed.

Second, the episode revealed poor judgment by those who handle large-scale investment. Entrepreneurs profited; typical policyholders in pension and insurance funds missed out. Members of the public have entrusted the care of their money into the hands of others, and they have the right to expect better.

From a Christian perspective, the key issue is again that of stewardship. Managers of investment funds are stewards, whether they like that description or not. Investing capital will never be risk-free, but it befits those who deal with other people's money to do so in a judicious and responsible manner, coming to an independent judgment rather than slavishly following trends. St Paul used the concept of stewardship when chiding the Corinthians, a church that displayed a comparable shallowness: 'Think of us in this way, as servants of Christ and stewards of God's mysteries. Moreover it is required of stewards that they should be found trustworthy.' (1 Cor. 4:1-2) By 'mysteries' he probably meant the gospel message that God is wanting to reveal to people.

What applies to handling the fundamental truths about God and the human condition also applies to investing people's money: a proper concern, both for faithfulness and fruitfulness, is called for. And just as church members need to be on their guard against false teaching, so fund managers need to be alert to those whom Warburton calls 'rogues, fraudsters, charlatans and hopeless romantics, most of whom are not capable of building or sustaining a viable and honest business' ('Golf courses', p.4). The relevant Pauline passage here is Eph. 4:14: 'We must no longer be children, tossed to and fro and blown about by every wind of doctrine, by people's trickery, by their craftiness in deceitful scheming.'

Paradoxes of Power

While the dotcom phenomenon ended sooner than was expected, we would be mistaken to conclude that the internet's impact on business, or vice-versa, is insignificant. Trends of rather more lasting significance can be found elsewhere – in some notable shifts of power – and have a paradoxical character.

A visit to www.cluetrain.com reveals something called The Cluetrain Manifesto. Like Martin Luther, the framers of the manifesto came up with 95 theses. Presumably the choice of number reveals a rudimentary knowledge of church history on the part of the authors. Here is a sample.

- Markets are conversations. (No.1)
- The internet is enabling conversations among human beings that were simply not possible in the era of mass media. (No.6)
- People in networked markets have figured out that they get far better information and support from another than from vendors. So much for corporate rhetoric about adding value to commoditised products. (No.11)
- Already companies that speak in the language of the pitch, the dog-and-pony show, are no longer speaking to anyone. (No.16)
- Companies need to lighten up and take themselves less seriously. They need to get a sense of humour. (No.21)

The Cluetrain Manifesto is also a book which grew out of the manifesto. Authors Rick Levine, Christopher Locke, Doc Searls and David Weinberger are American internet enthusiasts – two of them journalists, two with corporate experience. Essentially, it's a panoply of praise about the world wide web. They say: 'The web isn't primarily a medium for information, marketing or sales. It's a world in which people meet, talk, build, fight, love and play. In fact, the web world is bigger than the business world and is swallowing the business world whole. The vague rumblings you're hearing are the sounds of digestion' (p.120). This gives a good idea of the style in which the book is written.

Although *The Cluetrain Manifesto* sounds anti-business, the authors claim it's not: 'Business is just a word for buying and selling things. In one way or another, we all rely on this commerce, both to get the things we want or need, and to afford them. We are alternately the workers who create products and services, and the customers who purchase them. There is nothing inherently wrong with this set-up' (p.9). What they are passionately against is the way companies typically communicate with the public, the language of marketing and public relations. Much of what passes for corporate communication is so diluted, edited, packaged and targeted that any hints of real-life conversation are lost. Levine et al. bemoan the fact that most corporate websites look like brochures. Visitors have to click through screen after screen of 'fatuous self-praise' to find the few bits of useful information they really want. At least printed brochures don't take that long to download.

The Cluetrain Manifesto says such companies will have, and are having, to think again. The internet has recreated what existed over 200 years ago, before the era of industry and big business, markets where customers speak to each other. The internet is a place where people can talk to each other without constraint, without filters, censorship, official sanctioning, and – most significantly – without advertising. They communicate in a language that is natural, open, honest, direct, funny and often shocking. Among other things, they talk about the products and services on offer from the business world. They compare experiences, prices and opinions, bypassing the corporate spiel to distinguish the good deals from the bad. What is more, many corporate employees are joining in the conversations, in an unofficial capacity. The authors call for companies to join this exercise in authentic conversation. 'Marketing isn't going to go away. Nor should it. But it needs to evolve, rapidly and thoroughly, for markets have become networked and now know more than business, learn faster than business, are more honest than business, and are a hell of a lot more fun than business' (p.113). And in this, market expectations are solidly wedded to internet performance such as the availability of a software product for downloading or the security of a transaction in making a purchase.

Clearly, the authors are on to something important. Supportive or subversive messages can be broadcast to a vast audience, at the click of a mouse. Some companies have got wise to the possibilities and have developed websites that are genuinely interactive. Shell and BP (as mentioned on pages 46-7) are notable examples, displaying a level of transparency and engagement with their critics that was unimaginable ten years ago. Christians concerned with issues of truthfulness and transparency should surely applaud such developments.

Through being able to communicate easily, members of the public who have never met each other can play a useful role in each other's lives. The authors aptly illustrate this with an internet newsgroup where posting of sequential messages about the cost and quality of service received from a particular car manufacturer left everyone who took part a little bit wiser at the end.

Books like *The Cluetrain Manifesto* emphasise the power the internet puts in the hands of the ordinary person. (This assumes, of course, that he or she can afford to use the net – and though there is some cause for saying the net is socially exclusive, the numbers who are included increase all the time.) Anyone can create a website, enrol in a chat-room, and express their views. The internet makes for a more participative democracy, not just in a political sense – where it has clearly assisted the mobilisation of pressure-groups – but in a commercial sense in enabling a more varied input to the choices people make in the global marketplace.

The internet also provides small companies that cannot afford big marketing budgets a low-cost way to publicise their goods and services. Although it is obviously true that the more financial resources a company has at its disposal, the more it can spend on making a website look impressive, the overall effect is a levelling out of marketing penetration between companies. Let us not underestimate the empowering effects of the electronic revolution.

The contrasting trend about power on the net was highlighted at the conference by Simon Kershaw, who has worked in the computer software industry for the last 20 years. His paper was subsequently condensed into a short article, titled 'Monopoly and Competition: Power Concentration on the Net', and published in Vol.4:4 of *Faith in Business Quarterly*.

Kershaw recalled that the internet did not begin life as a commercial operation. It started in the Cold War atmosphere of the late 1960s, when the US Department of Defense wanted a computer network that had no central computer on which the rest of the network depended so that the network would survive the destruction of any particular computer. Because much of the system was implemented in the DoD by computer science graduates at American universities, it is not surprising that a parallel form was then developed for the academic community, networking universities, which became known as the internet. Military and academic uses therefore pre-date commercial use of the internet by nearly two decades. When companies got involved in the 1980s, they initially developed distinctive networks. Apple's eWorld and Microsoft's MSN, for instance, were both developed as independent networks unconnected to each other or to the internet. It is interesting that it was not until 1995 that Microsoft accepted that its own network would not prevail. Then the sleeping giant awoke. Microsoft changed tack and went for the internet in a big way. It's the establishment of one public internet that is potentially open to anyone that has created the potential for vast commercial use.

Among the big companies to have benefited from this, the corporations at the forefront of internet technology naturally loom largest. A few companies have pulled off a formidable concentration of power.

- *Cisco Systems* – founded in 1984, doubled in size every year afterwards until 1999, had revenues of $22 billion and profits of $3 billion in 2001, and was briefly the world's biggest company in terms of market capitalisation. Cisco makes routers, the devices that route data traffic from one computer to another, deciding on the best and quickest route around a network. They are the hardware building blocks of the internet. At the time of writing, Cisco has about two-thirds of the router market. Thus far it has kept a comparatively low profile, and has taken care to stay on the right side of the US regulatory authorities. Despite some recent setbacks, it is very ambitious
- *Microsoft* – embroiled in a long-running dispute with the American legal system over alleged abuse of power. Microsoft has always had a much higher profile than Cisco, not least because the firm's chairman, Bill Gates, courts publicity. Microsoft was already a big business by 1995 but became huge on the back of the internet. Its crucial change in strategy was to develop a browser – Internet Explorer, which has gradually eclipsed Mark Andreessen's Netscape – and to 'bundle' this with its Windows operating system. More generally, Microsoft has used its immense purchasing power to buy up many internet content providers as well as operating systems and software applications. Most people who buy a PC these days buy a host of Microsoft products with it. It was the bundling of Windows 98 and Internet Explorer that provoked anti-trust action, the outcome of which remains uncertain. In April 2001, Judge Thomas Penfield Jackson found Microsoft guilty of violating sections of the 1899 Sherman Anti-Trust Act, and of using its dominant industry position to monopolise the web-browser market. Three months later, a federal appeals court reversed his decision, though it did not exonerate the

company on all counts. There is certainly no sign that Microsoft's days of internet domination are over. Even if the company does end up being broken into two, each half would comprise a very powerful company in its own right. In the meantime, Microsoft continues to harness formidable talent, wield immense influence, and post record profits every year – even with a slowdown in the US economy

● *America Online (AOL)* – the internet service provider (ISP) that acquired Compuserve and Netscape in 1998, provides access to the internet in many countries for 20 million subscribers. In January 2000, AOL announced its merger with TimeWarner. This merger created a global media company, uniting the roles of access provider and content provider. These had previously been provided separately, and the concern is how the access provider uses content from the other part of the company. Will AOL, for instance, give what some might consider a disproportionate amount of space to entertainment and film rather than education and information? A large corporation may be able to control access by driving out smaller ISPs, and control popular content by owning most of it. Kershaw says: 'It is interesting that Rupert Murdoch, no stranger to the world of media power, and not usually thought of as a small business person, commented on the AOL/Time Warner merger by saying: "A lot of us used to be big fish in a small pond; now we are all minnows with two huge sharks" – the other shark being Microsoft.'

The jury is still out on what all this means for the consumer. Traditionally, a concentration of economic power that creates a monopoly or near-monopoly situation is seen as bad for the public – because lack of competition pushes up prices and inhibits technological advance. In the case of Cisco and Microsoft, the former is a real danger but the latter less so because innovation seems to be the air these giants breathe. With enlightened leadership at the helm, they have the potential to do much good, providing the internet with an infrastructure of products and services that make it easy

– even pleasurable – to use. But history teaches us to beware the corrupting tendency of power, and so does Christian theology. Sinful that we are, sooner or later the capacity for self-regulation breaks down and the resulting abuse of power means external sanctions have to be put in place.

So the internet demonstrates power at its most paradoxical. Anarchy of a sort reigns. The ordinary person and the little company can make their presence felt in a way that was hitherto rare. But their ability to communicate – to inform of their products, to express their opinions, to delight and to irritate – happens by permission of companies that are building up colossal market domination, presided over by the wealthiest chief executives and chairmen in the world. The irony of this seems lost on many internet enthusiasts.

Privacy

The tension between internal freedom and external control erupts in another major issue raised by the internet, personal privacy. Wherever we go, we leave a trail behind us of bits and pieces of information about ourselves that others are more interested in than we might realise. This is especially true of our purchasing habits. The collation and analysis of information makes possible some very precise targeting of customers. Tesco has staff who study your Club Card spending. From the pattern of purchases over an extended period they can learn quite a lot about you, such as the age of your children, whether you're a vegetarian, and your drinking habits. You may then be targeted with special discount vouchers. Similarly, how supermarkets are laid out – the location, order and proximity of products in relation to each other – is no accident. The optimum lay-outs are based on very careful research. The groups of products we typically buy are spread throughout the store, making it difficult for us to go through a full shopping list without making an entire tour of the place, and being enticed by various other goodies along the way. Once we start purchasing on the internet, the scope for consumer analysis, and a suitably worked out marketing response, is taken a stage further.

In the past, information on people was kept mainly on paper. This restricted how much data was stored and for how long. Because of the shortage of space, periodic clear-outs of paper took place. Digital technology is creating a radically different situation. Simon Peyton-Jones, a Microsoft researcher who spoke at our conference, explained why.

- Many of our everyday activities create permanent records. Every phone call, credit card transaction, e-mail, trip to the supermarket, bank transaction and visit to the doctor leaves behind an electronic digital trail
- Storing these records is extremely cheap. Indeed, computer disk storage is already so advanced that it is entirely feasible to keep all records for ever. A small laptop computer with 20 gigabytes of disk space is able to store 10,000 books of 1,000 pages each. Large centralised computers can store very much more
- Digital records are accessible from afar. Online digital records can be accessed over the internet without going near the organisation that holds the records. Responsible organisations go to considerable lengths to comply with the Data Protection Act and prevent unauthorised access to their records, but such chains are only as strong as their weakest link. Determined data-gatherers are extremely difficult to stop.

'In short, while privacy is not yet dead, there has been a shift in the quality and degree of privacy that we can take for granted,' Peyton-Jones said.

There are several dimensions to the privacy issue.

First, there is the increased amount of information being put in the hands of the marketers. As the Church of England report *Cybernauts Awake!* points out, websites log the host from which each page was requested, making it possible to identify who is reading what parts of the site. This not only allows an online bookstore, for example, to track which books you are buying, but also those which you are considering buying. Sophisticated software fits us into groups through the use of 'automated inference models'. Our digital trails can therefore result in us being targeted with special offers, based on the picture of our lives and particular interests that researchers are able to build up. How we respond to this will vary. Some people are glad of a personalised approach, in preference to the highly random marketing that results in being bombarded with all sorts of mail (postal and electronic) we regard as junk. Others feel highly uneasy about a marketing person they don't know who apparently knows so much about them – especially if the 'identikit' picture that is created is then sold by one company to another.

Second, the information may be incorrect. This is not just a matter of false implications being inferred from our trail. Data may be incorrectly entered into the computer, or errors perpetrated and perpetuated in the act of copying. At home, we receive a lot of unsolicited mail with basic details that are incorrect (e.g. my wife went through a phase of receiving material from several charities that addressed her as Hillinson, rather than Higginson) and this shows how readily erroneous information is passed on. The effects can be serious. A wrong postal code could affect our chances of getting our house insured. There are also cases of deliberate identity theft, where someone discovers some important piece of personal data (like your credit card number) and spends money in your name. Not only does this bring immediate financial loss. It also contributes false information to your 'data shadow'.

Third, companies have the means to exercise internal surveillance, checking that staff are not misusing e-mail or the internet. There are cases of employees being disciplined for spending hours visiting pornographic sites when they should have been working. The private space we think we inhabit when clicking away on a computer is actually open territory that an employer can enter at any time he is so inclined or has a reason to check up on us. Opinion at the conference was divided about this. For some privacy is a self-evident good, a 'right' we all obviously have, so any invasion of personal liberty is hard to justify. Others put much greater store by sharing and transparency, and believe that only people with something to hide need be worried about the loss of privacy represented by employer surveillance. Employees who use equipment for legitimate purposes are unlikely to be objects of suspicion. In fact, some of the tension between these positions can be resolved if the company is open with its employees that it reserves the right to investigate. Many employers use contracts that include regulations on use of the organisation's equipment and resources, and which assert rights of access to all communications where the employee is representing the company.

The forces responsible for law and order may exercise powers of surveillance in cyberspace. When Neil and Christine Hamilton were accused of sexual assault in August 2001, the police investigation extended to their e-mails. The relevant UK legislation (passed without much public attention in 2000) gives far-reaching investigatory powers to the police and secret service that include the requirement to hand over encryption keys if requested. Cryptography uses the keys to ensure allegedly untappable and unforgeable communication, thereby offering the potential for dramatically increased privacy.

Privacy is a serious moral issue, and the internet clearly poses new threats to privacy. I believe Christians should care about this, but it is an issue on which they need to steer their way carefully. The emphasis should not be so much on protecting personal rights as protecting the vulnerable.

So, to begin with, exalted claims for the good of privacy should be resisted. Too much privacy is unhealthy for us. In *Information Technology and Cyberspace*, David Pullinger (another conference contributor) points out: 'Absolute privacy – solitary confinement – remains one of the ultimate punishments' (p.104). Turned in on ourselves, without a requirement of public accountability, temptations to go astray run rife. But God sees what we do in secret. Jesus speaks of an ultimate accountability before him: '... for nothing is covered up that will not be uncovered, and nothing secret that will not become known.'

(Mt. 10:26) This need not necessarily be something to fear: total exposure can also be the hallmark of love. Are we not all naked before God?

Yes, one day we shall be naked before God, and there is a nakedness before each other (emotional as well as physical) that is also characteristic of our most intimate relationships on earth. But Peyton-Jones makes a telling point: 'Voluntary self-disclosure is fundamental to relationship. We measure the depth of our relationship with someone at least partly by what we are prepared to tell them about ourselves. Loss of privacy constitutes involuntary disclosure, which strikes at relationship. We may be naked before God, but we are not, and should not be, naked before each other, except when we choose to be' ('Privacy in Cyberspace', p.11).

Those of us who live a relatively privileged existence and have no particular secrets may feel quite relaxed over what we reveal about ourselves through use of the internet, but there are some who live a more perilous existence. Political refugees may need to create new personal identities for their own safety. Battered wives can be under threat if their whereabouts are discovered. People with a genetic predisposition for illness find it difficult to get insured if the full facts about their condition are known. Special measures may be necessary to protect individuals who are particularly vulnerable from those who roam the internet with malicious intent.

In addition, the value of *forgiveness* has a peculiar relevance in this context. When mistakes have been made and resources misused, should that stain stay on someone's record for ever? Is it appropriate that every visit to an inappropriate website should be registered and the data kept indefinitely? In many areas of our legal system there is scope for 'wiping the record clean' after a number of years. There is a case for doing the same thing with electronic records. Cyberspace has the capacity for perpetual memory, but as *Cybernauts Awake!* observes, it 'gives the potential for perfect forgetfulness, too; information could disappear without trace' (p.72). Hoarding detailed information about people going back years upon years shows an unwillingness to let people repent of their past and move on to better things. Technology gives us an awesome capacity for storing data, but it would be good for society to agree on appropriate time limits for keeping different types of information.

Business to Business

In the long run, B2B transactions over the internet are likely to prove even more significant than the transformation taking place in the way business relates to customers. Sophisticated systems can integrate information from customers, suppliers and other key partners. Processes and logistics are largely automated, creating a seamless chain of communications that delivers unprecedented standards of customer service – or so the patter goes.

Of course, the exchange of electronic data in business has been going on for some time. But because it involved proprietary hardware, bespoke software and non-standard protocols, and companies often differ in what they use, making it work effectively proved difficult. For many small suppliers it was an expensive headache. In contrast, the internet is a ready-made public system for electronic data interchange, with low-cost hardware and standard off-the-shelf software that is constantly being updated.

In a fully integrated internet supply chain, the idea is that everyone has relevant access to each other's prices, stock lists, dispatch times and delivery dates. By having access to more accurate information, companies are able to cut inventory and generally take inefficiencies out of the system. Purchasing orders are made much more quickly, saving on the dozens of faxes and the many meetings previously involved in their processing. The industry that sees most scope for generating huge savings is the car industry, not least because of its long and complex supply chain.

The internet gives a further twist to the issues of trust and power, highlighted in our discussion of managing the supply chain in Chapter 4. One observer has described integrated supply chains over the internet as a device 'to beat the hell out of suppliers' (*The Economist*, 4 March 2000, p.85). General Motors, Ford and DaimlerChrysler have joined forces to create the world's largest 'virtual' market, buying $240 billion worth of parts from tens of thousands of suppliers. One can well imagine many thousands of suppliers feeling apprehensive in the face of such formidable purchasing power. Many suppliers would rather their customers did not know everything there is to be known about their companies. They fear a resulting pressure on their profit margins. The possible gain to suppliers is that they too may be able to increase their power by joint action. By having access to more accurate information, particularly about future customer demand, they should be able to plan ahead better and tailor their inventory to what is required, thereby reducing their costs. In all this it needs to be remembered that the middle tier in the chain acts as *both* supplier *and* customer, posing the familiar ethical conundrum of whether they do to others as they wish that others do unto them.

It remains to be seen to what extent integrated supply chains become a reality. Interestingly the Japanese car manufacturers, who were at the forefront of the lean supply movement, are holding back on using the internet in this way. They are waiting to see how it works out for General Motors, Ford and company. One widespread concern is how secure such systems will be. There are fears of industrial espionage, that other companies – or just inquisitive hackers, who remain the scourge of the whole IT phenomenon – will infiltrate the system and discover sensitive commercial knowledge. Even more fundamental than the technical aspects, however, is the issue of trust between companies. As we saw in Chapter 4, moving from a low-trust to a high-trust culture is a slow process, and this may make progress on the level of internet integration slower than those who think only in terms of solving the technical problems imagine.

The B2B Analyst is a newsletter published weekly on the internet. Its 23 June 2000 newsletter says: 'In B2B e-commerce, "trust" is often a core principle in the mission statement for marketplace and exchanges. The challenge is that creating trust early on has little to do with being "e" or electronic. And everything to do with "p" for people, as significant human capital is required to stimulate and support "online" activity.' In other words, before businesspeople enter into deals and share sensitive information over the net, they like to know who they're dealing with. They like to experience the feel of a handshake, see the look in the other person's eye and hear the tone of their voice. There is still no substitute for a face-to-face relationship. The sharing of electronic information is an inadequate basis for trust.

Some commentators – including Christian commentators – are concerned that cyberspace is accelerating a breakdown in face-to-face communication, that relationships are becoming disembodied and impersonal. David Lyon, in an article in *Third Way*, bemoans this. Whereas a letter offers idiosyncratic handwriting, and a voice on the phone is modulated, e-mail is abstracted from the sender's bodily presence in an unprecedented way, Lyon says. He believes that cyberspace offers escape from reality, which has everything to do with the marvellous yet messy interaction of embodied persons. There may be some people of whom this is true: those, for instance, who use e-mail to excess, for whom it seems to have supplanted other forms of communication. But on the whole I think this danger is exaggerated. Many people's experience of e-mail, including my own, is that it has enabled us to keep in regular touch with a larger number of people than used to be the case – yet not at the expense of meeting with them. Rather, when the meeting takes place, it is possible to go further in the conversation more quickly on the basis of what has already been shared. The journal I co-edit, *Faith in Business Quarterly*, is a good example of this. There are four editors who live in different parts of the country. Most of our collaborative editorial work is done by e-mail, but we still find it invaluable to meet together once every three months – with much of the routine stuff having been done beforehand.

What is true of a small business venture like ours also applies on a much larger scale. Communication over the internet can perform many useful functions, including the sharing of ideas and especially the collation of information. But face-to-face meetings do something different. They generate the friendships – or at least the fundamental trust and respect – out of which business deals are made. Research shows they are also much more likely to resolve disagreements than are electronic exchanges. The internet may reduce the amount of direct human interaction in business, but it will not eradicate it. God has made us in such a way that we will continue to want to meet and need to meet.

Beauty and Terror

The range of important issues thrown up by the internet is very considerable. Because of its comparative novelty, there is still a sense of coming to terms with what they are and the Christian mind is therefore less formed in this area than on some of the other topics discussed in this book. It is certainly important to widen the area of discussion beyond pornography – which, to hear some Christians of limited horizons talk, one might think the only ethical issue of significance about the internet.

Nevertheless, pornography is worth a mention, for two reasons. Pornography is big business on the internet. The number of sites is said to run into six figures. To sample their wares in detail one has to declare oneself over 18 and not offended by such material, and pay out significant money, but there are plenty of salacious 'taster' sites which can be accessed by anyone. The significance of pornography on the net is not that it introduces a different, more hard-core type of material than has hitherto existed; it is comparable with what is found elsewhere. The concern rather is that pornography has become so accessible. Because access is only two or three clicks away, it may become a temptation to the private individual who would never take a magazine down from a top shelf or darken the doors of a sex shop. For those who do find this a serious temptation (and let's not pretend this is just a problem for children – there are adults who are addicted to pornography) the best answer is probably to use a software screener, such as SurfontheSafeside.com.

Pornography is also symptomatic of a wider phenomenon: the use of the internet for unsavoury purposes. John Naughton, author of *A Brief History of the Future: The origins of the internet*, says, 'The net gives racists, paedophiles and pornographers a distribution system beyond their wildest dreams' (p.45). One could throw Satanists into that list as well. But by the same token, he points out, it also 'gives freedom of speech its biggest boost since the US Constitution got its First Amendment.' I think Naughton gets the balance right when he says of the internet: 'A terrible beauty is born.' This is a phrase from W.B. Yeats' poem *Easter 1916*, and refers to the resurgence of Irish nationalism which followed an armed uprising against British rule on Easter Monday of that year. A terrible beauty is born. Like all powerful technologies, there lies within the internet an immense capacity for both good and evil. It is true of nuclear power. It is true of the internet.

So cyberspace has its aspects of terror. But it also contains a very real beauty. There is beauty in the way it facilitates communication, provides information and provokes some highly artistic creations. Certain websites, including some commercial ones, are a genuine pleasure to behold. The internet brings more people into contact with each other, opens up fresh markets, provides new job opportunities and encourages the entrepreneurial spirit.

All Things Are Yours

'So let no one boast about human leaders. For all things are yours, whether Paul or Apollos or Cephas or the world or life or death or the present or the future – all belong to you, and you belong to Christ, and Christ belongs to God.' (1 Cor. 3:21-23)

The context of this passage is the tendency of the Christians at Corinth to split into parties, identifying themselves strongly with different Christian leaders. Back in 1·12 Paul complains that they say 'I belong to Paul' or 'I belong to Apollos' or 'I belong to Cephas' or even 'I belong to Christ' – as if Jesus were a leader to be ranked alongside the others. There are, of course, equivalents in the world of information technology: for Paul read Bill Gates or Microsoft, for Apollos read Apple, for Cephas read Netscape or AOL. Very strong allegiances can develop to internet companies or the hardware, software or operating systems that service them. The Corinthians were boasting about their party allegiances, whereas Paul would far rather they boasted about the cross of Christ – the cross which he describes as the foolishness of God, wiser than the wisdom of men. Paul, Apollos and Peter are simply servants whom the Lord used to bring Christians at Corinth to faith (3:5). Summing up his argument, Paul says, 'So let no one boast about human leaders.' Christian leaders are to be received with appreciation (they are gifts from God to his church) but they are not to be adulated, nor to be put on unrealistic pedestals: that is good neither for them nor for the Christians who idolise them. Paul makes a remarkable statement in 3:21-22: '... all things are yours, whether Paul or Apollos or Cephas'. Leaders actually belong to their congregations, not vice-versa – a clear support, perhaps, for a view of leadership which inverts the traditional pyramid and supports the rest of the organisation.

But then Paul does an even more remarkable thing. He broadens out his list to include not just Christian leaders, but *all things*: the world, life, death, the present, the future. Gordon Fee in his commentary on 1 Corinthians says: 'These five items are the ultimate tyrannies of human existence, to which people are in lifelong bondage as slaves. For Paul the death and resurrection of Jesus marked the turning of the ages in such a way that nothing lies outside Christ's jurisdiction' (*The First Epistle to the Corinthians*, p.154). Christ is Lord of the world, not just the church. That is the clear message of other passages in Paul such as Colossians 1:16-17, where he says that Christ is 'before all things, and in him all things hold together'; 'for in him all things in heaven and on earth were created, things visible and invisible, whether thrones or dominions or rulers or powers – all things have been created through him and him.' Paul is describing the great cosmic forces of his age, and saying that all of them are ultimately under the authority of Jesus Christ. All of them find their true meaning and fulfilment when they are subject to him. And if Paul had been alive today, what might he have included among the great cosmic forces of our age? He might well have included the global market economy. He might well have included the world wide web.

Let's return to 1 Corinthians 3. If we really believe that 'all things are ours', that they belong to us, and we in turn belong to Christ, as Christ belongs to God, what might the implications be? We would be a lot more confident, much less fearful, about the way we face this world of ours. I say 'of ours' because that's what Paul says: 'All belong to you.' Christians should be people who grasp opportunities, and are known as such, not as those who shrink back in a state of timidity. There are too many shrinking violets in the church, not enough bold entrepreneurs. Maybe it's significant that I have never heard a sermon preached on this verse: the implications are too radical. But I have read a sermon on it, by Paul Tillich. Tillich says: 'Paul's courage in affirming everything given, his openness towards the world, his sovereignty towards life should put to shame each of us as well as all our churches. We are afraid to accept what is given to us; we are in compulsive self-seclusion towards our world, we try to escape life instead of controlling it. We do not behave as if everything were ours … . The reason for this is that we and our churches do not know as Paul did what it means to be Christ's and because of being Christ's, to be God's' (*The Boundaries of Our Being*, p.235). Challenging words, and we do well to ponder them.

My exhortation to the conference delegates in my parting message was that we should have a positive and determined frame of mind, taking Paul's words from 1 Corinthians 3 to heart. Cyberspace is ours. Like everything else, it belongs to God, and should be claimed for him – not just in the sense of proliferating Christian websites, though there is a place for that – but in the way Christians do business on the internet.

The internet should not be left to those who prey on weak and unsuspecting people and manipulate them mercilessly. The internet should be used responsibly, imaginatively, with a view to serving our fellow-humanity, and bringing glory to God.

11

INFLUENCING ORGANISATIONS FOR GOOD:
THE ROLE OF THE CONSULTANT

Today it sometimes seems as if the world is awash with consultants. In every organisational sector, consultants are on hand to offer advice – for a suitable fee. Even churches, dioceses and religious organisations are beginning to use them. During a two-year stint as president of the Cambridge Theological Federation, I was responsible for bringing in a consultant.

Consultants are fond of telling jokes at their own expense. Here is my favourite:

A shepherd is herding his flock in a remote pasture when suddenly a brand new Range Rover advances out of a dust cloud towards him. The driver, a young man in an Armani suit, Gucci shoes, Ray-Ban sunglasses and a Hermes tie leans out of the window and asks the shepherd: 'If I can tell you exactly how many sheep you have in your flock, will you give me one?'

The shepherd looks at the young man, then at his peacefully grazing flock and calmly answers, 'Sure!' The yuppie parks the car, whips out his notebook, connects it to a cellphone, surfs to a NASA page on the internet where he calls up a GPS satellite navigation system, scans the area, opens up a database and some thirty spreadsheets with complex formulae. Finally he prints out a 10-page report on his hi-tech miniaturised printer, turns round to the shepherd and says: 'You have here exactly 1,586 sheep!'

'That is correct. As agreed, you can take one of the sheep,' the shepherd says. He watches the young man make a selection and bundle it in his Range Rover. Then he says: 'If I can tell you exactly what your business is, will you give me my sheep back?'

'Okay, why not?' the young man answers.

'You're a consultant,' the shepherd says.

'That is correct,' the yuppie says. 'How did you guess?'

'Easy,' the shepherd replies. 'You turn up here although nobody called you. You want to be paid for the answer to a question I already knew the answer to. And you don't know anything about my business, because even now my dog is trying to get out of the back of your Range Rover!'

Origin of Consultants

The origins of management consultancy can be traced back to the 1890s, to Frederick W. Taylor and the start of the scientific management movement. Management consultants have been around in significant numbers for over sixty years. In the Second World War, consultancy was sufficiently important to be a reserved occupation. Paul Batchelor, a senior consultant with PricewaterhouseCoopers, says that even in the early post-war years consultants provoked powerful polarised reactions.

The positive image was the epitome of the Protestant work ethic, summed up as:

- Meticulous, hard-working, driving for success
- Able to bring fresh perspectives and generating a stream of ideas
- Constantly rooting out waste, raising productivity and cutting costs.

The negative image was that of corporate leeches, with consultants therefore seen as:

- Ruthless, fear-inducing
- Inhuman
- Management lackies.

These two images are still around, Batchelor says, as a long-standing early legacy.

Consultancy firms flourished during the boom years of 1955-70, suffered with the rest of industry during the 1970s, but have been operating on 'all systems go' with a few hiccups since 1980. Many of the largest consulting firms are specialist divisions of accountancy firms, or spin-offs from them. The nature of accountancy is that it entails advisory work. There is a natural progression from accounting and costing to giving advice to troubled companies on capital reconstruction and financial management. During the 1960s, accountancy firms started to cast their consulting brief wider, as managers needed help in such areas as production planning and control, sales and marketing, and recruitment. Then there was the arrival of the computer age. It has been said that most British consulting firms were poorly equipped for the impact of computerisation, but the typical manager knew even less about it – a situation consultants were quick to exploit. Andersen Consulting (now called Accouture), an offshoot of ill-fated accountants Arthur Andersen, has made advising on information technology a particular speciality.

The large consultancy firms are immensely prosperous. Some have exalted reputations. No consulting firm carries more weight in corporate boardrooms than McKinsey & Co. – it works with 750 of the world's 1,000 largest companies. Its stated goal (though not loudly trumpeted; that is not the McKinsey style) is to play an influential role in every significant economy in the world. McKinsey consultants are characterised by intellectual vigour, zealous dedication to their work, and adherence to a set of clearly defined values. Many have gone on to occupy top corporate posts, especially in the USA.

Questions Asked About Consultants

Not everyone is impressed by the big consultancy firms, however. Thomas O'Shea and Charles Madigan subject the industry to a critical appraisal in *Dangerous Company: The Consulting Powerhouses and the Businesses they Save and Ruin*. (It is not, however, a totally condemning view.) Most of the case studies the pair of journalists examine are American, but since the consulting firms they consider are international their findings have a wider relevance. They raise several searching questions in their book.

Do consultants provide value for money?
In short, does using a consultancy firm actually lead to an improvement in corporate performance? The answer, as you might expect, varies enormously. O'Shea and Madigan certainly point to some spectacular examples where the money does not seem to have been well spent. During the early 1990s, AT&T paid a variety of consulting firms (mostly four major ones) nearly half a billion dollars for the benefit of their advice. At the end of that process, most analysts agree, AT&T was as confused in its corporate strategy as it had been at the beginning, having tried a number of different ideas, none of which were notably successful. Over the same half-decade, Figgie International spent more than $75 million on consultants. Sales plummeted from $1.3 billion to $319 million; profits of $63 million became losses of $166 million; and the workforce of 17,000 shrank to 6,000. Perhaps not surprisingly, the firm refused to pay the consultancy firms many of the fees allegedly owing to them. However, my reading of this and other hair-raising cases cited by O'Shea and Madigan is that the criticism should not all be levelled at the consultants. The fault was partly that of top management, who left a lot to be desired and used consultants in a reckless and insufficiently focused manner.

Do consultants tell you the obvious?
The standard jokey definition of a consultant has become 'someone who borrows your watch to tell you what time it is

and then walks off with it.' The originator of this memorable comment is Robert Townsend in *Up the Organisation*. In some cases, walking off with the watch may be pretty much all the consultants are doing. Their reports and recommendations often have a dreary predictability. Someone in the client organisation could probably have come up with something comparable in substance, though not necessarily as polished in presentation. At Figgie International, senior management would have done much better to listen to dissenting voices from within their own ranks, such as the middle managers who saw and said that the consultants' recommendations were unworkable. Ironically, one of these got the sack but was later re-hired as a consultant when the company saw the error of its ways. O'Shea and Madigan urge companies to ask: 'Do I need advisers? ... Don't forget to assess the brilliance within your own company before you go trying to buy some from outside' (*Dangerous Company*, p.302). With that proviso, it has to be said that the virtues a good consultant may bring to a situation are often an objectivity and an awareness of best practice elsewhere. These things are not easily attainable by someone within the company.

Are consultants too sold on fashionable ideas?

Consultants are ideas people, and there is a fashion in ideas for improving corporate performance just as there is in any-thing else. Total quality management, just-in-time, business process reengineering, knowledge management – anyone who has worked in business for the last fifteen years will be familiar with catch-phrases like these and many more. Some consultancy firms commit themselves firmly to a particular idea, which they then apply willy-nilly to all their clients whether it's appropriate or not. There is no doubt that con-sultants play a major role in the adoption of marketable philosophies. At Figgie International, management and consultants alike were sold on the idea of 'world-class manu-facturing' without the phrase ever being properly defined. The Utopian connotations it carried actually seem to have got in the way of the company taking the small, gradual, detailed steps it needed to take in order to improve its manufacturing plant and processes.

Our consultation at Ridley included a rigorous critique of the then-fashionable concept of business process reengineering (often known as BPR), which is concerned with a radical redesign of a company's business processes. In the minds of the coiners of the phrase, Michael Hammer and James Champy, authors of *Reengineering the Corporation*, this was intended to improve efficiency, streamline or remove bureaucratic procedures, and improve job satisfaction through creating multi-skilled teams that accepted considerable responsibility. The idea appealed to a combination of vested interests:

- senior managers seeking short-term financial goals and looking to reduce costs
- powerful consultants seeking to expand business and latching on to a new idea
- software vendors seeking to sell more products and equating efficiency with better technology.

It's therefore not surprising that it caught on in a big way.

A few years down the line, and the overall results from BPR were not looking very good. Judged purely on financial criteria, some companies benefited, others declined, and a fair-sized group in the middle did neither. Judged by its impact on corporate morale, BPR fares rather worse. This is because it became interchangeable in many people's minds with *downsizing* – that dreaded word so characteristic of company life in the period 1993-6 (and which was partly a response to economic recession and increased global competition). Hammer and Champy claim that they never intended reengineering and downsizing to become synonymous. But James Champy implicitly accepts some blame in a later book, titled *Reengineering Management*. This opens with the statement that 'reengineering is in trouble. It's not easy for me to make this admission' (p.1) and switches the focus to managers, the individuals who need to bring about the desired change. The earlier book had been so process-centred it neglected the people element. The Work Structuring consultant Irwin Bidgood, who spoke on our consultation, made a similar point when he argued that business is a socio-technical system whereas BPR is only a technical solution.

Some of the popular business ideas peddled by consultants are helpful. Those that are, tend to last longer – though the ideas may need repackaging and dressing up in a new language if they are to maintain their freshness and impact. Other ideas are no more than passing fads, with a fleeting lifespan. In fact, no idea should be made the panacea for all evils or every company's situation. O'Shea and Madigan suggest that one of McKinsey's strengths is that it 'has tried to avoid the fads that are such meat and potatoes for newcomers to the consulting field. It offers the whole array of business services, but seems wedded to none of them in particular' (*Dangerous Company*, p.261).

Are consultants theorists rather than practitioners?

A major complaint among clients is the extraordinary disparity in expertise between the impressive senior consultant who wins the contract and the relatively inexperienced consultants who are often sent in to do the work. Many of the staff used by the big consulting firms are extremely young – in their twenties or early thirties. It is not unusual for them to have had little or no experience of mainstream business life, having joined the consultancy firm straight from university or after doing an MBA. The result may be someone who is good with words and adept at manipulating charts, graphs and other presentation tools, but lacks the worldly wisdom that the client was really looking for. Clearly everyone has to begin somewhere, and some young people have exceptional talent and learn unusually fast. But it is important that companies are given no false pretences about who will actually be doing the work for them. O'Shea and Madigan recommend insisting on a balanced team with a fair measure of experience represented.

The Ethics of Consultancy

The possibility that clients might be misled, wittingly or unwittingly, about the identity of the staff who will be working for them highlights the fact that consultancy, just like other areas of life, has its ethical dimension. In the UK, the Institute of Management Consultancy (IMC) has established a helpful code of professional conduct. As with most codes, the principles are clear. The challenge consists in their detailed application.

There are several issues which are potential problem areas for consultants.

Competence
The IMC code states: 'A member will only accept work that the member is qualified to perform and in which the client can be served effectively; a member will not make any misleading claims and will provide references from other clients if requested.'

This sounds straightforward, but in reality can be anything but. Whether a member firm considers itself well qualified to perform a piece of work will often be a marginal decision. A consultant may know a rival he thinks could meet the brief better, but it demands a considerable degree of self-confidence to tell the client that. However, one consultant I know told me of an occasion when he did this and the client was highly appreciative, maintaining the relationship and using the consultant for a more appropriate piece of work at a later date. On the one hand, being honest about your capabilities means you are more likely to secure the type of work you can do really well; on the other, it can be beneficial for you and your client to be stretched beyond your comfort zone. St Paul's words in Romans 12:3 are relevant here: 'Do not think of yourself more highly than you ought, but rather think of yourself with sober judgment, in accordance with the measure of faith God has given you.' Sober judgment suggests a realistic estimate, acknowledging limitations as well as strengths; but the 'measure of faith' God gives may also lead to taking on some bold assignments, confident that he will provide the resources to do a job well.

Fair pricing

Some may consider the notion of fairness irrelevant to pricing, on the grounds that a fair price is whatever the market allows and the client is willing to pay. Some consultants on our seminar thought it very important to charge high, because it meant their advice was more likely to be taken seriously. Others harboured doubts about that approach, believing it could deprive organisations of the consultancy services they desperately need – though of course one can charge differential rates. Whatever the rates, the basis of remuneration needs to be clearly agreed with the client in advance of commencing work. For an hourly or daily rate, honesty is expected of the consultant in accurately recording and reporting the length of time spent working on the project. The same applies to any additional expenses he or she may claim. It is very tempting to round figures upwards to one's own advantage.

Specially tailored advice

One way in which consultancy firms may skimp work, and therefore fail to provide value for money, is through treating different organisations as if they were the same. *Dangerous Company* details the case of a New York consultancy firm that had built a 'diversity practice' to help companies cope with the challenge of race and gender in the workplace. When Nissan USA complained that the recommendations it had received didn't seem particularly tailored to Nissan, it emerged that the consultancy had sent virtually the same report to all its clients over a two-year period – the names of the companies obviously excepted. Whilst there may be general advice on race and gender which most companies need to hear, it is hard to believe there aren't significant differences between where companies are at on these issues and how they need to tackle them. It is sad that so unethical a practice should emerge in a company dealing with key ethical questions. Such a blatant instance of duplicating work may be rare, but more diluted versions – giving minor variations on fairly standard advice – constitute a recurrent temptation to consultancy firms that harbour few scruples.

Confidentiality

The IMC code says: 'A member will hold all information concerning the affairs of clients in the strictest confidence and will not disclose proprietary information obtained during the course of assignments.'

This is fair enough – it expresses an ideal most consultants would aspire to – but it's a standard it is very easy to let slip. If all consultants adhered to it strictly it would be almost impossible to engage in any conversation with them about their work! One consequence of the confidentiality ethic is that consultancy firms are absolved from all external accountability in cases where the public might legitimately question what they have achieved. O'Shea and Madigan comment: 'This has a legitimate purpose in that clients don't want their secrets discussed. But it also provides a perfect excuse for not talking about anything that might be uncomfortable' (*Dangerous Company*, p.8). A more significant, yet related, dilemma is keeping different pieces of work entirely separate. For instance, consultants may not actually divulge pieces of information gained in dealing with Company A, but they realise the relevance of that information and feel strong pressure to use it when they give advice to Company B. The nature of consultancy is that it builds its knowledge base on the back of the clients it serves. The potential for conflicts of interest when a large consultancy firm is used by competitors in an industry is only too apparent.

Industrial espionage

This leads to another problem, which is that some companies may use consultants to discover privileged information about their competitors. The motive for this is not necessarily sinister, but may be part of a move towards benchmarking, i.e. carrying out a detailed comparison between the performance of different companies. If the information is not in the public domain, the basic moral position is clear: consultants should refuse such requests. The only way in which privileged information can be sought honestly is through approaching the targeted company directly and asking for it, disclosing both the purpose for which information is being sought and who the ultimate recipients of the information will be. It is possible that the company will consent to taking part in a benchmarking exercise, having an interest in securing such information itself. Be that as it may, industrial espionage is one example of the consultant's dilemma about whether to accept a brief which has potentially unethical aspects.

Moral mismatch

Consultants may see and hear behaviour in client companies that is out of kilter with their own ethical standards. The firm as a whole may be riddled with dishonesty, backbiting and intrigue. As a result the consultant thinks a drastic transformation in corporate culture is called for, though the area he or she is being paid to investigate is rather more limited. Alternatively, they may encounter dubious practice being perpetrated by a key individual. Calvert Markham cites an example: '...the marketing director of the client confides to you that he is about to change jobs, but does not plan to announce it until the annual bonus (which will be substantial in his case) is paid. The CEO – your client – at a subsequent meeting asks you if there are any foreseeable defections. Do you tell him about the marketing director?' (*Practical Management Consultancy*, p.64). There are many occasions when a high principled consultant must wonder whether to 'blow the whistle', either internally or – in cases where a company is guilty of a serious legal infringement – externally. In 1986-7 Olivier Roux, a consultant from Bain & Co. who acted as interim finance director at Guinness, was responsible for exposing the illegal payments and share-support scheme, leading to the imprisonment of Ernest Saunders, chairman of Guinness, and several other prominent businessmen. Roux blew the whistle in no uncertain manner, though his actions were tainted by the fact that he was himself involved in the practices he exposed.

Telling the client unpalatable truths

Consultants may reach conclusions they know will be unpopular with those that hired them. These may be organisational: the company's problems are far more serious and deep-seated, or the strength of the competition far greater, than the managing director imagined. Or they may be personal: the MD has an insensitive, autocratic style of leadership which is alienating most of his workforce. If the consultant is to provide the client with the objectivity that is supposed to be the profession's hallmark, a fresh and independent appraisal of what is going on, then the truth must be told. From the consultant's perspective this will be difficult, not only because most of us prefer telling people what they want to hear rather than what they don't, but also because it will probably jeopardise the prospect of repeat business. There are of course ways of cushioning uncomfortable news, by pointing out strengths in an organisation or leadership style as well as weaknesses. In the final reckoning, however, it is crucial that a clear message of warning comes through, and that consultants do not sacrifice integrity to self-interest.

What this amounts to is that being a faithful consultant is not a job for the faint-hearted. Once again the Old Testament narratives about the kings are surprisingly relevant. King David was not short of advisers or counsellors. This is the closest the Bible gets to the word 'consultant'. (Note that 'counsellor' is another possible translation of the Greek word *parakletos* used of the Holy Spirit in John 14.) During the dramatic and traumatic episode when David's beloved but wayward son Absalom plotted to overthrow him and David was forced to flee from Jerusalem, two of these advisers, Ahithophel the Gilonite and Hushai the Archite, played vital roles.

Ahithophel (whose counsel was reckoned equivalent to an oracle from God) proved disloyal. He went over to Absalom's side (2 Sam. 15:12), gave Absalom counsel to publicly sleep with his father's concubines, as a sign of open rebellion and utter shamelessness (16: 20-23) and then advised him to pursue David straightaway, while his father was 'weary and discouraged' (17:2). Hushai, in contrast, stayed loyal. He accompanied David out of the city, but was sent back by David and given instructions to feign friendship with Absalom and so 'defeat for me the counsel of Ahithophel' (15:34). Hushai successfully did this. When Ahithophel advised Absalom to go for David's jugular, the rebellious son was pleased with the advice, but – presumably because Hushai also had a formidable reputation – asked for his advice as well. Hushai advised against an immediate attack, on the grounds that David and his followers were valiant warriors who would fight like angry bears. He counselled Absalom to delay until he had summoned the whole of Israel to fight with him (17:5-13). This advice won the day: 'Absalom and all the men of Israel said, "The counsel of Hushai the Archite is better than the counsel of Ahithophel."' (17:14) Effectively Hushai bought vital time for David, and then sent secret word – not without difficulty – to David to mobilise for immediate battle. *The king was saved by a consultant.* Without Hushai's courageous, highly intelligent intervention, it is hard to see how David would have kept his throne – even if his actions do have a hint of industrial espionage, or a blatant conflict of interests about them. Desperate times call for unusual measures!

A striking illustration of courage in speaking the unspeakable is seen in 2 Samuel 12, the earlier – and better-known – story of Nathan the prophet. Prophets, men and women who spoke in the name of the Lord, also have an aura of the consultant. Some were social outsiders, but others, who operated under God-fearing kings, had a respected role as advisers at the royal court. (See Isaiah 36 – 39 for an outline of Isaiah's role two centuries later under King Hezekiah.) David was a God-fearing man who went sadly astray when he committed adultery with Bathsheba, wife of Uriah the Hittite, discovered that Bathsheba was pregnant, and then connived to get Uriah killed in battle. Nathan awakens David's conscience by going, unsummoned, to David and telling him a moving story about a rich man with huge flocks who stole a poor man's single ewe lamb. Thinking the story true, David's anger is kindled against the man, only for him to be stopped in his tracks by Nathan's astonishing reply: 'You are the man!' In an age when it was thought kings could get away with anything, this was courage of the very highest order. It is a story to strengthen the nerve of any consultant wondering whether to confront an apparently arrogant – but possibly persuadable – managing director with the news that solving the organisation's problems needs to start with him.

Some consultants may find this emphasis on ethics unfamiliar. It is of course possible that in much of their work they come across few moral dilemmas of any substance. Some consultants offer advice only on a narrow technical front. A small minority make business ethics their speciality, advising, for instance, on the adoption of a corporate code of ethics. But most consultants are involved on the broader canvas of an organisation's activities. In Paul Batchelor's view, four key business drivers underpin most consultancy work: managing cost; managing complexity; managing change; and satisfying customers. Each of these has significant ethical implications. You cannot be involved in any of these areas in any depth without engaging with fundamental questions of purpose, priorities and values. At the very least, managing cost, managing complexity, managing change and satisfying customers raise questions about how much a company values people and in what ways it shows this.

So consultants, whether they like it or not, are in the values business. They cannot, and should not, delude themselves into thinking that the work they do is values-free. I know of one consultancy firm that was prompted into working out its values by a client who wanted to know that they were; the client didn't wish to work with a consultant whose values were significantly different. By virtue of the advice that they give, consultants influence organisational life for good or evil. They can sensitise companies to the importance of values or they can encourage a hard-headed insensitivity. They can preach a simplistic message of one single bottom line or a more fully rounded gospel, whether that be phrased in terms of balancing the stakeholders, corporate social responsibility or the triple bottom line. They can perform the role of Ahithophel, counselling the practice of sleeping with the concubines of one's father (whatever a suitably offensive business equivalent of that might be) or they can wear the cloak of Nathan, arousing an individual or corporate conscience that has been deadened. They may perform their most important function as consultants precisely at those moments when they question the prevailing mind-set their client demonstrates. There is much to be said for asking the seemingly naive questions, such as:

- If you had a mission statement, what would it be?
- Are there alternatives to making people redundant?
- Do you have to regard your competitors as enemies, or is there scope for working collaboratively with them?

Questions like these may jolt clients into new ways of thinking.

Because consultants typically work for a variety of clients, they have scope for making an impact on organisational life across a diversity of fronts. For instance, Work Structuring, the consultancy run by Christian Schumacher, has carried its message of 'whole work' and 'processes of transformation' into manufacturing companies, hospitals and non-governmental organisations with, it seems, equal success. The most influential consultants put their ideas in print, or become celebrated public speakers – Peter Drucker and Tom Peters are the most famous examples. When we seek to assess who are the most influential people in the world today, we should not ignore the contribution of the management gurus.

Christians and Consultancy

My experience tells me that there is every reason to think that Christians are well represented in the consultant constituency. Perhaps persuading others is something that they find particularly congenial. In the light of what I have claimed about the influence of consultants, it makes eminent sense for Christians in the field to take careful stock of what they are doing. So the questions they may ask themselves typically include:

- In what directions are we seeking to 'move' organisations?
- Is the advice we give modelled on the best in secular thinking alone, or does it convey distinctively Christian insights?
- If the latter, to what degree might the consultant be explicit about this?
- Are there popular fads that Christian consultants should avoid – or which they should at least moderate by putting them in a broader context?
- Is being a consultant part of spreading or building the kingdom of God?

The concern to explore these questions is what brought a group of 17 consultants together at Ridley Hall for a two-day seminar on *Christians in Consultancy*. The aim was to clarify thinking on issues that are addressed regularly in consultancy work – in particular, assessing the potential Christian consultants have for influencing what is going on in the organisational world. The programme included a session on promoting Christian values that provoked considerable disagreement, but the fact that it exposed a difference of view was valuable and instructive.

On one side of the debate, some consultants felt there was no significant difference between Christian values and the best in secular values. For instance, believer and unbeliever alike agree that openness, teamwork, vigilance over safety and developing people are good things. Christians do not have a monopoly on wisdom and goodness, and should be humble enough to recognise these qualities in people who do not share their faith. God's Spirit is potentially capable of enlightening anyone, and this activity has often been described as 'common grace' in the Reformed tradition and 'natural revelation' in the Catholic one. Biblical support for this can be found in Romans 2:14-15, where

Paul speaks about Gentiles who do not have the law doing by nature what the law requires, showing that it is 'written on their hearts'. Interestingly, best-selling author Stephen Covey bases his Character Ethic on 'the fundamental idea that there are *principles* that govern human effectiveness – natural laws in the human dimension that are just as real, just as unchanging and unarguably "there" as laws such as gravity in the physical dimension' (*The Seven Habits of Highly Effective People*, p.34). Covey thinks these principles are not unique to any religion (he actually comes from Mormon Utah) but are a common denominator of them all. Indeed, 'they are self-evident and can easily be validated by any individual.'

Those who take this sort of view are liable to identify what is distinctively Christian not in terms of values but in terms of beliefs, notably in the God who is seen as the ground and guarantee of these values. Schumacher finds cycles in the world of work both of death and resurrection and of Trinitarian activity. These phenomena speak of the presence of God, if only we have eyes to see it. These ideas are mapped out in detail in his two books, titled *To Live and Work* and *God in Work*. Schumacher thinks that reforming the structures of an organisation in a humane direction, so that all may experience the satisfaction of 'whole work' – work which involves planning, doing and reviewing, and is involved with key processes of transformation – can be an important step in pre-evangelism, because it prompts people to question *why* things work better like this.

On the other side of the debate were those who felt that Christian values *are* distinctively different. The values of the kingdom of God are often in conflict with those of the world. They have a heavenly as opposed to an earthly origin. We should beware ideas that sound good, but which flatter in order to deceive – either because they are a public relations front or because they harbour dangerous 'New Age' heresies. In Corinthians, Paul talks about those who are 'false apostles, deceitful workers, disguising themselves as apostles of Christ. And no wonder! Even Satan disguises himself as an angel of light. So it is not strange if his servants also disguise themselves as ministers of righteousness.' (2 Cor. 11:13-15) If such charlatans exist in the church, we can expect to find a few peddling their ideas in the world of consultancy as well.

One consultant on the seminar spoke of his wish to see Christians offering 'clear, confident, assertive, worshipful lifestyles' in the workplace. Another passage from Paul would seem to support a distinctive approach: 'I appeal to you therefore, brothers and sisters, by the mercies of God, to present your bodies as a living sacrifice, holy and acceptable to God, which is your spiritual worship. Do not be conformed to this world, but be transformed by the renewing of your minds, so that you may discern what is the will of God, what is good and acceptable and perfect.' (Rom. 12:1-2, RSV)

What position one adopts in this debate is affected by many factors: temperament, one's particular experience of the working world, and theological perspective, among others. My own perspective is inevitably a personal one, and I make no claims that this was a consensus position reached by the seminar – though I think some participants would agree with it.

Christian and Secular Values

While I feel that there are elements of truth in each of the viewpoints described above, they both err toward one-sidedness. The first is monistic, failing to allow for real distinctions. The second is dualistic, exaggerating the differences between darkness and light – or at least the certainty with which we can distinguish them. The position I am drawn to is one that recognises a substantial overlap between Christian and secular values, but promotes certain concepts as characteristically Christian. This is not to claim that all Christians will subscribe to these values, nor that they will be absent from the thinking of all non-Christians – rather that Christians are *more likely* to emphasise them, or that the logic of Christian belief and discipleship points in that direction.

Many of the positions I think Christians ought to take on topical business issues are evident elsewhere in this book. I shall not here rehearse what I think to be an appropriate position on managing the supply chain, tackling corruption, or business and sustainable development. But I will add four areas where I suggest a significant values-contrast:

Secular	Christian
Honesty	Integrity
Care	Love
Fairness	Justice
Commitment	Balance

Each of these juxtapositions needs some explanation.

Honesty vs. Integrity

To attempt to hijack integrity as a characteristically Christian concept looks at first sight like barefaced effrontery. No word crops up more often than integrity in corporate mission statements. But I am not convinced that many of the organisations proclaiming their commitment to integrity have a very deep or secure grasp of what it means. Corporate understanding of integrity is often limited to a notion of honesty, which *is* a very important quality. The persistent and destructive tendency of human beings to be dishonest means that we should never take it for granted in organisational life. Integrity includes honesty, but means something more besides. It includes connotations of:

- moral courage
- consistency
- a readiness to give account in public of why you are doing what you are doing
- an unwillingness to compartmentalise life into some sectors where high moral standards apply and other sectors where they don't.

Integrity suggests a life that is well integrated. A biblical study of the word integrity (which is used several times in the Old Testament wisdom literature) supports this wide-ranging, holistic understanding.

Care vs. Love

Concern for people is certainly present in the language and behaviour of secular organisations. 'Our people are our greatest asset,' some say, and it is not always an idle piece of window-dressing. There *are* companies which are genuinely concerned about the welfare of their clients and the development of their employees. This concern is often expressed in the word 'care' – a positive word, but cool in comparison with the warmer and more far-reaching notion of love. The nearest that modern management jargon comes to using this word is in the cryptic context of the acronym TLC (Tender Loving Care!). Even if 'love' is too awkward a word or too prone to misunderstanding to be useable in a typical organisational context, the content of the word is something the Christian should not be willing to abandon. Love implies a sympathetic understanding of people, a readiness to give time to them, and a willingness to go the extra mile; all qualities that are often in short supply in today's world. Love in corporate action might mean an unusual expenditure of effort in helping redundant employees find new jobs. It might mean 'forgiving' someone for a well-intentioned action which badly misfired. It might mean being unafraid to display personal warmth and affection.

Fairness vs. Justice

Fairness is often used in an organisational context. There is a demand for equal opportunities, free of distortions caused by bias about race, gender, sexual orientation or disability. Companies vying for a contract ask for fair consideration of their tenders. Workers doing similar types of job expect to be paid similar wages. These are common examples of what most people understand by fairness. The issues raised tend to be restricted to the internal workings of a self-contained system. Justice includes all this but asks deeper, more searching questions. It resists the tendency to justify huge discrepancies in pay simply by reference to the laws of supply and demand. It raises the question of whether the market mechanism needs to be tempered by correcting influences in favour of poor and disadvantaged people. We must acknowledge that Christians are not always prominent among those raising considerations of justice, but the prophetic tradition contained in the Bible suggests that they should be. It is a word that ought to be heard more frequently in a business context.

Commitment vs. Balance

Organisations expect and demand considerable levels of commitment from their employees these days. For those with full-time jobs – especially managers – the hours spent at work have got longer. Christians should certainly be prominent for their whole-hearted attitude and willingness to roll up their sleeves and do a job well. Indeed, the implications of practising the sort of self-sacrificial love mentioned above are that certain tasks take longer, because standards of service are set very high. The other side of the coin, however, is that Christians should question an obsessive, idolatrous attitude to work that fails to allow employees time and space for other things in life.

In a survey I did of 50 corporate mission statements and codes of ethics, I came across only two that referred to employees' families, saying something like this: 'We encourage our employees to strike a balance between their responsibilities to the company and to their home life.' That is a sobering statistic. Equally disturbing is the report I heard of an investment bank which deliberately recruits single or divorced people because it believes married people are unlikely to be able to give the round-the-clock commitment that it craves. I know one Christian partner in a leading accountancy firm who sees fighting the long-hours culture as *the* major expression of his witness at work. It may cost him his chance of becoming a senior partner, but that is the price he is prepared to pay for affirming the importance of family relationships.

The juxtapositions outlined above should not be regarded as a comprehensive list. Others could be suggested. Taken together with the rest of this book, they indicate that the relationship between Christian and secular values is a matter of some subtlety. There is substantial overlap, but the extent of the overlap will vary according to organisational setting. In this respect I find one of the images Jesus used about the nature of Christian discipleship, that of *salt* (Mt. 5:13), instructive. Salt was often used in the ancient world as a preservative, to stop food going bad. Sometimes a proclamation of Christian values may have the function of providing a moral warning. But salt also has the effect of giving additional flavour and taste. Sometimes the Christian dimension has more the feel of a top-up; it enhances a value system or corporate ethos which is already basically good.

If consultants give advice that directs organisations in a direction compatible with Christian values, how overt should they be about this? Again, our gathering of consultants did not come up with any straightforward answers. Some felt that being open about their value-base was a help to their clients, because it encouraged clients to think about the basis of the values *they* wished to promote. The unashamed way in which New Age consultants promote their ideas in the work-place prompted different responses. On one hand: 'If they can do it, why should Christians be so inhibited?' And on the other: 'Do we really want to follow their example?' Perhaps the most appropriate approach is one which combines astuteness with openness: commending Christian values – garbed in neutral language – because they are likely to be effective, but always being prepared to 'ground' them in a Christian world-view.

The Rise of the Sole Practitioner

There is some evidence that consultants are having to work increasingly hard to prove their worth. Most clients are highly sophisticated managers with a healthy dose of scepticism about the trite or fashionable solutions on offer. To be successful, consultants need to have outstanding analytical and interpersonal skills, as well as relevant industry knowledge. Companies often want consultants who are prepared to roll up their sleeves and be actively involved in the implementation of the changes they recommend. And when consultancy is good, it can be very good indeed. High quality consultancy is worth its weight in gold: when good counsel leads to a dramatic and sustained improvement in organisational performance, or a decisive change in strategy that gives a clear market advantage, the fees which consultants charge no longer look so exorbitant.

O'Shea and Madigan suggest that some of the best value-for-money consultancy is being provided by small- and medium-sized consultancies: firms which do not carry so many overheads and do not charge as much as the McKinseys and Accoutures of this world, but give excellent service in certain carefully defined areas. When it comes to hiring a consultant, a company needs to be clear exactly what it is looking for, and be prepared to look beyond the big names to see who else might be able to fit the bill – and hopefully charge less.

A small consultancy may actually consist of just one person; sometimes acting on their own, sometimes in association with two or three others: hence the trading practice whereby the word 'associates' often follows an individual's name. The changing patterns of work that characterised the 1990s certainly contributed to the rise in number of consultants. Three ideas stand out here: *outsourcing, downsizing* and *portfolio lifestyle*. As companies have focused on core competences and core processes, they have outsourced many other functions. So there is an increased propensity to buy in extra services, which will often have a consultancy flavour to them. As companies come under pressure to cut costs, they have taken out levels of management and retired people early. So downsizing swells the ranks of able people who still have much to offer the organisational world, and consultancy seems the obvious way to offer it. As the concept of the portfolio lifestyle has grown in popularity, people have warmed to the mix of paid work, leisure and voluntary activity it typically contains, and consultancy is the type of work that fits most easily with this lifestyle. So the contemporary marketplace has large numbers of independent consultants jostling for business with established consulting firms.

Most of the consultants who attended our seminar were in this category: sole practitioners, working in discreet areas and seeking to identify a market niche. Some had already achieved notable success, while others were waiting for a breakthrough. Becoming a consultant is no automatic passport to prosperity. For the independent consultant, there is often a lack of steady income: months when next to nothing comes in, followed by a couple of lucrative projects.

At the end of the *Christians in Consultancy* seminar, the group decided that they had enjoyed meeting together so much they would continue doing so. Since then Ridley Hall has hosted a meeting of the Christian Consultants Group three times a year. No agenda is set, but the 24-hour meetings always include three key ingredients: sharing personal news and concerns, praying for one another, and discussing issues of common interest to consultants. There is a pool of about twenty-five consultants, of whom half will attend any one meeting. The group has developed its own momentum, and is constantly adding to its number. Its popularity is a mark both of the fact that consultants enjoy discussing ideas, and that being a sole practitioner can be a lonely and vulnerable existence. The Christian Consultants Group provides a relaxed and friendly setting for peer support, encouragement and challenge. The group also set the agenda for the seminar that is the topic of the next chapter.

12

CHANGING PATTERNS
OF WORK:
THE PORTFOLIO LIFESTYLE

Charles Handy popularised the word 'portfolio' in his best-selling and highly influential book *The Age of Unreason*, written in 1989.

'To re-invent work in its fullest sense we need another word. "Portfolio" might be that word. There are artists' portfolios, architects' portfolios, share portfolios. A portfolio is a collection of different items, but a collection which has a theme to it. The whole is greater than the parts. A share portfolio has balance to it, mixing risk and security, income and long-term gain in proper proportions; an artist's portfolio shows how one talent has more than one way of displaying itself.

'A work portfolio is a way of describing how the different bits in our life fit together to form a balanced whole. "Flat people", as E.M. Forster called them, were those who had only one dimension to their lives. He preferred rounded people. I would now call them portfolio people, the sort of people who, when you ask them what they do, reply. "It will take a while to tell you it all, which bit would you like?" Sooner or later, thanks to the re-shaping of the organisation we shall all be portfolio people. It is good news.' (*The Age of Unreason*, p.146)

Lifestyle

The phrase has certainly caught on. Portfolio lifestyle is widely used of the person who is based at home, works not for one employer but provides a service to a variety of parties, mixes fee work with free work (to use more of Handy's terminology) and often builds in a decent amount of time devoted to family, friends and leisure activities. This is the lifestyle being pursued by increasing numbers of people, especially those who have come to the end of their time in a 'core' job. For some it is a way of easing gracefully and gradually into retirement, between, say, the ages of fifty and sixty-five. For others it is a lifestyle consciously and deliberately chosen much earlier in their careers.

Portfolios of work are not new. The response of many women upon hearing of the concept is to retort that this is something they are already doing.

Max Comfort, author of the lively and useful book *Portfolio People*, writes: 'Through the ages, working women have (without thinking about it, let alone labelling it) managed a "portfolio" of tasks. They have had to look after the needs of often large families, manage the household finances, act as the family "therapist" and counsellor, look after animals, make and repair the family's clothes and maybe, in their "spare" time, take a part-time job. This was often quite menial, cleaning, cooking, bar work, waiting or part-time factory work. Many were outworkers, often on low piece-rates' (*Portfolio People*, p.18). Comfort adds the comment: 'Little has changed, I can hear the women readers observe.'

Indeed, I am inclined to think it is only because men find themselves forced into a similar position that, to bolster their self-esteem, they have to dignify the lifestyle with a title. But what also distinguishes them from the majority of home-based women is that, because many of them have come out of well-paid jobs, they are accustomed to charging a handsome fee for their services – and are in a position to do so. They are more likely to gravitate to a consultant-type job than to menial work. The re-positioning of men's work, however, may also have some effect on that of their female partners. Handy suggests: 'As more men re-balance their portfolios it should be increasingly possible for more women to put serious bits of paid work into their portfolios' (*The Age of Unreason*, p.151). Women are increasingly taking the initiative in doing that anyway.

Through hosting the Christian Consultants' group, which meets regularly at Ridley Hall, as well as through running a conference on *The Portfolio Lifestyle* in June 1999, I have come to know many portfolio workers well. I have also interviewed a sample of them – male and female – about their way of life. The questions I asked them were these:

- What activities make up your portfolio lifestyle?
- What factors led you to take up these particular activities?
- To what extent do these activities entail (a) continuity and (b) change with your previous working life?
- Do you feel that your portfolio lifestyle enables you to use your gifts more fully and creatively?

The answers to those questions, integrated with reflections from the conference and insights from several books that have been written about portfolio working, form the basis for this chapter. The various named individuals are all taken from my sample. Throughout, I have tried to bring a distinctively Christian understanding to bear on the joys and opportunities, the snags and the pitfalls of what people are experiencing as they venture into what is, for many, new territory.

Gifts

John told me that a motivating factor in his portfolio lifestyle was the need to 'stir up the gift' within him. The reference is to 2 Tim. 1:6 and is well worth reading in full. Paul says to Timothy: 'I am reminded of your sincere faith, a faith that lived first in your grandmother Lois and your mother Eunice and now, I am sure, lives in you. For this reason, I remind you to stir up the gift of God that is within you through the laying on of my hands; for God did not give us a spirit of cowardice, but rather a spirit of power and of love and of self-discipline.' And 1 Tim. 4:14 says something similar: 'Do not neglect the gift that is in you, which was given to you through prophecy with the laying on of hands by the council of elders.' If we ask what gift that was in Timothy's case, the answer is probably provided by the preceding verse: '... give attention to the public reading of scripture, to exhorting, to teaching.' Timothy's gift had to do with his calling as a preacher and teacher of the Word of God.

There are, of course, many other God-given gifts. Gordon Fee in his commentary on Timothy defines gift neatly as 'gracious endowment'. Endowment suggests something that is bequeathed, a long-term investment or furnishing of a person with particular qualities. Gracious emphasises the fact that such furnishing comes from God, that it is part of God's big-heartedness to equip people lavishly with such qualities. In Romans 12 and 1 Corinthians 12, Paul lists many of the gifts which are useful in a church context: prophecy, service, teaching, exhortation, generosity, compassion, words of wisdom, tongues, healing. Some of these gifts are relevant to a secular working context, but there are others: a fine eye for financial detail, skill in resolving conflict, and dexterity with one's hands. In quoting 2 Tim. 1:6, John was thinking chiefly of the expertise he had as a result of working for 35 years in the energy industry.

Paul tells Timothy to *stir up* God's gift to him. The verb is a metaphor for rekindling a waning fire. The New Revised Standard Version translates it 'rekindle', while the New International Version more vividly says 'fan into flame'. The fire was still burning, but it was in danger of going out. Gifts can suffer from neglect, from failure to practise them, and from lack of opportunity to use them. They are precious. They shouldn't be taken for granted, and the parable of the talents teaches that there is a calling to account by God for how they are used. A shift to a portfolio lifestyle provides the opportunity for re-evaluating what one is doing with these gifts. It could offer the time and impetus to 'stir up' a gift which has lain dormant for several years.

A question that many people wrestle with is: What is my gift? Or rather, what are my gifts? Most of us have several. Where does my gifting chiefly lie? There are two main ways of answering this.

One is a *subjective* approach, in terms of being honest with ourselves about our passions, the things that really enthuse and excite us. What do we really treasure? Remember what Jesus said: 'For where your treasure is, there your heart will be also' (Mt. 6:21). So if we are pondering the direction we might take in our portfolio lifestyle, it's well worth asking two more questions: Where do you really invest your creative energy? Where do you *want* to invest your creative energy?

Who Do You Think You Are?

Put like that, the answer may be blatantly obvious. You *know* what motivates you. You know what you'd *really* like to throw your energy into. The problem is you'd never previously been able to see yourself having the time to do it nor had any prospect of being paid to do it! Think again – it may now be a genuine prospect. For others, deeply harboured desires have been suppressed for so long that the answer remains elusive. There are various techniques to help you in identifying the focus of your creative energies. In *Portfolio People*, Max Comfort recommends a series of mental exercises, including 'The Seven-Year Vision' and 'The Portfolio Airways Pre-Flight Check-list', designed to help people identify what really makes them tick and what their true ambitions and aspirations are. In *More than a Job: Creating a Portfolio Lifestyle*, Jani Rubery suggests thinking about our past and identifying the patterns, people and particular events which have shaped our lives to date. I recently had a session with a career development consultant. Through giving me cards with a word or phrase to sort into different piles, he helped by getting me to separate different activities, aspects and areas of life into groups of 'Very

Important', 'Quite Important', and 'Not Important'. It clarified the things I most enjoyed doing – such as influencing people with ideas!

An organisation offering a lot of support in this area is SIMA (UK) Ltd., run by Nick Isbister. He has developed the *Who Do You Think You Are?* coaching programme, built upon a proprietary process called the System for Identifying Motivated Abilities (SIMA), which helps people understand who they are and what they really want. The process is very simple: it asks you to recall events in your life that you have enjoyed and done well. Your 'achievements' (i.e. the things that you feel most proud of or that show you at your best) are a great guide to your strengths. Through a series of guided explorations of what these are telling you, a picture is built up of your gifts. This creates awareness of how you operate when you are at your best. Through personal coaching, the implications of this are then explored and worked through. Nick has trained over 150 coaches worldwide to use this technique. It helps people to identify the things they do well, and most enjoy doing; the abilities and activities they find absorbing and engaging, and to which they gravitate almost without thinking. Nick also runs workshops that help people re-examine their priorities. He believes people should know what their gifts are and give these in service to others. An exercise I've experienced Nick use in a group is 'The Currency of Life'. He gives people a piece of paper with a large circle containing about twenty smaller circles, representing such areas as clients, family, sport, etc. He then gives them each 50 twopence coins and invites them to distribute these as appropriate in terms of how much time and energy they are investing in those different areas. This can be a very revealing exercise, if carried out honestly.

Who Do Others Say You Are?

The other way of answering that question is more *objective*, or perhaps I should say more external. It pays less attention to what we feel and more attention to how others see us. Charles Handy describes how a 48-year-old accounts director with an advertising agency came to him asking for advice about finding another job. Handy asked him what he was good at, and the man said he didn't really know. So Handy gave him a task: ' "Ask twenty people you know well, at work or outside work, to tell you just *one* thing you do really well." The man came back in a fortnight looking puzzled but happy. "I've got a list of twenty things," he said. "Quite surprising some of them. Funny thing, though, none of them mentioned running an account group." ' (*The Age of Unreason*, p.149). The experience had been quite illuminating for him.

Something similar happened to me at Ridley Hall. Ridley is built round a series of staircases, which comprise significant social and worshipping units. Twice a week during term we meet as staircase groups for times of worship, both formal and informal. On one occasion a student on my staircase distributed blank cards, and got us all to write a couple of sentences about each of the other people on the staircase – something positive that we'd really valued about that person during the course of the past year. We took our time about it so that we wrote things specific to each person: not just 'a jolly good chap' or its equivalent. Each person ended up with about twelve cards in a little brown envelope. The results were most enlightening. In my case, two words (not necessarily words I would have expected) kept recurring in the students' descriptions of me. I had to take notice: 'This is how others see me!' You may find this an exercise worth doing with a group who know you well.

Barnabas – A Man Seen Through the Eyes of Others

A notable biblical character worth considering in this context is Barnabas. The fascination of his character is that the New Testament contains nothing about him of an autobiographical nature: we see the man simply as others saw him. We first encounter Barnabas in Acts 4:36-37: 'There was a Levite, a native of Cyprus, Joseph, to whom the apostles gave the name Barnabas (which means 'son of encouragement'). He sold a field that belonged to him, then brought the money, and laid it at the apostles' feet.'

We do not know whether Barnabas saw himself as a 'son of encouragement'. We do not know whether he liked his new name. He may have inwardly seethed – as people often do about a nickname, however complimentary – or protested in vain: 'Call me Joe!' We do know that once the apostles had given him the name he was stuck with it, and both this and all the subsequent references to Barnabas in the book of Acts amply justify it. When Barnabas went to Antioch, he encouraged all the Christians there to remain true to the Lord with all their hearts (Acts 11:23). This track record probably weighed in the minds of the church leaders at Antioch when they responded positively to the call of the Holy Spirit: 'Set apart for me Barnabas and Saul (Paul) for the work to which I have called them' (Acts 13:2). We can imagine Barnabas proving an invaluable steadying influence on Paul (a man of great evangelistic fervour and acute theological intelligence, but also the possessor of a volatile temperament) during the ups and downs of the missionary journey that followed (Acts 13-14). When the two men came to set out on a second missionary journey, however, 'no small disagreement' broke out between them. The reason was that Paul had lost patience with their previous companion, John Mark, who had abandoned them in Pamphylia on the first journey. Barnabas insisted on giving him another chance (Acts 15:37). Presumably Barnabas saw in Mark abilities or potential that Paul did not see – at that time, anyway. The apostles discerned Barnabas correctly: there's no doubt that he was a great encourager.

As well as identifying personal skills and characteristics, others may also be able to help in discerning our suitability to the portfolio lifestyle *per se*. It does not suit everyone. Some of my interviewees had warmed to it more than others: there are advantages and disadvantages. It is clear that going portfolio involves a *giving up*, both in a negative and a positive sense.

Giving Up

There are things people often miss by going independent or becoming self-employed:

- *Security*

  Being employed by someone else does confer the benefit that a regular salary is paid into the bank account every month. Some of my sample are earning significantly less money than they used to. Even when employed on a lucrative project, the independent consultant has the worry of where the next work is coming from – so that doing productive work and marketing one's services compete for attention. Max Comfort suggests a 3/2 week where three days are spent doing the fee earning and two days are spent on maintaining and marketing the business, including time for refreshing and energising oneself. Ram Gidoomal, the successful Asian entrepreneur and consultant who spoke at our conference, recommended securing six months of fee-generating work before launching out independently.

- *Support*

  John, who used to work for a big public company, has had to learn to do many things himself for the first time. He's had to adjust to coping without a secretary, booking his own air flights, typing his own letters and mastering word processing skills. Even the more commercial aspects of negotiating fees and contracts, or collecting and chasing fees, may be something one is now having to do for the first time; in a big organisation, this was delegated to others. Developing expertise over a wide range of activities demands a steep learning curve.

- *Structure*

  Being employed provides a strong incentive to a structured lifestyle. It makes people get out of bed, have their breakfast, travel to work and sit down at their desk, all to a regular time pattern. The portfolio lifestyle puts an overwhelming premium on self-motivation. When working at home it is very easy to fritter time away taking the dog for a walk, mowing the lawn and drinking endless cups of coffee. There is nothing wrong with these activities but a whole day spent in doing them is not likely to yield much cause for satisfaction!

● *Being part of a team*
Operating on your own, for much of the time at least, can be quite lonely. So there may be nostalgia for the cama-raderie of working at a project together, and the shared satisfaction of bringing it to completion. Bryony found team-working the thing she missed most, not least because she felt she had team-working skills which were now under-utilised. When working from home there may still be plenty of contact with people, but much of it over the phone or via e-mail rather than face-to-face. In a later book, *The Empty Raincoat*, Charles Handy admits that not all his pre-dictions in *The Age of Unreason* worked out as sunnily as he'd imagined: 'Teleworking is fine in technological theory but lonely in reality. That asset which is yourself can atro-phy in isolation. We independents need somewhere other than the home, somewhere where there are colleagues not clients, somewhere where we can find the companionship and gossip of the old office or factory but without the boss. Somewhere where we can exchange experience and con-tacts. We need a club' (*The Empty Raincoat*, p.217).

I know an Anglican vicar who got wise to the fact that his parish contained a high number of self-employed people working from home who were feeling quite isolated. He organised a monthly soup-and-bread lunch where they come together for companionship. As is the way with such people, they haven't just made good friendships but also developed useful business contacts.

But there is also a positive side to *giving up*. There are things people said they were very glad to be rid of in going portfolio:

- *An uncongenial corporate ethos*
  Some people leave corporate life because they find they've
  grown increasingly at odds with the company they work
  for. Richard, who'd spent many years with a financial services company, mentioned several factors. The pressure on
  him as finance director when things were going wrong had
  become unacceptably high; the strategic direction was mistaken in his view; the culture of the company had changed;
  he no longer saw eye to eye with the people at the top.

- *Politicking*
  Corporate life is not always characterised by teamwork and
  convivial friendship. In some companies, managers put most
  of their creative energy into jockeying for position amongst
  and against each other. They are preoccupied with forging
  tactical alliances, covering their backs and boosting their personal prestige. The more independent spirits just get sick of it.

- *The boss*
  For many people, dissatisfaction with a job is personalised.
  There is a particular manager or colleague who gets under
  their skin and makes life difficult. They may have reached a
  stage of life where they long to be in charge themselves, to
  wield significant influence, but there's an obstacle that
  prevents them doing so: they've hit the 'glass ceiling' in
  corporate terms. Going independent offers scope for cir-
  cumventing the problem.

- *The treadmill*
  A conventional job may provide structure and security, but
  it often means being stuck in a rut – and not a very pleasant
  rut at that. Many businesspeople are tired of the daily com-
  mute, the long hours, leaving home at 6.30 in the morning
  and returning at 8.30 or 9 in the evening. Most have no great
  regrets about giving that up. Bill, who used to 'endure
  fume-ridden journeys on the tube', spoke about the pleasure he now takes in morning walks on the cliffs near his
  home on the Norfolk coast.

So in contemplating and evaluating the portfolio lifestyle on a personal basis, these aspects warrant careful consideration. What sort of 'giving up' is entailed? Is it a positive giving up, a negative giving up, or some sort of mixture of the two?

Being Stretched

Going portfolio is likely to involve being stretched. Again, there are different dimensions to this:

- *Applying existing skills in new contexts*
  This creates challenge, but with plenty of stimulus. Bill, who used to work for a major high street bank, is a consultant in organisational development, but not with financial services. The opportunities that have opened up have been with other types of organisation. Nevertheless, there is continuity in that he worked in management development during his time with the bank. Bryony had a background in sales and marketing, but now specialises in one-to-one counselling and facilitating workshops. The marketing aspect has disappeared, except that she found it very useful initially in knowing how to market herself. Richard has focused his accountancy skills in working with a number of charities, including a fast growing educational charity. This has represented a new environment, but he has relished the challenge it has posed for him.

- *Developing new skills*
  Alison studied part-time for two years to get an MA, and that has developed her consultancy work in a different direction. She has combined this with buying and developing a small shareholding, and discovered the joys and frustrations of being a farmer. Iain has developed skills in handling databases and organisational finance through being treasurer to a quarterly journal: not paid work, but what Charles Handy would call gift work. It has become a significant part of his developing portfolio. Wherever the

lack or reduction of support staff has been a significant aspect of the move to portfolio working, this has meant learning new skills to some extent.

● *Marital adjustment*
The portfolio lifestyle makes a difference to family life. It will probably mean a husband and wife seeing far more of each other than they have been used to, especially if one previously worked long hours and the other was based at home. This may bring great joy and satisfaction, but it can also bring unexpected strains. They may rather have enjoyed their separate lives and now find themselves getting under each other's feet. Whether welcome or unwelcome, a portfolio lifestyle will stretch the marital relationship, taking it in new and challenging directions. Handy devotes a section of the relevant chapter in *The Age of Unreason* to 'portfolio marriages'. He sums up some research he did on the marriages of successful managers: 'There is no optimal pattern for a marriage. All patterns are possible. It seems essential to have a joint understanding of what the pattern is, how and when it might change, what the consequences are of living in a certain pattern and what are the costs and benefits. People clearly can change their pattern if both partners want to. Separation and divorce often seem to occur because one partner wants to change the pattern and the other does not' (*The Age of Unreason*, p.163).

● *Juggling*
There is a being stretched simply in terms of what I call 'juggling': the business of keeping all the different balls in the air without letting any of them fall to the ground. David Pullinger describes juggling as 'a common metaphor for maintaining continual action in a number of projects, attempting to apportion attention so that none loses momentum or direction' (*Information Technology and Cyberspace*, p.91). Jani Rubery says: 'Whatever we do in life, it is important that we strive for balance in our spiritual

growth, physical and mental health and emotional fulfil-ment. Because a portfolio requires juggling a number of roles, achieving this equilibrium can be very demanding' (*More than a Job*, p.67). Self-employed people may be able to organise their time so that different days are devoted to dif-ferent areas of work (or life), but there are still days when demands come from all directions, or it's difficult to know what should take priority.

The self-knowledge accumulated through psychometric tests like Myers-Briggs can be useful here. Generally speaking, a 'P' is happier having lots of different balls to juggle, while a 'J' prefers to have a clear focus, to get on with a clearly defined task and do it. That doesn't mean only certain personality types are suited to the portfolio lifestyle. We can change and develop; and being stretched beyond our comfort zone is often the route to personal growth and fulfilment. Pullinger recom-mends a process of 're-collection of self' at the end of each day (*Information Technology and Cyberspace*, p.98). He cites research done by psychologists which shows that people sleep better when they avoid the fresh stimulus of telephone and other forms of distant communication in the half hour before they go to bed. Far better to unwind by considering what has been done during the day, what lies ahead the next day, and com-mitting both in prayer before God.

On the business of juggling, a businessman who spent his final working years as an independent consultant always found great inspiration from Colossians 1:17, the verse from that memorable passage about the person of Christ: 'He is before all things, and in him all things hold together.' Paul is talking about the role of Christ in creating and sustaining the universe, in providing its focal point and underlying purpose. If all things hold together in Christ on a cosmic level – to pursue the image, if he is able to juggle the really big balls successfully – then Christians should be confident that he is interested in helping us to hold our bit of that world together.

All the same, it is important that Christians should not be glibly triumphalist. My sample did not pretend that they had their lifestyle 'sussed'. Sometimes Christians, just like everyone else, come unstuck. They get over-stretched, take on one commitment too many, or make a mess of something. It's crucial to be honest enough to admit it, and to learn from the experience.

Among the interviewees, one left me feeling sadder than most. Alan gave up full-time employment, principally to pursue his ambition to write for a living. He is an aspiring writer of drama and children's books. To support himself until the writing was established, he developed a training consultancy – and also got involved in lots of other things, including being trustee of a local community project. The book writing has been put on the back-burner. In his case, the very diversity of portfolio living seems to have made it more difficult to focus on the one thing he really wants to do. Like giving up, being stretched may have its negative side as well as its positive.

Letting Go

Notwithstanding that example, going portfolio may involve real scope for *letting go* in the sense of letting your hair down and allowing yourself real scope for relaxation and recreation. My respondents came up with an interesting selection of hobbies, including becoming a cycling fanatic (and a lot fitter with it), puppet-making, round-Britain sailing, and Jitterbug Jive dancing. The portfolio lifestyle will probably offer more time to devote to recreational activities, or at least the flexibility to do them at times when many people cannot. I hope we can indulge ourselves in this way without feeling guilty about it.

In the process, of course, people often find that they have gifts or talents in the recreational area which blossom and grow. Through spending more time on the golf course, you may reduce your handicap from 24 to 14 – or even 14 to 4! You may become a superb photographer; your garden may be the envy of all your friends. But if not, don't worry about it. One of the things that distinguishes leisure from work is freedom from the pressure of constant self-improvement. We need a non-utilitarian view of leisure that takes pleasure simply in the way things are, which rejoices in the goodness of God's creation and can laugh at our own limitations. One of the things I most admire about my father-in-law is that even on the days when he's playing golf badly, when he comes to the 15th tee – which has the most spectacular view on the course – he always stops to enjoy it. He literally purrs with delight and simply praises God, rejoicing in the vista stretching out in front of him.

Stewards of God's Grace

The shift to a portfolio lifestyle may also change the amount of time and the nature of investment given to explicitly Christian work. I struggle to know how best to sum this up but find myself returning to a favourite verse, 1 Pet. 4:10: 'Like good stewards of the manifold grace of God, serve one another with whatever gift each of you has received.' Whatever Christians do in terms of service in the world – and that is the major focus of this book – they also have a responsibility to put their gifts to positive use among God's people. We are called to be *good stewards of God's grace*.

Again, I was struck by the variety of expressions this took among my respondents, emphasising the fact that God's grace is truly manifold – a word that can be translated as multi-coloured. In terms of the gifts on offer, the church should be as colourful as a kaleidoscope.

● For Patrick, changing from full-time to part-time employment created the space for him to volunteer as a church-warden. He previously had a pastoral role in the church, but believed that God wanted him to 'serve at tables' for a while – a reference to the seven deacons who dealt with the food distribution in Acts 6. In this capacity, he was able to help in mending relationships, after an unhappy interregnum and while the new vicar was establishing himself. He certainly wouldn't have been able to do that if he'd still been working full time in the City. There are many behind-the-scenes jobs like churchwarden which are hardly glamorous, but can be very important – and we should expect to see a sprinkling of portfolio workers among those who do them

- Several in my survey had been involved in pioneering Christian initiatives. I'm convinced that para-church organisations are at the centre of many of the most exciting things happening in the church today. I found no less than three people involved in Christian publishing, including the director of a local Christian bookshop; the initiator of a spiritual renewal movement in her diocese; the trustee of a Christian self-catering holiday house; the organiser of a fellowship group for the spouses of Christian MPs; and the prime mover in an initiative to bring senior business leaders together in a 'city under God'. I was struck by the energy, enterprise and enthusiasm people had invested in these different initiatives. They seemed to show Christian portfolio workers at their best, really making things happen

- Overtly Christian work may take the form of participating in mission. Going portfolio can also mean grasping more opportunities for sharing one's faith. Alan now regularly appears on the radio, doing what he calls 'defending the Faith'. Bryony, a gifted evangelist, spends up to two weeks a year involved in missions around the country. This prompts two questions worth posing to everyone. Does 'going portfolio' increase or decrease my capacity for witnessing to the gospel? Does it bring me into more situations or less where I can speak to other people about what Christian faith and values mean? Portfolio workers may be challenged to adjust their balance of activities – or even, perhaps more importantly, their mix of relationships – in the light of those questions.

A Widespread Temptation

Portfolio workers are, almost by definition, avid networkers. Whenever they get together in a group, they are on the look-out for contacts who might be useful to them: a person who has similar interests, or with whom they might enter into a joint venture, or – who knows – other influential people that they would really like to meet.

Several delegates on our conference identified the pressure this creates as a real temptation. How do we avoid 'using' people? How do we avoid pigeon-holing some people as interesting and others as not? We have probably all had the experience at a party of talking to someone who is paying little attention to us, constantly looking over our shoulder at the person they'd really like to meet. We've probably done that ourselves; it's a widespread social phenomenon. Being a portfolio worker, experiencing that constant pressure to widen your circle of contacts and land the next profitable project, exacerbates the tendency.

The world gives mixed advice on this score. Business books I've read recommend using others without any inhibitions, targeting the people who can benefit you most. Richard Koch links this with giving a superior service to one's most valuable customers (*The 80/20 Principle*, ch.6). Max Comfort argues differently. Though he thinks we are all basically driven by self-interest, he is alert to the pleasure (the 'bits of magic') that can come through human interaction. 'Being in touch, sharing anecdotes, swapping ideas and suggestions, even with someone on the other side of the globe that we're never likely to meet, is an essential part of business maintenance ... Try to engage the person's interest, locate their "hot spot", ask questions about what they do and share a bit of yourself' (*Portfolio People*, p.154). He also narrates a story told by Peter Caddy, a former commanding officer in the RAF and co-founder of the Findhorn Foundation in Scotland, from his days in the catering business. 'When a "down and out" left the tea-room after nursing a single cup of tea for the whole afternoon, the manager of the establishment insisted on opening the door for him and thanking him for his custom. Whatever his appearance or his background, he was a customer' (p.143).

Clearly, Christians should be in the vanguard of those who treat everyone as important. All human beings are made in the image of God. None should be used as a mere means to an end. But believing that is no foolproof protection against the temptation to do so. We need to develop a way of engaging with people that values them simply for who they are, while remaining open to benefits that may accrue from a developing relationship. Jani Rubery comments: 'There is a time for honest agenda-driven networking, but there is also a time for getting to know people for the sheer fun of doing so' (*More than a Job*, p.57). Sometimes a person who knows us well – like a marriage partner – can see better than ourselves if we're getting the balance right in this area.

In any case, snap judgments about people's usefulness to us are often mistaken. The key contact and the good advice may come from unexpected sources. Let's remember 2 Kings 5, the story of how Naaman, commander of the Syrian army, heard from a captive slave-girl that help for his leprosy problem might be found in the neighbouring land of Israel. Through the king of Syria, he sends a distinctly peremptory request for help to the king of Israel. But the advice he needs – washing in the river Jordan – is not to be found from kings but from a Jewish prophet, Elisha; and even when Naaman receives the advice, he would never have heeded it but for the intervention of his servants, who tell him to swallow his pride and do what Elisha has said.

Portfolio workers find networking to be a *humbling* experience. They are constantly surprised by where the next good contact comes from.

13

SPIRITUALITY AND THE WORKPLACE:
A NEW PARADIGM AT WORK?

Judi Neal is a passionate woman, and her passion is for work. 'There are so many things I want to do, I've just got to get started, because the day is moving,' Judi, director of the Association for Spirit at Work, says enthusiastically. She stays awake until 3 am most nights, and then sleeps just five hours, rising at 8 am.

Judi's Story

'When I was still in corporate America, I slept nearly eight hours, but it was never enough,' she explains. 'I always felt tired and I drank coffee to get me going even though I didn't like it.' Judi, who has a PhD in organisational behaviour, was working as organisational development manager for a large defence systems corporation in Illinois. In the course of her work, she learned that the company was breaking the law by making faulty ammunition that was sold to the US government as if it met government specifications. Because she couldn't get management to listen to her concerns, she ultimately blew the whistle on the company. Within six months, she left her job, feeling forced out through intimidation, threats and harassment.

Judi was unemployed for a year. Eventually, she was asked to teach a course on women and management at a university in Connecticut. That opened new doors. 'In this new job, I made the commitment to be as authentic as I could possibly be, to be true to my spiritual values regardless of the cost to my career, and allow myself to be guided in the ways I could be of service in the world instead of trying to plan out the details of my life.'

In 1993, while teaching management full-time, Judi founded the Center for Spirit at Work. She felt inspired to provide support to others who, like her, may feel 'alone and crazy' while trying to be fully authentic and align their values and their work. In due course, Judi left the university to devote herself full-time to this endeavour. (Source: www.workand-soul.com)

I mentioned the resurgence of interest in spirituality in the workplace near the end of Chapter 1. The number of conferences, research projects, books, academic papers, organisations and web-sites devoted to the subject is multiplying fast – both nationally and internationally. In the USA, the Association for Spirit at Work (as Judi's organisation is now called) has proved very influential. The association's vision is 'to make a difference in the world by expanding the role of business in transforming society.' Its website (www.fourgate-ways.com) says: '[The Association] provides support for those who share this vision and who see work as a spiritual path. We will feel that we have been successful when a critical mass of organisations are committed to caring for the environment, are deeply respectful of local cultures, and are committed to the full development of all human beings who are connected to or impacted by the organisation. We are committed to being an inclusive organisation, embracing people from all faith traditions, as well as those who do not practice or adhere to any particular faith or religion.'

The understanding of humanity and work which drives this vision is spelt out in the association's Values and Beliefs Statement: 'We adhere to values of integrity, collaboration, and trust in our relationships with employees, customers, stakeholders, and the Divine. We believe that human beings are an integration of body, mind, emotion and spirit, and that it is our essential nature to evolve and develop to higher levels of awareness and consciousness. Work provides a marvellous opportunity for us to practise our spiritual principles and to benefit from our contemplative practices in daily life. It also provides an opportunity to grow and develop to our full potential. We believe that organisations that nurture this holistic approach to human development are more likely to be effective.'

This association has a fast-growing membership list, not just in the United States but in this country and further afield as well.

A Weekend in Ballarat

While on sabbatical in Australia and New Zealand, I soon became aware that spirituality at work is not just an American and British phenomenon but is alive and well down under. There too discussion groups, seminars and conferences are burgeoning. My first-hand encounter with the movement took place during a gloriously sunny December weekend at a conference, entitled *Redefining Success and Reinvigorating the Workplace*, at Ballarat University in Victoria. This was organised by a network called Spirituality Leadership and Management (SlaM), which sounds more top executive than it actually is. 'Spirituality and the Workplace' would be a more accurate description. The conference was attended by about 150 people. Subsequently in New Zealand I met Alastair McKenzie, an ordained lecturer from Christchurch. We compared notes and it emerged that he had recently attended a conference in New Zealand with a very similar style and ethos to the one I attended in Ballarat. From this I conclude that many of the trends apparent in Australia are characteristic across the Tasman Sea as well.

The meaning of the word spirituality is elusive. Michael Joseph is a Christian facilitator and coach who has done extensive research into the current revival of interest in the subject. In particular he has analysed the words and phrases most often used in discussions about spirituality. He concludes that the theme uniting many disparate understandings is *interconnectedness*. (See his paper 'Spirituality in the Workplace – What are we talking about?' in *Faith in Business Quarterly* 4:3.) Spirituality is about being connected, and four dimensions of spirituality are repeatedly mentioned:

- *Connection with self*
  Key phrases mentioned in this connection are purpose, way of being, faithfulness to core beliefs, getting in touch with who we are and being who we are
- *Connection with others*
  There is a strong focus on mutual self-giving, compassion, intimacy, harmony and common purpose
- *Connection with nature*
  Obvious concepts here are unity with creation, ecological concern, drawing inspiration from the beauty of nature, and the four elements of earth, air, fire and water
- *Connection with God or a higher power*
  There is a reaching after the divine, variously understood and described, but evident in such ideas as the sacred, the ground of our being, a higher consciousness, Gaia, or a world soul.

All these elements were evident at the Ballarat conference, with perhaps the first and the third most prominent. The papers and workshops on offer included 'Spirituality as a Factor of Personality: Its Effect on Psychological Wellbeing', 'Applying the Enneagram Theory to Motivate Individuals', 'Profitability through Clean, Green Business Practices – A Breath of Fresh Air', and 'The Beat of the Heart – A New Cosmology for Business Accessing Authenticity through Play, Rhythm and Deep Ecology'.

Most of the delegates were academics, trainers or consultants. There were some 'coal-face' workers, but not many. What struck me equally forcibly was how few were committed

Christians. I made a deliberate attempt to search them out, and I reckon they were in single figures; maybe six or eight. I encountered something that we are getting used to in this country as well: most delegates expressed a profound interest in spirituality but were either indifferent or hostile to religion, especially institutional religion. Spirituality was in, religion was out. At the same time I felt this was a little disingenuous because many delegates professed to being Buddhists or articulated ideas found in Eastern religions. Hostility to religion was mainly concentrated on Christianity, which was seen as tarred by an oppressive colonial past and regarded as distinctly *passé*. However, I must emphasise that the typically friendly character-trait of Australians meant I never experienced personal hostility when people discovered my background and beliefs. The attitude was rather one of curiosity that a theological college lecturer should be interested in attending such a conference.

Actually, I concluded that the most substantial difference was not between those delegates who were and weren't professing Christians. It was between those who believed in a god or higher power who is immanent only (within us), and those who believed in a God who is immanent and transcendent (outside and beyond us). Joseph's fourth dimension of spirituality was the most contentious. When we hit that point of difference, we really did seem to be understanding utterly different things in our discussion of spirituality. I would describe only those who believe in a transcendental deity – at Ballarat, a minority group – as *theists* in the traditional understanding of the word.

How Should Christians Respond?

I found Ballarat a fascinating counterfoil to a conference I organised on *Spirituality and the Workplace* at Ridley Hall in June 2001. The weather was similarly sunny, the company was equally congenial, and many of the same themes emerged. But the Ridley conference had a different make-up and a different agenda. Almost all the delegates were Christian, and the main aim was to identify an appropriate Christian response to the growing interest in spirituality at work.

Until now, Christians have been uncertain how to respond, having often felt their backs to be against the wall. Confronted for so long by the unrelenting march of secularism and materialism, Spirituality at Work is a movement that appears as if it might be sympathetic to their concerns. There's a formidable argument that Christians should welcome the movement, because it represents a long overdue advance on the dualistic, reductionist view of the world and the workplace that has dominated much of the modern era. But there's a strong counter-argument. 'Spiritual' is a word that can carry overtones of *spiritualist*, and should not be affirmed uncritically as depicting what is good and comes from God. Some Christians see Spirituality at Work as first and foremost a pagan movement, the work of sinister spirits who should not be confused with the Holy Spirit. So a real dilemma exists. Should Christians support the Spirituality at Work movement because we have a fundamental sympathy in aim, or is the underlying incompatibility too great?

Both these perspectives found articulate expression at the Ridley conference. Their main exponents were on one side Bob Cumber, a consultant and former banker, and on the other David Welbourn, an experienced industrial chaplain. Their papers were subsequently written up and published in *Faith in Business Quarterly* 5:3.

Spirituality and the New Age

Cumber, who researches New Age influences in the business community, was particularly concerned to trace links between the current interest in spirituality at work and New Age thinking. Cumber sees New Age thinking, which is difficult to define in any precise way, as a smorgasbord of ideas and concepts, many of which have become so mainstream over the last 10 or 15 years that few people now bat an eyelid at them.

'New Age is a coming together of those with a common interest in finding a new way forward to save the future of the planet – rejecting the Christian era and seeking a time of peace, harmony, wholeness and restoration. The chosen route is frequently derived from a blend of occult concepts with Eastern religions and beliefs – notably monism (all is One) and pantheism (all is God); an awareness of the supernatural and a rejection of materialism' ('Spirituality and the New Age', *Faith in Business Quarterly* 5:3, p.11).

This spirituality has a 'pick and mix' basis and can indeed be tailored to suit each individual. A strong thread of self-actualisation and self-fulfilment pervades it. There is a desperate hungering after success, even if success is defined in other than conventional business terms. Cumber has encountered numerous New Age practitioners working in training and development, and in organisation development. He believes many are genuine seekers after truth.

'They are genuine, lovely people who want to add value to the world and help individuals and businesses succeed in a frighteningly rapidly changing world. They are often prophets in their own time and wise beings who see the dangers of ignoring environmental issues, of failing to treat people with dignity or of following short-term rather than long-term options. They truly believe that, given the right insight, wisdom and perception, individuals, teams and organisations can achieve their true potential. They will use a wide range of methodologies to achieve this' ('Spirituality and the New Age', p.14).

Their means are many and various, but include crystals, astral projection, transcendental meditation, feng shui, neurolinguistic programming, new consciousness, positive thinking and a search for inner peace. The busy and hard-pressed appear ready to grasp at each and every potential saviour. That people are prepared to consider personal and spiritual solutions – and not just financial and practical answers – is, on one level, highly encouraging. However, if we should seek to live in God's world in God's way, Cumber thinks the sad reality is that many of these journeys will lead people to half truths and they'll miss the real treasure.

Feng Shui

Feng Shui is a practice that has acquired extraordinary popularity in the business world – especially, it seems, among those most sober and hard-headed of business institutions, the banks. Feng Shui is based on an ancient Chinese philosophy that has its roots in the Taoist concept of *chi*, the electromagnetic energy which embodies the *yin* and *yang* forces that are basic to the functioning of the universe. This energy encompasses the five elements of wood, fire, earth, metal and water; and these elements need to be in the correct congruence with each other if the *chi* is to flow in a positive rather than negative way. Feng Shui consultants suggest ways to improve the environment – and enhance the harmony – in any home or business, advising a reconfiguration of shapes, colours, materials and furnishings in order to benefit an individual's career, wealth, health and relationships. A visit to a Fengh Shui website offers the following tips for how to arrange your office:

- Always place the fax machine, telephone and computers in the 'wealth area and future wealth area', to gain more business.
- Do not have any cactus or sharp looking plants in your office as these plants have small sharp leaves and therefore cause *shar* (or slow-moving) *chi* in the office.
- Do not place a paper cutting machine next to the main door; its cutting function is likely to cause staff to back stab and fight each other.

A recent use of Feng Shui, which featured on national television, concerns the fact that losing football teams at the Millennium Football Stadium in Cardiff had all used the same dressing room. Feng Shui experts believed this was because of its proximity to electrical equipment, and gave the room a thorough 'cleansing'. Unfortunately for the next occupants of the dressing room, Cambridge United, it failed and they lost the LBV Vans Trophy final 4-1 to Blackpool. As an occasional watcher of the team, I think this actually says more about the current desperate straits of Cambridge United (bottom of the Division Two table in 2001-2) than whether or not Feng Shui actually works!

There is a central insight within Feng Shui that is wise and appealing. Some ways of physically ordering space are conducive to working well and other ways are not. But from a Christian perspective, there is also much that is superstitious or based on a dubious world-view. In the obsession with finding geophysical explanations for personal and organisational health, a danger looms that individuals will abdicate personal responsibility for themselves and their relationships. The blame for back stabbing in the office cannot simply be put down to where the paper cutting machine is positioned.

Cumber cited Danah Zohar as an example of a business consultant with an eclectic approach to spirituality. Zohar teaches in the Oxford Strategic Leadership Programme at Oxford University and is a visiting fellow at Cranfield School of Management. With her husband, Ian Marshall, she is the author of SQ: Spiritual Intelligence the Ultimate Intelligence, an exploration of their personal philosophy and spiritual understanding with a psycho-scientific explanation of something they've dubbed Spiritual Intelligence (SQ). They define this as 'the intelligence with which we address and solve problems of meaning and value, the intelligence with which we can place our actions and our lives in a wider, richer, meaning-giving context, the intelligence with which we can assess that one course of action or one life-path is more meaningful than another' (SQ, pp.3-4). SQ is for them the necessary foundation for an effective functioning of both IQ (intellectual intelligence) and EQ (emotional intelligence, a concept developed in the mid-1990s by Daniel Goleman).

Many Christians might agree with Zohar's diagnosis of Western culture. 'As a culture, we are going mad. Why? It is the argument of this book that the reasons are mainly spiritual, that our personal and collective mental instability follows from the peculiar form of alienation from the centre – alienation from meaning, value, purpose and vision, alienation from the roots and reasons for our humanity' (*SQ*, pp.170-1). Christians are likely to join in her apparent lament: 'Formal religion and its ethics no longer hold sway, family structures are fluid and constantly changing, and our sense of community and tradition has broken down. Somebody has moved all the moral goalposts and we don't know any longer what game we are playing, never mind what constitutes its rules' (*SQ*, pp.199-200). But they are likely to be somewhat perplexed by her solution. Our spiritual intelligence is sometimes described as a 'God-spot' in the brain, but answers to the questions of who God is, what he is like or even whether he exists remain strangely elusive in Zohar's writing. She embraces ideas from the whole spectrum of world religions, including Christianity, but in a random manner. Thus she:

- quotes with approval St Paul's teaching on love in 1 Corinthians 13, but pairs it with the humanistic psychotherapy of Carl Rogers
- takes her understanding of Jesus not from the New Testament Gospels but the Gnostic Gospels, where Jesus encourages his disciples to dance with him – interpreted by Zohar as feeling the active force of their spiritual intelligence
- cites Jesus' saying 'the kingdom of God is within you' but understands this ultimately in terms of a capacity we all have deep down to reintegrate and heal ourselves.

SQ turns out to be the soul's intelligence, by which – through appropriate nurture and cultivation – we can make ourselves whole. Using a combination of spontaneity and discipline, we can live with an uncertain world and find an inner poise with respect to it, even forging 'a new ethics based on our own innate spiritual intelligence' (p.200). In some ways it is an attractive ideal of humanity that Zohar aspires to, and not everything about it should be dismissed. She applauds the notion of servant leadership, and devotes several pages to expounding it (pp.258-63). But in her final analysis, the idea of Christ dying on the cross so that all might know eternal life has the status of a myth, and she is at pains to deny that there is any 'grand redemption'.

The eclectic approach typified by Zohar has the appeal of appearing to treat different religions even-handedly. Insights, images and rituals are adopted piecemeal from them all. (Within that, however, I detect a clear preference for the Eastern religions of Hinduism, Buddhism and Taoism.) But this approach is symptomatic of a consumerist attitude to spirituality: buying into all the bits you like best, irrespective of their mutual coherence. In the process, some important questions about truth are jettisoned. The world's religions have their common ground – notably the three great monotheistic faiths of Judaism, Christianity and Islam – but they also have areas where they disagree. They cannot all be equally close to the truth. Whether, for instance

- Jesus was the incarnate Son of God, the 'Word made flesh' as the Prologue to John describes him
- Jesus died on the cross for the salvation of the world, and decisively altered for the good humanity's relationship with God
- Jesus was raised from the death, as a foretaste and assurance of eternal life

  are tenets of belief which *matter*.

They should not be seen as subordinate to a higher common denominator called 'spirituality'. Christians cannot rest content with a cavalier approach to claims about fundamental truths.

Spirituality and the New Paradigm

David Welbourn traces the origins of the current interest in spirituality at work rather differently to Bob Cumber. He does not deny New Age influences, but sees the shift from an old to a new *paradigm* as more significant. A paradigm is a mind-set, a world-view or particular way of seeing 'life, the universe and everything'. Paradigms can change. When that happens, we talk about a paradigm shift occurring: an obvious example is the cosmological revolution caused by the discovery that the earth moves round the sun rather than the other way round. Welbourn believes a major paradigm shift has occurred in both physical science and management science in recent decades.

As long as Newtonian physics held sway, a mechanistic view of the universe prevailed. God, if taken into account at all, could be relegated to the position of a celestial watchmaker, whose only role was to set things going in the first place. The work of Einstein showed that the world was more complex than that. It removed the notion that the universe is fundamentally predictable. While there is predictability at the macro-physical level, there is an unpredictable randomness at the sub-atomic level. The universe produces novelty: new forms of life are emerging all the time. A holistic view of reality has also emerged. Everything is part of one vast, interlocking and complex system.

'Paradoxically, while scientists were unlocking more and more of the secrets of the universe, they were becoming inclined to acknowledge a profound mystery at the heart of things. They admitted the universe cannot really be described; the best we can do is to use models and metaphors,' Welbourn says ('The New Paradigm', *Faith in Business Quarterly* 5:3, p.18). This has led to a new openness to religion and theology among scientists – so long as believers accept that they too are on a voyage of discovery, and are open to truths emerging from other disciplines. In many ways it is the more mystical kind of religion that is most conducive to this dialogue with science. Mystics stress the utter mystery and unknowability-in-itself of the divine, while at the same time claiming an intimate relationship with it. 'This mystical attitude has often been reflected in the scientific community. Today, more than ever before, scientists find themselves astounded by the elegance and beauty of the universe, while at the same time wondering at the inherent mystery and elusiveness at the heart of reality,' Welbourn claims ('The New Paradigm', p.19).

He thinks that the same transition from reductionism to openness to other levels of human inquiry, from a narrow 'parts mentality' to a more systems-based, holistic approach, is observable in the changing face of management science. The early days of management thinking were dominated by F.W. Taylor and his 'scientific' analysis of work into functions of optimal efficiency. Organisations were thought of as quasi-machines, and understanding of the whole sought from study of the parts. Behavioural science in the 1950s and 1960s showed a greater interest in the human contribution, but was still fairly reductionist in its understanding of humanity. Welbourn sees the new paradigm as penetrating the world through the Organisational Transformation movement, which became influential during the 1980s. Drawing especially on a book called *Transforming Work*, edited by John Adams, he draws up a contrast between the old and the new paradigms. (See diagram on p.290, taken from 'The New Paradigm at Work', *Faith in Business Quarterly* 4:1, p.11)

It is clear that the new paradigm represents a new openness to spiritual realities. Business schools, management writers and organisational consultants have increasingly taken on board insights from the right-hand side of the table, even if they do not all use or understand it as a total package. There is a growing emphasis on the importance of aligning corporate goals with the deeper spiritual aspirations of the company's staff. This is partly to ensure their commitment and peak performance, but is also seen as something intrinsically worthwhile and desirable.

Partakers in the Divine Nature

Welbourn also comments on the Spirituality At Work movement from a theological perspective. Like Cumber, he notes a tendency in the movement to locate the divine *within* human beings, but is more relaxed about it. At the conference he put forward a thesis: 'The views of the divine currently being expressed are largely an attempt to rediscover the reality of divine immanence. Expressed another way, people are crying out for what amounts to a reinstatement of the Holy Spirit, who for centuries has been – in the Western church – the

OLD PARADIGM	NEW PARADIGM
1. Cartesian/reductionist/mechanistic view of reality	1. Holistic/ecological/systemic view of reality
2. The world regarded as divisible, separate, simple and infinite	2. The world regarded as a complex, interconnected, finite ecological-social-psychological-economic system
3. Monochrome view of reality with same kind of laws applying throughout	3. Different laws apply at different levels of reality
4. The world is to be manipulated and controlled	4. The world is to be surrendered to and enjoyed
5. Emphasis on form and function	5. .Emphasis on energy and flow
6. Reason is the only reliable guide	6. We need intuition as well as reason
7. Change thought to happen in a mechanical, linear sequence, and regarded as predictable	7. Change conceived as having multiple causes, as being subtle and unpredictable
8. Events and situations classified and their outcomes controlled through the application of known laws	8. Each situation or event is unique and their outcomes are not controllable simply by applying general laws
9. Human attitudes and feelings can be disregarded	9. Confidence, expectation and love are critical aspects of causality
10. True knowledge is disinterested, dispassionate	10. All knowledge is 'interested knowledge'
11. People regarded simply as employees of the organisation	11. People treated as multi-dimensional persons with a life outside the organisation
12. Fulfilment is sought from material rewards alone	12. Fulfilment is sought through the opportunity to pursue lofty (even cosmic) objectives in line with people's deepest spiritual values
13. People are brought into line through rules and regulations	13. Alignment is achieved through commitment to a common vision
14. The leader controls the whole show	14. The leader's role is to inspire and teach
15. Problems are solved from the top	15. Problems are solved participatively with staff at all levels making their special contributions
16. Management is a science	16. Management is a performing art

Cinderella of the Holy Trinity'. ('The New Paradigm', p.20) The Western church has tended to emphasise the transcendence of God: the God who stands over against the world, and created all that there is out of a substance that is not divine. But that is not the sole understanding of God found in Christian theology.

Welbourn draws attention to elements in New Testament writings which emphasise the divine within us. There is a strong theme of both Jesus and the Holy Spirit indwelling believers in the Gospel of John (especially chapters 14 and 15). Paul speaks of Christians as members of the body of Christ. Perhaps the most remarkable statement indicating a convergence of the human and the divine is found in 2 Peter 1:3-4, which says that 'His divine power has given us everything needed for life and godliness' and holds out the promise that we 'may become partakers in the divine nature'. This passage is not often preached on in the Christian West, but the Eastern Orthodox Church is a different story. There the idea of human deification – human beings coming to be like God – is prominent. Typical of this view is the Eastern Orthodox theologian Vladimir Lossky, who supports the concept both from 2 Peter 1 and the writings of the early Church Fathers, e.g.:

- Clement of Alexandria, for whom Christian perfection consists in the knowledge of the good and assimilation to God
- St Athanasius, who speaks of the deification to which created beings are called
- St Basil, who wrote: 'The Holy Spirit deifies by grace those who still belong to a nature subject to change'
- St Cyril, who was dominated by the idea of deification as humanity's supreme goal; by virtue of the incarnation, we become sons of God by participation
- St Gregory of Nyssa, who in commenting on the text 'Blessed are the pure in heart, for they shall see God' argues that the state of blessedness does not consist in the fact that something is known *about* God, but in having God within oneself

- St Gregory of Nazianzus, whose prayer was: 'Let the Spirit possess me, Let him lead me by the hand, intellect and tongue to what is due and what he wants ... I am a divine organ, and instrument of the word, which is tuned and played by the good artist, the Spirit.'

This mystical strand, which highlights the capacity and desire of the Holy Spirit to penetrate and transform human beings, is also found in Western Christianity, but it is particularly strong in the East. Welbourn believes the Spirituality at Work movement, and the new paradigm that lies behind it, are helping Western Christians to rediscover an important part of their heritage: 'An aspect of God in which Christianity has always theoretically believed – God within, the divine as immanent, God the Holy Spirit' ('The New Paradigm', p.21). He thinks that the emphasis on the idea of God within need be judged unsound only if it purports to represent the whole of God.

It seems to me, however, that many of today's spokespeople for the spirituality movement are doing precisely that. If they speak of God at all (often, as we have seen, other phrases are used) it is a God who is *merely* immanent. The transcendent dimension is missing. Classical Christian theology speaks of God as both immanent and transcendent in a balanced way. If the God of the spirituality gurus is not a personal, relational God who is creator and redeemer of the world, then a significant gulf in understanding exists. I do not believe the early Church Fathers would find they had much in common with them. While the two St Gregorys and others believed that human beings could travel a long way on the road to become like God, they saw a precondition for this as recognising the gulf between God and us created by human sin. It is no natural affinity that we have to be like God. Only God's saving initiative in Christ makes such aspirations possible.

It is certainly true that God's wind – an analogy used of the Holy Spirit – blows where it chooses (Jn. 3:8), and that God is actively concerned in the lives of all people, not just Christian believers. In Acts 10, God gave a fresh revelation of his purposes to Peter and the early church through a Roman centurion, Cornelius, a devout, generous, God-fearing man, but at that time neither a Jew nor a Christian. He was a serious searcher after truth, and hence presumably open to the promptings of the Holy Spirit. There may be people today in the Spirituality at Work movement who are like him. But we also need to be aware that not everyone who uses the words 'spirit', 'spiritual' or 'spirituality' is in that category. 1 John 4:1 warns: 'Beloved, do not believe every spirit, but test the spirits to see whether they are from God; for many false prophets have gone out into the world.' The New Testament persistently speaks about the Holy Spirit in a Trinitarian connection; in other words, in close association with the two other members of the Trinity, God the Father and God the Son. In 1 Corinthians 2 the spiritual person is described as someone in whom the Spirit of God dwells; and the Spirit imparts wisdom, but it is wisdom not 'of this age or of the rulers of this age' (2:6) but the wisdom revealed in a crucified Christ. Similarly Romans 8, that wonderful chapter on the transforming power of the Spirit, is shot through with Paul's infectious excitement about the love God has demonstrated in the person of Jesus.

The Jury is Still Out

How should Christians respond to the Spirituality at Work phenomenon? Is the movement here to stay? For David Welbourn, the answer to these two questions is closely linked. He is distressed at the prospect of some Christians flatly rejecting the movement, and asks them to apply the 'Gamaliel test' of Acts 5:33-39. After citing a number of messianic movements that had come to nothing, the well-respected Pharisee Gamaliel gave a wise piece of advice to his Jewish colleagues, who were intent on suppressing the early Christian movement. He urged them: 'Leave these men alone! Let them go! For if their purpose or activity is of human origin, it will fail. But if it is from God, you will not be able to stop these men; you will only find yourselves fighting against God.' This is fair comment. Time will tell whether the Spirituality at Work movement has real, God-given substance to it, or whether it is ephemeral.

At present, the jury is still out. I for one remain to be persuaded either way. I will simply point to contrasting pieces of evidence on both sides of the debate.

On the one hand, several people in business have told me that the Spirituality at Work movement is creating a new openness among people to talking about issues that really matter. It has become more acceptable to talk about issues of faith, values, purpose and identity in a corporate context. Welbourn attests this himself as an industrial chaplain. 'For years we industrial chaplains have been trying to articulate the relevance of Christian faith and values to business life. And we've had a very hard task on our hands, largely because of the dearth of common conceptual ground. That task is considerably easier now that spirituality is on business's own agenda. It is now *business* books, not just books on ethics or theology, which are highlighting and promoting all the values and many of the concepts we ourselves are committed to,' he says ('The New Paradigm', p.22). A senior human resources director in a pharmaceuticals company said something similar to me. This is welcome news. If the Spirituality at Work movement leads to fruitful debate, discussions in which Christians can both identify shared spiritual ground but also explain a distinctive Christian understanding, we would be foolish not to applaud and welcome this development. Christians should grasp the opportunities now coming their way with both hands, but also sensitively and humbly.

On the other hand, I am not convinced that this interest in spirituality necessarily runs very deep, or that the terminology of spirit and spirituality is something that the majority of people in corporate life are yet comfortable with. Most of the running in the movement is not actually being made by practising businesspeople. Welbourn undertook a sabbatical study project on the subject in California, home of several key American figures in the movement, but had difficulty discovering companies where spirituality was on the boardroom agenda. As I have already mentioned, the vast majority of delegates at the Ballarat conference in Australia were academics, trainers and consultants. People who manage, make and market things were largely notable by their absence. The Ridley Hall conference had a fairly similar make-up of delegates to Ballarat, with a slightly higher proportion of business practitioners. A major international conference on *Living Spirit – New Dimensions in Work and Learning* took place at the University of Surrey in Guildford on 22-24 July 2002. A fascinating range of papers and workshops were on offer, grouped into four areas: 'Living Spirit at Work', 'Transpersonal Realities', 'New Age and Esoteric Spirituality' and 'New Leadership'. The leaders of these workshops, according to their CVs, include:

- several different kinds of consultant, facilitator, coach and mentor
- management trainers, personal trainers and professional development trainers
- psychologists, psychotherapists and gestalt therapists
- a playwright, a theatre director and an artist
- a methaphysical practitioner, a motivational speaker and a spokesman for the holistic movement
- a ceremonialist, a Shamanic practitioner and a Reiki master
- two 'interfaith' ministers.

What emerges from this is a picture of enthusiasts for Spirituality at Work: people who make their living out of ideas, whether new ones or old ones with a new slant. They love formulating ideas, trying them out, persuading others and helping put them into practice. They doubtless have much that is interesting and stimulating to offer, but they are people on the periphery of business rather than working at its heart day to day. The director for centralised operations in the Lloyds TSB Group ran a workshop. He stood out as someone quite exceptional, precisely because he did come into that mainstream category. I suspect that Spirituality at Work will prove to have a shelf-life longer than the average fashionable idea only if it is adopted by more such people – in short, if there is momentum from people in business with sensitive spiritual antennae who can convince their colleagues of its relevance to their ongoing work.

14

THE REVIVED IDEA OF VOCATION:
CALLING IN THE BUSINESS WORLD

You may have journeyed into strange and unfamiliar territory while reading this book. Having the worlds of faith and business drawn together is probably a new experience, as a yawning chasm has been allowed to develop between the two. We began by exploring the marginalisation of Christianity by business, and now we've traversed the chasm and reached the other side – the marginalisation of business by Christianity.

Hostile Territory

This is the oft-quoted testimony of William, a Christian sales manager.

'In the thirty years of my professional career, my church has never once suggested that there be any type of accounting of my on-the-job ministry to others. My church has never once offered to improve those skills which could make me a better minister, nor has it ever asked if I needed any kind of support in what I am doing. There has never once been an inquiry into the types of ethical decision I must face, or whether I seek to communicate the faith to my co-workers. I have never been in a congregation where there was any type of public affirmation of the ministry in my career. In short, I must conclude that my church does not have the least interest in whether, or how, I minister in my daily life.'

What this and similar stories show is that the institutional churches are indifferent to business, suspicious of business or actively hostile to it.

It's not fashionable to say anything good about business in church circles. I know, because I've felt pretty much on my own in doing so for the last 12 years. A striking demonstration of the church's discomfort is the difficulty it has in including the world of business in its times of corporate prayer. Often, people in particular occupations will be prayed for – but which ones? My extensive research with a wide range of groups, from every type of denomination, shows a persistent trend:

- Frequently – clergy, church workers and missionaries
- Quite often – those in the so-called 'caring professions', teachers, doctors, nurses and social workers
- Every now and again – those in positions of national leadership or responsible for the maintenance of law and order, politicians, police, the armed forces
- Almost never – those involved in the commercial world, e.g. accountants, engineers, bank managers and salesmen.

The church does not pray for business people: perhaps because it regards their activities with embarrassment; perhaps because it never occurs to leaders of worship to pray for them; perhaps because it does not know *what* to pray for them. Probably a combination of all three.

And yet within these congregations are many people who work in business. It's not that business is unrepresented in a typical group of church members. Churches depend on the giving of businesspeople to make ends meet. Anglican clergy depend for their pension provision on investments in stocks and shares made by the Church Commissioners. Some of the people ensuring that business remains off the church's agenda are in business themselves. It is almost an unconscious conspiracy between clergy and laity. Much of the church's corporate prayer is now led by lay people, and they largely follow the patterns established by clergy in the style and content of their prayers. The marginalisation of business by Christianity is a curious affair, deeply riddled with irony.

Just as we needed a historical perspective to understand the marginalisation of Christianity, so too for the marginalisation of business by Christianity. We need to see how we have come to the current situation. The two processes of marginalisation are necessarily linked, so we must retrace a little of the ground covered in Chapter 1. But then the story takes off in a different direction, tracing the notion of vocation or calling: two words that should be regarded as synonymous, because they mean the same thing.

'Calling is the truth that God calls us to himself so decisively that everything we are, everything we do, and everything we have is invested with a special devotion and dynamism lived out as a response to his summons and service,' Os Guinness says (*The Call*, p.4). That truth has been obscured or lost to view during long periods of the church's history. It was to rediscover this truth, and to explore its relevance for the present day, that the Ridley Hall Foundation held a conference on *Vocation: Christian Calling in the Secular World*, in June 1998.

The Biblical View of Calling

In the opening presentation at the conference, Steve Walton, then a lecturer at St John's College Nottingham and now at London Bible College, summed up the New Testament understanding of vocation in terms of a fourfold usage. He spells this analysis out in detail in his book *A Call to Live*. Since the conference, I have been interested to find both Os Guinness and Paul Stevens, author of *The Abolition of the Laity* (a rather misleading title for a masterly study of vocation, work and ministry in a biblical perspective), come up with similar categorisations independently of each other.

The fourfold call comprises:

(i) The call to *belong* to Jesus Christ

This is the primary summons to discipleship. Jesus called the fishermen James and John from their nets to follow him (Mk. 1:19-20). When challenged by the scribes and Pharisees about his habit of eating with disreputable people, he replied: 'I have come to call not the righteous but sinners' (Mk. 2:15-17). St Paul says of the Christians at Rome that they 'are called to belong to Jesus Christ' (Rom. 1:6). Timothy is reminded of 'the eternal life, to which you were called and for which you made the good confession' (1 Tim. 6:12). The Greek word for church is *ecclesia*, which literally means 'called out ones'.

(ii) The call to *be holy*

Jesus' followers (just like Old Testament Israel) are to be a people wholly dedicated to God. Paul tells both the Roman and Corinthian Christians right at the start of his letters to them that they are called to be *hagioi*, a Greek word that can be translated either 'holy' or 'saints' (Rom. 1:7, 1 Cor. 1:2). He begs the Christians at Ephesus 'to lead a life worthy of the calling to which you have been called' (Eph. 4:1). Note that the context in which he uses this language is almost always corporate: Paul is concerned with the quality of life of Christians as a group.

(iii) The call to *let God be God*

This involves recognising the initiative of God: that he has his purposes and will not be thwarted in carrying them out. Our responsibility is therefore one of living actively under his sovereign power. God 'gives life to the dead and calls into existence the things that do not exist' (Rom. 4:17). The 'gifts and the calling of God are irrevocable' (Rom. 11:29). John writes: 'See what love the Father has given us, that we should be called children of God; and that is what we are.' (1 Jn. 3:1) When used in this way, the language of calling often has the effect of assuring us that God will bring his work in human beings and the world to completion – but never in a way that lets us off the hook and leaves us as passive bystanders.

(iv) The call to *do*

Here calling is linked with carrying out various tasks and roles. Paul twice describes himself as 'called to be an apostle' (Rom. 1:1; 1 Cor. 1:1). As an apostle he was sent by God to lead others to faith in Christ. Once he had been converted, this 'became the mainspring of his life. It was this that motivated him and made him tick' (*A Call to Live*, p.75). Within that calling, there were specific missionary projects that God called Paul – with colleagues – to undertake. One example, already noted in Chapter 12, is Acts 13:2, where the Holy Spirit says to the church leaders in Antioch, 'Set apart for me Barnabas and Saul for the work to which I have called them.' In Acts 16:10 Paul and another companion – apparently the author Luke himself – attempt to cross over to Macedonia, 'being convinced that God has called us to proclaim the good news to the.'

Walton noted that this final category of references is the smallest, and that it is difficult to find New Testament passages which speak unambiguously of calling in an everyday working context. In one passage, 1 Corinthians 7:17-24, Paul uses call language for the 'place in life' or 'station' (slave or freeman; married or single) that we occupy. This is a passage I shall come back to later. But the language of calling about individuals performing specific functions is found in the Old Testament.

Unsung Heroes

A fascinating snapshot of ordinary people working as God intended is found in Exodus 35:30-36:1. Bezalel and Oholiab are two of the unsung heroes of the Bible. Nobody teaches about them in Sunday School, yet the practical contribution they made to the life of the pilgrim people of God was immense. Bezalel was a skilled carpenter, metalsmith and engraver. He led the work on the tabernacle and its precious cargo, the ark of the covenant. Oholiab was his assistant, specialising in design, weaving and embroidery. Notice three key points from this passage:

- God is described as having both called Bezalel by name and filled him with his Spirit. The latter phrase is used sparingly in the Old Testament. Usually it is reserved for individuals in the roles of prophet, priest or king, but here we find it used about the skills of the craftsman. God's Spirit encompasses the fashioning of material things. That Spirit is potentially available to anyone 'to whom the Lord has given skill and understanding to know how to do any work.' (Ex. 36:1, NRSV)
- God equipped Bezalel and Oholiab for their work. The qualities mentioned include ability, intelligence, knowledge, craftsmanship, skills in specific materials, and – not least – inspiration to teach (35:34). Whether it is done on a one-to-one basis, the apprentice learning by observation of the master craftsman at work, or whether it happens in a more didactic way, the expert imparting knowledge to pupils in a group, the gift of teaching is one of priceless value
- The emphasis on artistic design (35:32, 35) appears to put a strong premium on creativity. These men did not work to stereotyped formulae. The Spirit of God released their imaginations to create something striking in its originality. They used a great variety of colours, materials and forms in the making of the tabernacle and all it contained.

A few years ago we carried out a radical refurbishment of our chapel at Ridley Hall. New seating, lighting and furnishings were installed. We held a service to mark the reopening of the chapel, and invited all the people who had worked on the building (carpenters, electricians, embroiderers, etc.). I preached on this passage, partly because I wanted to affirm these people in the work they had done for the college. They were very appreciative; some said it helped them to see their work in a different perspective.

Isaiah 45:1-7 is another remarkable passage. Here the object of God's calling is Cyrus, the Persian king whose defeat of Babylon led to the end of the Jewish exile. The God of Israel says to Cyrus: 'I call you by your name.' When this phrase is used in the Old Testament it means more than simply giving a name: it means charging with meaning and purpose. Cyrus had a purpose in the designs of God. Even though he was not himself a believer, he warrants the title 'anointed' or 'chosen one' (Is. 45:1).

> For the sake of my servant Jacob, and Israel my chosen,
> I call you by your name, I surname you, though you do not know me.
> I am the Lord, and there is no other; besides me there is no god.
> I arm you, though you do not know me. (45:4-5, NRSV)

Much of the time the Bible simply accepts human work in a matter-of-fact sort of way. The psalmist wrote: '... man goes out to his work, to his labour until evening' (Ps.104:23). It is as natural and routine an activity as that the lions should roar (v.21) and the sun should rise (v.22). Different occupations all have their part to play in the functioning of society and the furthering of God's purposes. The ease with which the biblical writers accepted them is shown in their readiness to use working metaphors about God himself. The Bible repeatedly uses vivid images drawn from human life to talk about God. Some of these are political (e.g. king), some familial (e.g. father), and some relational (e.g. lover). But many are drawn from the world of ordinary work. In a highly suggestive book, titled *God the Worker: Journeys into the Mind, Heart and Imagination of God*, Robert Banks draws to attention no less than eight biblical pairings:

- God as Composer and Performer
- God as Metalworker and Potter
- God as Garmentmaker and Dresser
- God as Gardener and Orchardist
- God as Farmer and Winemaker
- God as Shepherd and Pastoralist
- God as Tentmaker and Camper
- God as Builder and Architect.

Reflecting on the biblical passages Banks cites can lead us into a richer and more profound understanding of God. But it can also enrich our understanding of the various occupations put to metaphorical use. For example, a potter who meditates on Jeremiah 18 might well come away pondering the awesome creative potential entailed in the reworking of clay.

Superficially, Jesus might seem to be indifferent to the value contained in ordinary human work. He called his closest disciples away from their everyday occupations such as fishing and tax collecting to follow him on his wanderings as an itinerant rabbi. He does not seem to have been bothered about the disruptive effect this caused. Imagine the annoyance Zebedee must have felt when his sons James and John, key players in the family fishing business, suddenly stopped mending the nets and left him in the boat with his hired men (Mk. 1:20). The call to a highly personal style of discipleship overrides normal domestic and occupational loyalties.

Several qualifications are in order, though. What was demanded of Jesus' 12 closest disciples was not necessarily expected of all his followers. One tax collector, Levi (Matthew), upped and left his tax booth (Mk. 2:14), presumably not returning for at least the three years of Jesus' earthly ministry. Another, Zacchaeus, may well have remained in post, collecting taxes in a different way, cured of the element of personal greed (Lk. 19:1-10). And while Jesus' call to the fishermen was radically disruptive, it was not radically discontinuous. Jesus never said to them: 'Why did you waste your time fishing?' On the contrary, he often used their fishing boats – as a pulpit to preach from, as a means of escape from the crowds, and as a way of getting from one side of the lake to the other. But more significantly, he underlined a continuity between the job they knew so well and the task he now called them to: 'Follow me, and I will make you fish for people' (the politically correct revision of 'fishers of men'). He used their occupation as an analogy. The picture he conjured up is one of a great shoal of people waiting to be caught for the kingdom of God. In that pursuit, many of the qualities needed for catching fish are relevant to 'catching' people: courage, patience, perseverance, flexibility and teamwork.

The language Jesus habitually used, especially in his parables about the kingdom of God, the central theme of his teaching, positively throbs with illustrations taken from everyday work. It features farmers going out to sow (Mk. 4:3-9), merchants purchasing precious stones (Mt. 13:45-46), builders working out their estimates (Lk. 14:28-30), and middle managers faced with the sack providing for their future (Lk. 16:1-8) – to name only a few examples. Jesus certainly engaged in a major critique of wealth, repeatedly warning against the tendency to idolise money. But he took for granted a world of work and exchange where buying and selling were everyday human activities. The need to count the cost, increase one's talents, and take risks with one's resources, attitudes that could be taken for granted on an earthly level, were carried over into Jesus' understanding of how we relate to God and the destiny he has in store for us. Jesus affirmed the world of work, even in the act of widening people's horizons and drawing people into a vision of something much bigger.

Paul's Working Illustrations

Paul is little less reticent about employing illustrations from the working world. Consider the passage where he is exhorting his young colleague Timothy: 'You then, my child, be strong in the grace that is in Christ Jesus; and what you have heard from me through many witnesses entrust to faithful people who will be able to teach others as well. Share in suffering like a good soldier of Christ Jesus. No one serving in the army gets entangled in everyday affairs; the soldier's aim is to please the enlisting officer. And in the case of an athlete, no one is crowned without competing according to the rules. It is the farmer who does the work who ought to have the first share of the crops. Think over what I say, for the Lord will give you understanding in all things.' (2 Tim. 2:1-7, NRSV)

Here Paul draws lessons from three different spheres of life, military, sporting and agricultural. Each makes a slightly different point. The example of the soldier teaches endurance and concentrated service, the athlete teaches discipline, and the farmer teaches perseverance. Taken together, they illustrate aptly what it means for Timothy to be *strong* in the grace that is in Christ Jesus (v.1).

Another passage where Paul uses examples from different occupations is where he is arguing the case for himself and colleagues like Barnabas to be paid for their work in proclaiming the gospel (a right, however, that he ultimately does not insist on). He points out: 'Who at any time pays the expenses for doing military service? Who plants a vineyard and does not eat any of its fruit? Or who tends a flock and does not get any of its milk?' (1 Cor. 9:7, NRSV)

In other words, soldiers, farmers and shepherds all enjoy some perks resulting from the work they do. It is a wonderfully lavish use of illustration. Why use one when three will do? I cannot help thinking that if contemporary preachers employed workplace analogies so readily, not only would they communicate more effectively but it would also help people to see that what they do at work is significant in the eyes of God.

The Active and Contemplative Lives

In the early church, the positive view of ordinary work which is found or implied in many parts of the Bible was not immediately lost to view. But before very long, Christian thought was affected by the prevalent attitudes in Greek and Roman culture. To the Greeks, work was a curse and something beneath the dignity of a free person. Physical work, especially, was regarded as degrading to human dignity. The Greek social structure supported such an outlook, for it rested on the premise that slaves and artisans did the work, enabling the élite to devote themselves to the exercise of the mind in art, philosophy and politics. The Roman view was not much different. Cicero wrote: 'The toil of a hired worker, who is paid only for his toil and not for artistic skill, is unworthy of a free man and is sordid in character ... Trade on a small retail scale is equally sordid' (*De Officiis*, 1:42, p.150).

Few Christian writers have been as dismissive as that, but by the fourth century they were tending to see activities that involved manual labour (like farming) or the exchange of money (like trade) as second-rate. Eusebius of Caesarea, the principal historian of the church from the apostolic age down to the early fourth century, is a clear exponent of this point of view. According to Eusebius, two ways of life were given by Christ to his church – the 'perfect life' and the 'permitted life'. One is spiritual and dedicated to contemplation: 'It is above nature, and beyond common human living. Wholly and permanently separate from the common customary life of mankind, it devotes itself to the service of God alone.' Those following the perfect life 'appear to die to the life of mortals, to bear with them nothing earthly but their body, and in mind and spirit to have passed to heaven.' The other way of life is earthly and dedicated to action: '[It is] more humble, more human, permits men to have minds for farming, for trade, and the other more worldly interests, as well as for religion.' A kind of secondary grade of piety is attributed to such people. (*Demonstration of the Gospel*.)

Not all the theologians who followed in Eusebius' wake held such an élitist view. Augustine has words of praise for farmers, craftsmen and merchants. Thomas Aquinas affirmed work as a natural right and duty, and drew up a hierarchy of what he regarded as respectable professions and trades. He even said: 'To live well is to work well.' But both Augustine and Aquinas still treated these activities as inferior to the contemplative life. 'The one is loved, the other endured,'

Augustine said. The distinction between the active life and the contemplative life was crucial and runs through most of the Middle Ages.

The word 'calling' therefore became reserved for those holy people who felt called to separate themselves from everyday human activities and relationships in order to devote themselves to a life of prayer. Many monastic orders were founded during the medieval era. In the hierarchy of callings, priest came high, but monk and nun came even higher. To spend your time in contemplative prayer, absorbed in the vision of God, lost in wonder, love and praise – that was the highest calling anyone could aspire to. Os Guinness notes that monasticism began with a *reforming mission* as 'it sought to remind an increasingly secularised church that it was still possible to follow the radical way of life required by the gospel. It finished with a *relaxing effect* – the double standard reserved the radical way for the specialists (the aristocrats of the soul) and let everyone else off the hook' (*The Call*, p.33). Guinness calls this the Catholic distortion of calling: the double standard which reinforces a sacred-secular divide, and which is found in many other churches today apart from Catholic ones.

It is important to note that even in monasteries the everyday stuff of life could not be ignored altogether. Indeed, most monks and nuns spent some of their time doing physical work. Some of them refused to divorce the tasks that they did from the life of prayer. St Benedict had a very positive view of everyday work; it was he who coined the phrase 'to work is to pray'. The Rule of St Benedict integrated tasks of manual labour, services of worship and times for biblical reflection around the overriding theme of the praise of God. The most famous expression of this attitude is found in *The Practice of the Presence of God*, the spiritual classic written by the Carmelite monk Brother Lawrence.

'The time of business does not for me differ from the time of prayer; and in the noise and clutter of my kitchen, while several persons are at the same time calling for different things, I possess God in as great tranquillity as if I were upon my knees at the Blessed Sacrament,' Brother Lawrence writes.

Admirable as this is, there's not much evidence from the medieval era that this integrated view of work and worship made much impact on ordinary people in the outside world. The church did little in its teaching to encourage them to see their work as a sphere in which they could serve their neighbour and glorify God. The church was locked into a way of regarding occupations as first or second class, similar to the way it saw the single or celibate life as superior to the married state.

Around 1500, this way of thinking was challenged by two great movements. The first was the Renaissance, a remarkable flowering of artistic talent in all its many dimensions. Great painters and sculptors like Michelangelo Buonarroti and Leonardo da Vinci display an overriding confidence and exuberance in their work. Subconsciously, it sings the praises of the kind of individual, craftsmanlike and artistic labour at which they excelled. This work necessarily required the handling of materials. Non-agricultural manual labour thereby derived a new status: a dignity which the word craftsmanship carries still.

Luther and Calvin

The second great movement was the Reformation. Here pride of place must undoubtedly go to Martin Luther. His revolutionary understanding of 'calling' broke the medieval mould. Luther railed against the monastic life, and affirmed the equal status of all Christians as they respond to God in faith. He said all works are measured before God by faith alone: 'Indeed, the menial housework of a manservant or maidservant is often more acceptable to God than all the fastings and other works of a monk or priest.' Calling becomes a basic category for understanding Christian existence. The primary calling is to respond to God's offer of salvation. The secondary calling is to accept as God-given the duties which come through occupational, social and family positions, and to fulfil them ungrudgingly and wholeheartedly.

'For Martin Luther and subsequent reformers, the recovery of the holistic understanding of calling was dramatic. Writing about the "Estate of Marriage" in 1522, Luther declared that God and the angels smile when a man changes a diaper. William Tyndale wrote that, if our desire is to please God, pouring water, washing dishes, cobbling shoes, and preaching the Word "is all one" … . Little wonder that the cultural implications of recovering true calling were explosive. Calling gave to everyday work a dignity and spiritual significance under God that dethroned the primacy of leisure and contemplation. Calling gave to humble people and ordinary tasks an investment of equality that shattered hierarchies and was a vital impulse towards democracy,' Guinness writes (*The Call*, pp.34-35). It opened the door to regarding every task or job as important in God's eyes. Luther considered that there were only a few jobs that were beyond the pale, notably robber, prostitute, and for some of his life at least, usurer – a lender at interest. The medieval dichotomy and hierarchy between the active and contemplative lives had been assaulted head on.

John Calvin's teaching on vocation corresponds closely to Luther's. Calvin saw work as 'a dignified and glorious means of praising and affirming God in and through his creation, while adding further to its wellbeing' – sentiments which sound surprisingly modern. His strong belief in God's providence led him to urge contentment in one's work: 'In all our cares, toils, annoyances, and other burdens, it will be no small alleviation to know that all these are under the superintendence of God … . This, too, will afford admirable consolation in following your proper calling. No work will be so mean and sordid as not to have a splendour and value in the eye of God' (*Institutes of the Christian Religion*, 3.10.6). Like Luther, Calvin thought that contentment should issue in a readiness to stay in the same station in life. A key text for both of them was 1 Corinthians 7:20, where Paul says: 'Every one should remain in the calling in which he was called.' Calvin comments: 'Each should be content with his calling and persist in it, and not be eager to change to something else. … Paul wishes to correct the thoughtless eagerness which impels some to change their situation without any proper reason. ... He condemns the restlessness which prevents individuals from remaining contentedly where they are.'

These views rapidly crossed the English Channel. A book of homilies dating from around 1552, published to assist the clergy in instructing the people, says: 'It is the appointment and will of God, that every man, during the time of this mortal and transitory life, should give himself to some honest and godly exercise and labour, and everyone follow his own business, and to walk uprightly in his own calling.' William Perkins said vocation or calling was 'a certain kind of life ordained and imposed on man by God for the common good' (*Works of William Perkins*, p.903).

The Puritan Tenets

In the writings of the sixteenth and seventeenth century English Puritans a high view of work and a worldly view of vocation are themes which are sounded again and again. A whole stream of quotations from influential writers like Perkins and Richard Baxter could be cited, but it is unnecessary to belabour the point. Leland Ryken's book *Work and Leisure in Christian Perspective* marshals the evidence from the Puritans impressively. This teaching can be summed up in a series of key propositions:

1. Christians are saved by the grace of God. We cannot earn our own salvation. Daily life is the arena where we express our gratitude to God by the quality of the lives we live.
2. It is important to work hard. God has commanded us to labour for our daily bread, and we should be diligent in performing our duties. Idleness was seen as a snare of the devil and roundly condemned.
3. Although one of the motives for working was to provide for oneself and one's family, the focus of work should be service to others. Work expresses the mutual dependence of people upon each other.

4. Vocation involves the idea of stewardship. (The biblical grounds for understanding stewardship in terms of caring for the earth are discussed in Chapter 9.) The Puritans focused on a more personal application: making good use of the time, talents and money which God has given us. A prominent modern Christian who endorses this idea enthusiastically is the businessman, civil servant and politician Sir Fred Catherwood, author of the aptly named book *God's Time, God's Money*.

5. Work should be done 'as unto the Lord,' in keeping with Paul's words in Colossians 3:23: 'Whatever your task, work heartily, as serving the Lord.' George Herbert gave lasting expression to this in his great hymn:

Teach me, my God and King,
In all things thee to see,
And what I do in any thing,
To do it as for thee.

All may of thee partake:
Nothing can be so mean,
Which with this tincture (for
    thy sake)
Will not grow bright and clean.

A servant with this clause
Makes drudgery divine:
Who sweeps a room, as for
    thy laws
Makes that and the action fine.

This is the famous stone
That turneth all to gold:
For that which God
    doth touch and own
Cannot for less be told.

An Anglican clergyman, Herbert was not himself a Puritan, but he shared their thinking in this area.

6. Every legitimate type of work, which provides some useful service to other people, can be a genuine God-given vocation.

It is evident that development of the idea of vocation in the world was closely bound up with what became known as the Protestant work ethic. It is fashionable these days to deride the Protestant work ethic: for some, it even occupies the status of a bogeyman. In its original form and context, however, it was an extremely positive way of thinking. The tragedy is that as time went on, as the eighteenth century replaced the seventeenth and the Puritan influence decreased, the notions of vocation and work became subtly twisted. An insidious process of distortion set in. The result was that by the end of the nineteenth century, almost all the major ideas of the Reformers and Puritans had been turned on their head. So let's look at them again, one by one.

The Secularisation of the Protestant Work Ethic

1. The psychological evidence suggests that it is very difficult for people fully to accept God's grace – even for people who place a strong notional emphasis upon it. A gracious God seems too good to be true. The temptation to seek assurance of salvation through our own efforts is a besetting one. Weber's argument has a measure of plausibility: the Protestant habits of working hard and accumulating wealth came to be motivated partly by a desire to see evidence of God's blessing in one's life, and therefore to feel more secure about one's eternal destiny. This should not be oversimplified in terms of replacing justification by faith with justification by works. It was more a case of subconsciously seeking *assurance* about justification through one's works.

2. Working hard could be taken to extremes. Workaholism is not a recent invention. The fear of idleness became obsessive. Isaac Watts is rightly praised for his great hymn 'When I survey the wondrous cross', but he also wrote the following song for Charity and Sunday schools:

How doth the busy little bee In works of labour or of skill
Improve each shining hour I should be busy too
And gather honey all the day For Satan finds some mischief
From every opening flower. still
 For idle hands to do.

The association of idle hands with Satan and mischief proved extremely pervasive. Although the Puritans set aside Sunday as a day of complete rest, rest was almost entirely absent from the rest of the week. As the Industrial Revolution took over, men, women and children were often made to work in factories and mines 14 or 16 hours a day.

3. The motive of working for others' benefit was gradually replaced by a strong ideology of self-interest. The notion of dependence on others gave way to an emphasis on self-reliance. This is illustrated by the sort of proverbs or aphorisms popular in the eighteenth century: 'Early to bed and early to rise, makes a man healthy, wealthy and wise.' 'God helps those that help themselves.'

4. The notion of stewardship remained strong, but stewardship not carried through fully can end up as a disguised form of selfishness. John Wesley taught a simple philosophy: 'Earn all you can, save all you can, give all you can.' There were, of course, some notable industrialists-turned-philanthropists who carried this out to the letter. In nineteenth century USA, Andrew Carnegie started life penniless but made a fortune in the steel industry, and then spent the last 18 years of his life giving away $480 million to worthy causes. He had promised when he was thirty-three and an up-and-coming business-man that he would do this. John Laing is an early twentieth century English example of a Nonconformist businessman who did something similar. He made his money in the construction industry, and the trusts he founded continue to support a large number of evangelical causes. But not every-one proves true to these fine intentions. Many earn all that they can and save all that they can, but don't get around to giving all that they can. If they no longer believe in God or care about other people, this is hardly surprising, but even for those who retain a Christian commitment, the lure to hold on to most of what you've got remains strong.

5. With the gradual decline of religious belief and practice people no longer worked to glorify God. Throughout the eighteenth and nineteenth centuries, secularisation was pro-ceeding apace, although the number of churchgoers was still high compared with what it is now. Even for believers, working 'as unto the Lord' can become an empty phrase

devoid of any real meaning. In relation to work, the worship of God and the call of God were gradually replaced simply by the duties and roles of society. Os Guinness notes a process by which 'the original demand that each Christian should have a calling was boiled down to the demand that each citizen should have a job' (*The Call*, p.40). He calls this the typical Protestant diversion – elevating the secular at the expense of the spiritual – and regards it as every bit as serious as the Catholic distortion of elevating the spiritual at the expense of the secular. Without a lively sense of the presence of God, of a creator being to whom we are responsible, vocation is a hollow concept. As Guinness succinctly puts it: 'There is no calling unless there is a Caller' (*The Call*, p.20).

6. Even where the word 'vocation' survived, there was a gradual restriction in its application. As the commercial impulse became stronger and it became clear that many people in business were motivated principally by self-interest, there was a reaction against using the language of calling in that context. In church circles, the medieval distinction between sacred and secular occupations reappeared in a slightly different form. Monks were no longer at the head of the list; missionaries were. They were followed by church leaders or people who worked full-time for overtly Christian organisations. People might have a vocation to one or other of the caring professions – doctor, nurse, teacher, social worker, probation officer. Some might even have a calling to be politicians. An unofficial, dimly acknowledged but nonetheless real gradation of jobs set in. What is crystal clear is that somewhere along the line (perhaps around the beginning of the twentieth century) working in business slipped out of view. It disappeared from most people's understanding of the limits of the word 'vocation'.

Professions

'Caring professions' is no casual turn of phrase. Profession is another key word in the arena of work, and it demands special attention. It derives historically from the professing, or taking, of religious vows. These vows were not exclusive to monastic orders or priests.

One of the earliest occurrences of the word 'profession' is in the Hippocratic Oath, which dates from the fourth century BC. The religious nature of the oath is that doctors swore 'by Apollo Physician, by Asclepius, by Health, by Panacea and by all the gods and goddesses, making them my witnesses.' Among the duties they vowed faithfully to perform was an obligation of confidentiality: 'And whatsoever I shall see or hear in the course of my profession, as well as outside my profession in my intercourse with men, if it be what should not be published abroad, I will never divulge, holding such things to be holy secrets.'

In pre-industrial Europe, certain occupations came to acquire the status of professions. The main four were the clerical profession, the medical profession, the legal profession and those of commissioned status in the armed forces. These might seem to have little in common, but they shared elements in what they 'professed':

- Learning – professionals, typically, are those who have devoted a considerable amount of time to study, in order to master a substantial body of information and knowledge
- Advice – professionals, typically, are those who give advice to others, and who claim to be objective in so doing. Their specialist knowledge – and, with the passage of time, experience – provide the basis for this claim
- Morality – professionals, typically, share a moral code which may either be explicit or implicit in its formulation. Every profession has its norms and part of the training consists in socialisation into these norms
- The Right to Self-Regulation – professionals, typically, claim a competence and integrity which enables them to regulate their own profession. Members who fail to live up to the expected standards of competence and ethics will be disciplined – even, in serious cases, expelled – by their professional bodies.

In the two centuries or more since the Industrial Revolution, the number of occupations claiming professional status has mushroomed. They include some who operate either in or on the periphery of the commercial sector: architects, engineers, surveyors, accountants, etc. The nineteenth century saw the rise of professional institutes. On the whole, the professions were well paid jobs but they did not offer especially lucrative careers. Part of their attraction lay in the status and respect they could command. Because there was a connotation of public service attached to them, the professions still had some of the veneer we have noted in the word 'vocation'.

In the world of business, a social distinction in Britain therefore emerged between:

(i) professionals; who claimed specialist knowledge, who 'professed' the capacity to give objective advice; and who had a commitment to high moral standards

(ii) the rest; which included both semi-skilled workers or unskilled workers and the managers who organised the way they worked. Employers and employees might be divided in many ways, and were often at loggerheads with each other. Yet what they had in common was that they were collectively tarred by their involvement in trade or manufacturing. Britain grew prosperous on the back of the Industrial Revolution, but the British Establishment – so-called educated opinion – never really welcomed industrialists into its fold. It is significant that engineers, despite the fact that they set up professional institutes, have struggled to attain a status on a level with law or medicine. The reason is that by the nature of their work, they are too close to the grubby business of manufacturing. This is in stark contrast to their position in Germany, where they are celebrated for the ingenuity that is actually implicit in the very word engineer.

In contemporary society we have reached a situation where we have three words – vocation, profession and occupation – that overlap to some extent but retain significantly different connotations. 'Vocation' has reverted to its medieval usage to some extent. It tends to be reserved for a select band of jobs that demonstrably help other people and do not pay particularly well. 'Profession' includes most of these, but covers a wider range of jobs united by the various elements I have just outlined. 'Occupation' is a much more general term and includes virtually any job that occupies people – though it is customarily used to indicate more settled work than simply casual labour.

Before we return to 'vocation', it is important to note some recent developments in the professional field. One is that professionals these days are much less embarrassed about charging high fees for their services and earning a lot of money. The public perception is that their motives may be less altruistic than they used to be, and their advice may be less objective. In addition, their right to self-regulation is coming under criticism and challenge. We live in a society where it is increasingly difficult to command respect automatically, and the professions are coming under pressure to be more publicly accountable.

Volf's Critique of Work as Vocation

Can the idea of vocation be reinstated, returning it to Christians doing all sorts of work even in the area of business? I certainly hope so. But the way to do this is not simply by repeating the brave assertions of Martin Luther as if nothing significant had happened during the last 500 years. We need to take seriously the criticisms of Luther's teaching. One of the most cogent critiques of Luther on vocation is by the Yugoslav theologian Miroslav Volf in his book on theology and work, *Work in the Spirit*.

Volf has two main criticisms of the Lutheran view.

First, Volf thinks this understanding of work as vocation is indifferent to the phenomenon of human alienation of work. It offers no criticism of dehumanising ways in which work may be organised, such as mindless repetitive work on an assembly line. If even the 'lifting of a single straw' is a 'completely divine work', as Luther once said, Volf sees no reason why 'the same description should not apply to the most degrading types of work in industrial and information societies' (*Work in the Spirit*, p.107).

Second, Volf thinks that the understanding of work as vocation provides too static a view of human existence. Remember that the key verse for Luther was 1 Corinthians 7:20: 'Every one should remain in the calling in which he was called.' Paul said this in a context of crisis, where 'the form of this world is passing away' – he may have expected the second coming to take place shortly. Paul therefore argued that slaves should be content to remain slaves, and single people should not aspire to get married. Luther and Calvin both interpreted this verse to mean one should stay content with the situation where one finds oneself – in particular, they should normally stay in the same occupation. Volf thinks this idea of vocation is simply not applicable to an increasingly mobile society. Most people in Western societies do not keep a single job or employment for a lifetime, but often switch from one job to another several times in the course of their active life.

I think these criticisms need taking on board, but there is no reason to abandon the idea of vocation in doing so. God's calling to a specific occupation might well include a call to bring about reform and change in that area of work. It might well include the transformation through the power of the Spirit that plays so large a part in Volf's theology of work. There is also no intrinsic reason why the concept of vocation need not be interpreted more dynamically. The fact is, God can call us to many different areas of activity within a lifetime. He did so in the lives of both St Paul and Martin Luther. There is no doubt that the changing patterns of work are pointing increasingly in this direction. This may pose a threat, but can provide an opportunity as well to live a richly varied life in which God uses us in many different ways – as the chapter on the portfolio lifestyle demonstrates.

Volf wishes to replace calling with the concept of *charism*, or gift, because he thinks this has a much sounder New Testament basis. Passages like Romans 12 and 1 Corinthians 12 teach that all Christians have been equipped with gifts, which

are to be used for the benefit and building up of the church.
Many of these gifts (e.g. teaching and administration,
mentioned in Rom. 12:7) are clearly of wider relevance in society. People with well-developed skills in interpersonal
relationships or clarity and vividness of communication are
invaluable in numerous contexts. Volf thinks the matching of
gift to task should guide Christians making a career choice,
not some dubious notion of divine calling.

He clearly has an important point here. Where a sense of
vocation is unaccompanied by any evidence of the necessary
attributes (whether that be pastoral sensitivity in someone
wanting to join the clergy or manual dexterity in someone hoping to become a craftsmen), individuals should ask
themselves seriously whether they have misunderstood God's
purposes for them. Vocation and gift should ideally be complementary concepts. There is no need to play one off sharply
against the other, as Volf does. Indeed, there is good reason to
think that gift by itself is inadequate as a sustaining motive.

My rationale is simple. We can all think of situations at
work that everyone finds uncongenial, tasks for which scarcely anybody would claim a gift. Who actually enjoys telling a
group of employees that their services are no longer required?
Yet the fact is that there are times when – for the organisation's
good, or because the nature of work has changed – people
have to be made redundant. Someone has to be the harbinger
of bad news. Usually it falls to the line manager or the personnel manager; it is part of the job expectation that they carry
out this function. For Christians who are seeking to discharge
unpleasant responsibilities like this as faithfully, sensitively
and truthfully as they can, the conviction that God has *called*
them to the particular task may play a very important part in
steadying the nerves and carrying them through.

A Call to Business

The concept of vocation has been around for 2000 years. I have
tried to identify the main strands in this history and make

some sense of them as a necessary prelude to thinking through what God's call might mean in the world today. In particular, is it legitimate to claim that some people might have a call to business?

I believe the answer is an unequivocal yes. If business has an important role in God's purposes, in terms of making good use of God-given resources, adding value and creating wealth – as I believe it does – then it makes abundant sense to see God as calling individuals with the relevant skills and aptitudes to this crucial task. But such an affirmation needs clarifying and expanding otherwise Christian businesspeople may be led astray, conforming uncritically to the status quo and the ways of the world.

Calling should not be equated narrowly with doing a particular job. We must beware the 'Protestant' distortion of calling to which Guinness so perceptively alerts us. Particular jobs come and go, but God calls us to something bigger. Nor is it sufficient to construe calling in terms of affinity with a certain business sector, though it may well make sense for many to confine themselves to one sector – and thereby build up specialist expertise. For calling to be authentic it needs to be bound up with a holistic, God-given vision for a sector of business life. I once heard a senior Christian banker expound his philosophy of banking, saying that he saw the role of banks as providing venture capital and managing the element of risk. Two simple phrases, yet containing a great profundity – and some way removed from the driving forces in most banking operations today. Where banks are primarily concerned with providing venture capital and managing the element of risk, they make an invaluable contribution to society; and the shape of a genuine vocation is present, the detail waiting to be filled in.

Company mission statements occasionally hit on profound truths. They could serve as vocational straplines – if they are truly believed, genuinely acted upon and do not simply serve as a clever public relations exercise. I like the mission statement produced by GlaxoSmithKline following the merger of Glaxo Wellcome and SmithKline Beecham. This reads:

'GlaxoSmithKline – one of the world's leading research-based pharmaceutical and healthcare companies – is committed to improving the quality of human life by enabling people to do more, feel better and live longer.' It would be difficult to improve on this as a description of what pharmaceutical companies should be about. Enabling people to do more, feel better and live longer: we can all say amen to that. Keep that in the forefront of your vision and any worker in the pharmaceutical industry has a vocation to be proud of – but how easy it is to be diverted from these noble aims into something far less worthy. Christians constantly need to remind themselves of the big picture. Their faith should equip them to alert others to the big picture.

The final lesson is to remember that work is a secondary vocation. The Protestant Reformers taught this, but, as we have seen, their teaching got distorted in the centuries that followed. The primary vocation is to heed the call of Jesus and follow him. Work should be seen in the overall context of discipleship. We are called to serve and honour God with every fibre of our being, in all areas of life: family, local or wider community and leisure pursuits, as well as the work that takes up most of our time, and the church, which too easily becomes the dominating focus of our 'Christian' activity. Vocation needs to be integrated into an all-embracing understanding about God's claim on the whole of our life.

POSTSCRIPT:
WHAT'S THE BIG IDEA?

'What's the big idea?' That's the question that one of my colleagues, Mike Thompson, asks our ordinands about every
sermon they plan or deliver. His point is that every message
from the pulpit should have at its heart a central thrust that is
clear, memorable and unmistakable.

If the same yardstick applies to books, then *Questions of
Business Life* may at first sight be found wanting. What I offer in
these pages is not one big idea, but a whole series of smaller ones.
This is not a one-sided, black and white sort of book. It neither
condemns business for its many faults nor exonerates it on all
counts. It is intended to be a carefully reasoned book with subtle
nuances. I argue that contemporary business gives ground for
hope on certain counts (there are genuinely encouraging developments taking place) and cause for concern on others (there are
negative trends that are proving disturbingly persistent).

Examples of trends which are positive include:

- the heightened sense of corporate social responsibility
  being demonstrated by some multinational companies
- the increasing adoption of a partnership approach in customer-supplier relationships
- the heightening awareness of the pervasive evil of corruption,
  and the progress being made by various initiatives to combat it

- the positive opportunities opened up by the development of the internet.

Examples of trends which are negative include:

- the sense of loyalty having become an outdated concept in many corporate settings
- the tendency, encouraged by advertising, for people to ground their identity in material possessions
- the political and business failure to act decisively enough to reduce reliance on fossil fuels.
- the widespread exercise of stewardship in a greedy and exploitative direction, in relation to capital, people and the environment.

With each of those trends, however, there are clear countervailing tendencies. With none of the topics considered in this book is the wind all blowing in the same direction. That is why I emphasise the importance of attending closely to detail.

There *is* a big idea, however. It is latent in, and lurking behind, all the attempts at fairly balanced judgment. It concerns the relevance of the Christian faith to what is going on in the business world. To further demonstrate this, I will allude briefly to a subject I have not treated fully in this book – leadership. The one seminar run by Ridley Hall in the last six years that is not accorded a chapter in this book was titled *Transforming Leadership*. Because the seminar covered much of the ground dealt with in my book of the same name, published in 1996, I felt there was a danger of too much duplication. Nevertheless, given the importance of leadership in organisational life, and since I teach a module on it, I keep close track of current thinking on leadership in the business world.

Stealing our Clothes?

Chapter 3 frequently mentions the work of the Centre for Tomorrow's Company. The 'tomorrow's companies' encouraged by the Centre are marked by a strong sense of shared vision and values, and relationships of mutual trust with key stakeholders – the so-called inclusive approach. In 1999, the Centre for Tomorrow's Company published *Leadership in Tomorrow's Company*, written by Philip Sadler. This 38-page booklet aims to answer the question: What kind of leadership will inspire and enable tomorrow's companies to compete successfully in tomorrow's world?

Sadler's response is to treat the reader to a succinct and discerning survey of recent research and writing on leadership. He goes along with the widely accepted distinction between management (which is concerned with controlling and problem-solving) and leadership (which is about motivating and inspiring: aligning people so that they are committed to the realisation of a shared vision). To exercise leadership it has often been thought necessary to have a charismatic, 'larger than life' personality. But research shows that while some transformational leaders have been of this type, such as Jack Welch of GE, other equally effective ones have not, for example Donald Petersen of Ford.

Whatever their personality type, the key issue facing future leaders is 'unlocking the enormous human potential by winning people's emotional support,' Sadler says. 'Our leaders of the future will have to be more competent, more articulate, more creative, more inspirational and more credible if they are going to win the hearts and minds of their followers.'

In the second half of the booklet, he examines some concepts of leadership that have a common focus on releasing human potential. The first concept is the learning leader. Drawing on Peter Senge's *The Fifth Discipline* and John Neill's inspirational example at the car parts firm Unipart, Sadler talks about leadership as the process of nurturing people's commitment to, and capacity for, learning at all levels of the organisation.

Leaders will encourage this by:

- being open about their own need to learn
- asking challenging questions and stimulating intellectual curiosity

- acting as coach or mentor and establishing facilities like learning resource centres
- fostering a culture which is supportive of learning.

The second concept is one that recurs throughout this book – stewardship. Sadler cites a book of that name by Peter Block, who states that stewardship is 'the willingness to be accountable for some larger body than ourselves – an organisation, a community'. It is to do with 'our choice for service over self-interest', with being 'willing to be deeply accountable without choosing to control the world around us'. This accountability reaches in all directions, and includes answering to one's subordinates. Block sees leaders as stewards who are responsible for clarity rather than control.

The third concept is the servant leader. Here Sadler draws on the work of Robert K. Greenleaf, whose thinking has continued to exercise considerable influence since his death in 1991. In Greenleaf's view, servant leaders are marked by listening, empathy, healing, awareness, persuasion, conceptualisation, foresight, commitment to the growth of people and building community. Sadler mentions C. William Pollard as a company CEO who is a strong advocate of servant leadership. Pollard is chairman of American firm ServiceMaster, which has been nominated the best service company in the Fortune 500 for the last ten years. ServiceMaster has achieved 25 years of consecutive growth in revenues and profits, yet retained a strong values base throughout and is renowned as a company which practices what it preaches.

At this point in my reading I had to put the booklet down and laugh, because ServiceMaster is a company with an explicitly Christian ethos. One of the four planks of its mission statement is 'to honour God in all we do' yet Sadler makes no mention of this. Moreover, each of the three leadership concepts Sadler calls 'relatively recent' are, in their origins, profoundly Christian. In the *Transforming Leadership* seminar, we took five biblical models of leadership and applied them to the secular world. They included – surprise, surprise – servant, steward and sage. The latter is a close equivalent to the learning leader. (The other two, just for the record, were shepherd and seer.)

Reading Sadler's booklet reminded me of an experience in the early 1990s, at an early meeting of MODEM (Managerial and Organisational Disciplines for the Enhancement of Ministry). Gillian Stamp, professor of Social Studies at Brunel University, told the gathering: 'The organisational world is stealing your clothes.' There was silence as the audience, mostly clergy, absorbed this profound insight. She was referring to the fact that the best in modern management theory is essentially Christianity in secular guise. As I have just shown, *Leadership in Tomorrow's Company* is a vivid illustration of this.

It would be churlish to criticise Sadler for failing to highlight this Christian heritage. The fact is that Christians have been lamentably slow to make connections between their own understanding of leadership and the wider world. Most books written by Christians on the subject don't go beyond the sphere of leadership in the church. If we are unwilling to push our heads above the parapet and make a contribution to modern management thinking, complaints about stealing our clothes are apt to sound rather plaintive. We never made it clear they were our clothes in the first place.

But there is more to be said. Yes, the concepts of the leader as learner, steward and servant can all be gladly owned by Christians. But that does not mean we should uncritically swallow the stew into which these familiar ideas have been mixed. An authentically Christian view on business does not consist simply of agreeing with the 'best' ideas that other people are coming up with. There will nearly always be a distinctive, slightly off-beat perspective that should lead Christians to ask questions about current orthodoxy. So I have serious questions to ask about each of Sadler's three 'wise men':

- Senge's emphasis on continuous learning is welcome (let's not forget that 'learn' is the root meaning of the word disciple) but there is a curious vacuum at the centre of it. The price of his fascination with the learning process is a relative neglect of residual content. Are there no great truths about organisational life to be passed on, no abiding truths about human nature? The Christian concept of the leader as teacher has rather more to say about what is taught, more confidence that there is some trustworthy deposit worthy of transmission.

- Block is correct to see accountability as fundamental to the notion of stewardship, but then confuses accountability with responsibility. The two overlap, but they are not the same. As Jesus' teaching in Luke 12:42-48 illustrates, stewards are those who are both under authority and in authority. They are accountable to people above them and responsible for people below them. Steward is a model that perfectly describes the position of a middle manager, but it has a wider relevance as well. The Christian concept of the leader as steward is a protection against organisational fuzziness.

- Greenleaf produces an admirable description of many key features of servant leadership, but he underplays the hard side of being a servant. For Jesus, servant leadership meant being prepared to take up a cross – literally so. In organisational life, there are times when the leader has to accept that 'the buck stops here', that there are costly responsibilities it would be unfair to delegate to anyone else, and he or she needs to set a self-sacrificial example. The Christian concept of the leader as servant insists that the *tension* contained in putting these two words together is kept firmly in view.

A Constructive, Critical Contribution

What I have outlined in this response to Sadler's booklet is something that should be characteristic of the Christian contribution to business more widely. There is both a constructive and a critical role to be played. Christians should be known as people who affirm the good things that are happening in corporate life. They should be people who don't shelter behind superficial plaudits, and who ask the deeper questions. From the resources of their faith, they ought to be well equipped for this. Jesus said his disciples are the salt of the earth. As I pointed out in Chapter 11, salt has a variety of functions. In the ancient world it acted as a preservative, stopping food from going bad. But it also provides extra tang and taste, enhancing everything that is good. Christians in business – as in other areas of life – should have a good strong salty flavour.

Sadly, that is far from the reality in many places today. Christianity has been effectively marginalised by business. Business has been scandalously marginalised by the Christian Church. It is imperative that we reverse both these processes of marginalisation. There are a few isolated examples of this beginning to happen, and I hope the Ridley Hall Foundation has made a small but significant contribution over the last few years. On one topical issue after another we have found that a robust and imaginative biblical theology, allied with the well informed, practical understanding that businesspeople bring, has a refreshing and often unexpected relevance to the work they do. This has emerged as we have gathered Christians and others to probe the topical issues together: to think interactively, constructively and critically, about the way that faith impinges upon the business world.

The baton now needs to be taken up, not just by other specialist organisations in the area of faith and work, but by the Christian church more widely. Church leaders need to take the lead in equipping their members with a wide-ranging working theology. Church members need to take the lead in apprising their leaders about what is happening in the working world. Out of the dialogue that ensues, clear direction needs to come about how Christians should seek to be influencing the corporate world. Marginalisation has to stop.

That's the Big Idea.

BIBLIOGRAPHY:
books and articles consulted and cited

John D. Adams, *Transforming Work*, Miles River Press, 1984.

James Allcock, 'Issues Raised: Response on the Final Afternoon', *Faith in Business Quarterly* 1:4, December 1997.

Tim Ambler and Andrea Wilson, 'Problems of stakeholder theory', *Business Ethics: A European Review*, 4:1, pp.30-35, 1995.

John Argenti, *Your Organisation: What is it For?*, McGraw-Hill, 1993.

John Argenti, 'All Things to All Men: The Surest Route to Perdition', *Strategy*, March 1997, pp.4-5.

Robert Banks, *God the Worker: Journeys into the Mind, Heart and Imagination of God*, Judson Press, 1992.

Craig Bartholomew and Thorsten Moritz (eds.), *Christ and Consumerism: A Critical Analysis of the Spirit of the Age*, Paternoster Press, 2000.

Richard Basham, 'The Roots of Asian Organised Crime', *IPA Review* Vol.48/4, 1996, pp.11-16.

Zygmunt Bauman, *Intimations of Postmodernity*, Routledge, 1992.

Peter L. Berger, 'The Gross National Product and the Gods: The Idea of Economic Culture', *The McKinsey Quarterly*, 1994, No.1.

R.J.Berry (ed.), *The Care of Creation: Focusing Concern and Action*, IVP, 2000.

Peter Block, *Stewardship: Choosing Service over Self-Interest*, Berrett-Koehler, 1993.

John Calvin, *Institutes of the Christian Religion*, Eerdmans (1-volume ed.), 1995.

Sir Fred Catherwood, *God's Time, God's Money*, Hodder & Stoughton, 1987.

James Champy, *Reengineering Management: The Mandate for New Leadership*, HarperCollins, 1995.

Sang-Goog Cho, 'Korean Economy: A Model Case of a Miraculous Growth?', unpublished paper, September 1993.

Andrew Clayton, 'Child Labour in the Third World', unpublished paper.

David Clutterbuck, *The Power of Empowerment: Release the Hidden Talents of your Employees*, BCA, 1994.

Church of England Board for Social Responsibility, *Cybernauts Awake: Ethical and Spiritual Implications of Computers, Information Technology and the Internet*, Church House Publishing, 1999.

Max Comfort, *Portfolio People: How to Create a Workstyle as Individual as You Are*, Century Business, 1997.

Stephen R. Covey, *The Seven Habits of Highly Effective People: Restoring the Character Ethic*, Simon & Schuster, 1992.

Peter Curran, *All the Hours God Sends? Practical and Biblical Help in Meeting the Demands of Work*, IVP, 2000.

John Davis, *Greening Business: Managing for Sustainable Development*, Basil Blackwell, 1991.

Ulrich Duchrow, *Global Economy: A Confessional Issue for the Churches?*, WCC Publications, 1987.

Ulrich Duchrow, *Alternatives to Global Capitalism: Drawn from Biblical History, Designed for Political Action*, International Books, 1995.

Sir John Egan, *Rethinking Construction: The Report of the Construction Task Force* (The Egan Report), Department of the Environment, Transport and the Regions, 1998.

Gordon D. Fee, *The First Epistle to the Corinthians*, Eerdmans, 1987.

Gordon D. Fee, *1 & 2 Timothy, Titus*, Hendrickson, 1989.

Daniel Finn, *Just Trading: On the Ethics and Economics of International Trade*, Abingdon Press, 1996.

R. Edward Freeman, *Strategic Management: A Stakeholder Approach*, Pitman Publishing, 1984.

R. Edward Freeman and William M. Evan, 'A Stakeholder Theory of the Modern Corporation: Kantian Capitalism', published in Tom L. Beauchamp and Norman E. Bowie, *Ethical Theory and Business*, 4th ed., Prentice Hall, 1993.

R. Edward Freeman, 'The problems of stakeholder theory: some further directions', *Business Ethics Quarterly* 4:4, pp.409-423, 1994.

Milton Friedman, 'The Social Responsibility of a Business is to Increase its Profits', *New York Times Magazine*, No. 33, pp.122-126, September, 1970.

Francis Fukuyama, *Trust: The Social Virtues and the Creation of Prosperity*, Penguin Books, 1995.

Yiannis Gabriel and Tim Lang, *The Unmanageable Consumer*, Sage, 1995.

A.G. Gardiner, *Life of George Cadbury*, Cassell & Co., 1923.

Kenneth Goodpaster, 'Business ethics and stakeholder analysis, *Business Ethics Quarterly* 1:1, pp.53-71, 1991.

Timothy Gorringe, *Capital and the Kingdom: Theological Ethics and Economic Order*, SPCK, 1994.

George Goyder, *The Just Enterprise*, Andre Deutsch, 1987.

Mark Goyder, 'The Inclusive Approach', *Faith in Business Quarterly* 1:3, pp.12-13, 1997.

Mark Goyder, *Living Tomorrow's Company*, Gower, 1998.

Stephen Green, *Serving God? Serving Mammon? Christians and the Financial Markets*, Marshall Pickering, 1996.

Mark Greene, 'Jingle Hell or Shooting the Messenger? Reflections on the Vilification of Advertising', unpublished paper, 1996.

Mark Greene, 'Ads 'R Us', *eg*, no.5, March 2001.

Robert Greenleaf, *Servant Leadership: A Journey into the Nature of Legitimate Power and Greatness*, Paulist Press, 1977.

Brian Griffiths, *Morality and the Marketplace*, Hodder & Stoughton, 1982.

Brian Griffiths, *The Creation of Wealth*, Marshall Pickering, 1984.

John Griffiths, 'A World Away from Ronald McDonald', *Third Way*, October 1995, p.13.

Os Guinness, *Fit Bodies, Fat Minds*, Hodder & Stoughton, 1995.

Os Guinness, *The Call: Finding and Fulfilling the Central Purpose of Your Life*, Word Publishing, 1998.

Michael Hammer and James Champy, *Reengineering the Corporation*, Nicholas Brealey, 1993.

Charles Hampden-Turner and Fons Trompenaars, *The Seven Cultures of Capitalism*, Piatkus, 1993.

Charles Hampden-Turner, *Corporate Culture: How to Generate Organisational Strength and Lasting Commercial Advantage*, Piatkus, 1994.

Charles Handy, *The Age of Unreason*, Century Hutchinson, 1989.

Charles Handy, 'What is a Company For?', *RSA Journal* Vol.CXXXIX, March 1991.

Charles Handy, *The Empty Raincoat: Making Sense of the Future*, Arrow Books, 1995.

Richard Harries, *Is There A Gospel for the Rich? The Christian in a Capitalist World*, Mowbray, 1992.

Paul Hawken, Amory B. Lovins and L. Hunter Lovins, *Natural Capitalism: The Next Industrial Revolution*, Earthscan, 1999.

Noreena Hertz, *The Silent Takeover: Global Capitalism and the Death of Democracy*, William Heinemann, 2001.

Richard Higginson, *Called to Account: Adding Value in God's World*, Eagle, 1993.

Richard Higginson, *Transforming Leadership: A Christian Approach to Management*, SPCK, 1996.

Richard Higginson, *Mind the Gap: Connecting Faith with Work*, CPAS, 1997.

Richard Higginson, 'Shareholder vs Stakeholder Theory: A Review of the Literature', *Faith in Business Quarterly* 1:3, 1997.

Thomas Hobbes, *Leviathan* (ed. R. Tuck), Cambridge University Press, 1991.

John Houghton, *Global Warming: The Complete Briefing*, Lion, 1994.

Will Hutton, *The State We're In*, Vintage, 1996.

Michael Joseph, 'Spirituality in the Workplace – What are we talking about?' *Faith in Business Quarterly* 4:3, 2000, pp.3-5.

John Kay, *Foundations of Corporate Success*, Oxford University Press, 1993.

Simon Kershaw, 'Monopoly and Competition: Power Concentration on the Net', *Faith in Business Quarterly* 4:4, 2000, pp. 20-22.

Naomi Klein, *No Logo*, Flamingo, 2001.

Richard Koch, *The 80/20 Principle: The Secret of Achieving More with Less*, Nicholas Brealey, 1997.

John Laird, *Money, Politics, Globalisation and Crisis: The Case of Thailand*, Graham Brash, 2000.

David Landes, *The Wealth and Poverty of Nations: Why Some are So Rich and Some are So Poor*, Little, Brown & Co., 1998.

B. Langtry, 'Stakeholders and the moral responsibilities of business', *Business Ethics Quarterly* 4:4, pp.431-435, 1994.

Sir Michael Latham, *Constructing the Team: Final Report of the Government/Industry Review of Procurement and Contractual Analysis in the UK Construction Industry* (The Latham Report), Stationery Office, 1994.

David Lea, 'Corporate and public responsibility, stakeholder theory and the developing world', *Business Ethics: A European Review* 8:3, pp.151-162, 1999.

Marc Lewis, *Sin to Win: Seven Deadly Steps to Success*, Capstone, 2002.

Vladimir Lossky, *The Mystical Theology of the Eastern Church*, St Vladimir's Seminary Press, 1976.

David Lyon, 'Memory and the Millennium: Time and Social Change at the Fin de Siècle' in Timothy Bradshaw (ed.), *Grace and Truth*, Eerdmans, 1998.

David Lyon, *Jesus in Disneyland*, Polity Press, 2000.

David Lyon, 'Yours Virtually', *Third Way*, May 2000, pp.23-26.

Calvert Markham, *Practical Management Consultancy*, 3rd ed., Accountancy Books, 1999.

Chris Marsden, 'Corporate Citizenship', *Faith in Business Quarterly* 1:4, pp.15-17, 1997.

Paul Marshall, *A Kind of Life Imposed on Man: Vocation and Social Order from Tyndale to Locke*, University of Toronto Press, 1996.

David Martin, *Tongues of Fire: The Explosion of Protestantism in Latin America*, Basil Blackwell, 1990.

Alan Mitchell, 'Raising the Stakes', *Marketing Business*, pp.28-30, Dec. 1996-Jan. 1997.

Geoff Moore, 'Tinged shareholder theory: or what's so special about stakeholders?', *Business Ethics: A European Review* 8:2, pp.117-127, 1999.

George Moody-Stuart, *Grand Corruption: How Business Bribes Damage Developing Countries*, WorldView Publishing, 1997.

George Moody-Stuart, 'Corruption', in Chris Moon and Clive Bonny (eds.), *Business Ethics: Facing up to the Issues*, Economist Books, 2001.

David Murray, '"Looking to the Interests of Others": Some Biblical Considerations', *Faith in Business Quarterly* 1:3, pp.9-11, 1997.

David Murray, 'What Spirit? Cautionary remarks on workplace spirituality', *Faith in Business Quarterly* 4:1, pp.16-17, 2000.

Laura Nash, *Good Intentions Aside: A Manager's Guide to Resolving Ethical Problems*, Harvard Business School Press, 1990.

John Naughton, *A Brief History of the Future: The origins of the internet*, Weidenfeld & Nicolson, 1999.

J.T.Noonan, Jr., *Bribes: The Intellectual History of a Moral Idea*, Macmillan, 1984.

Michael Northcott, *Life after Debt: Christianity and Global Justice*, SPCK, 1999.

James O'Shea and Charles Madigan, *Dangerous Company: The Consulting Powerhouses and the Businesses They Save and Ruin*, Nicholas Brealey, 1997.

Chris Patten, *East and West: China, Power and the Future of Asia*, Macmillan, 1998.

Gordon Pearson, *Integrity in Organisations: An Alternative Business Ethic*, McGraw-Hill, 1995.

Simon Peyton Jones, 'Privacy in Cyberspace', *Faith in Business Quarterly* 4:4, 2000, pp.9-11.

John Plender, *A Stake in the Future: The Stakeholding Solution*, Nicholas Brealey, 1997.

Gordon R. Preece, *The Viability of the Vocation Tradition in Trinitarian, Credal and Reformed Perspectives: The Threefold Call*, Edwin Mellen Press, 1998.

David Pullinger, *Information Technology and Cyberspace: Extra-connected Living*, Darton Longman & Todd, 2001.

John Ramsey, 'Partnership of unequals', *Supply Management*, 28 March 1996, pp.31-33.

RSA Report, *Tomorrow's Company*, 1995.

Jani Rubery, *More than a Job: Creating a Portfolio Lifestyle*, Paternoster/Spring Harvest, 2001.

Leland Ryken, *Work and Leisure in Christian Perspective*, IVP, 1987.

Philip Sadler, *Leadership in Tomorrow's Company*, Gower, 1999.

Save the Children, *Big Business, Small Hands: Responsible Approaches to Child Labour*, 2000.

Christian Schumacher, *To Live and Work: A Theological Interpretation*, Marc Europe, 1987.

Christian Schumacher, *God in Work*, Lion, 1998.

Peter M. Senge, *The Fifth Discipline: The Art and Practice of the Learning Organisation*, Century Business, 1990.

Richard Sennett, *The Corrosion of Character: The Personal Consequences of Work in the New Capitalism*, W.W. Norton, 1998.

Stan Sesser, 'A Reporter at Large: Opium War Redux', *New York Reporter*, September 1993, pp.78-89.

Shell Report 1998, Profits and Principles – does there have to be a choice?

Shell Report 1999, People, planet and profits: an act of commitment.

Shell Report 1999, Dealing with Bribery and Corruption: A Management Primer.

Shell Report 2000, People, planet and profits: how do we stand?

Shell Report 2001, People, planet and profits.

Vandana Shiva, *Biopiracy*, South End Press, 1997.

Adam Smith, *An Inquiry into the Nature and Causes of the Wealth of Nations*, Penguin Classics, 1986 (1st ed. 1776).

Max L. Stackhouse, Dennis P. McCann and Shirley J. Roels, with Preston N. Williams (eds.), *On Moral Business: Classical and Contemporary Resources for Ethics in Economic Life*, Eerdmans, 1995.

Elaine Sternberg, *Just Business: Business Ethics in Action*, Warner Books, 1994.

Elaine Sternberg, The Stakeholder Concept: A Mistaken Doctrine, Foundation for Business Responsibilities, *Issues Paper* No.4, 1999.

R. Paul Stevens, *The Abolition of the Laity: Vocation, Work and Ministry in a Biblical Perspective*, Paternoster, 1999.

Christopher Sunderland, *In A Glass Darkly: Seeking Vision for Public Life*, Paternoster, 2001.

Keith Suter, *Global Agenda: Economics, the Environment and the Nation State*, Albatross Books, 1995.

Lester C. Thurow, *The Future of Capitalism: How Today's Economic Forces Shape Tomorrow's World*, Nicholas Brealey, 1996.

Paul Tillich, *The Boundaries of our Being*, Collins Fontana, 1973.

Fons Trompenaars, *Riding the Waves of Culture: Understanding Cultural Diversity in Business*, Nicholas Brealey, 1993.

Elizabeth Vallance, *Business Ethics at Work*, Cambridge University Press, 1995.

Rob van Drimmelen, *Faith in a Global Economy: A Primer for Christians*, WCC Publications, 1998.

Miroslav Volf, *Work in the Spirit: Toward A Theology of Work*, Oxford University Press, 1991.

James Walvin, *The Quakers: Money and Morals*, John Murray, 1997.

James Walvin, 'Why were the Quakers especially good in business?', *Faith in Business Quarterly* 3:4, 1999, pp.8-13.

Peter Warburton, 'Golf courses on the moon: is investment in the internet doomed to disappoint?', *Faith in Business Quarterly* 4:4, 2000, pp.3-8.

Steve Walton, *A Call to Live: Vocation for Everyone*, Triangle, 1994.

Derek Warren, 'Blue Circle shows that dialogue really works', *IPA magazine*, November 1999.

Max Weber, *The Protestant Ethic and the Spirit of Capitalism*, Unwin, 1971 (1st ed. 1905).

David Welbourn, 'The New Paradigm at Work', *Faith in Business Quarterly* 4:1, pp.10-15.

David Welbourn, 'The New Paradigm: Its Outworking in Science, Religion and Workplace Spirituality', *Faith in Business Quarterly* 5:3, Autumn 2001.

John Wesley, 'The Use of Money', *Sermons on Several Occasions*, Epworth, 1944.

David Wheeler and Maria Sillanpaa, *The Stakeholder Corporation: A Blueprint for Maximising Stakeholder Value*, Pitman, 1997.

William Wolman and Anne Colamosca, *The Triumph of Capital and the Betrayal of Work*, Addison-Wesley, 1997.

Christian Wolmar, *Broken Rails: How Privatisation Wrecked Britain's Railways*, Aurum Press, 2001.

James P. Womack, Daniel T. Jones and Daniel Roos, *The Machine that Changed the World*, Free Press Paperbacks, 1990.

James P. Womack and Daniel T. Jones, *Lean Thinking: Banish Waste and Create Wealth in Your Corporation*, Simon & Schuster, 1996.

Clive Wright, 'Resolution of Conflicting Stakeholder Interests', *Faith in Business Quarterly* 1:4, pp.22-25, 1997.

Robert Wuthrow, *God and Mammon in America*, The Free Press, 1994.

Simon Zadek, *The Civil Corporation: The New Economy of Corporate Citizenship*, Earthscan, 2001.

Danah Zohar and Ian Marshall, *SQ: Spiritual Intelligence the Ultimate Intelligence*, Bloomsbury, 2000.